THE DREAM NEVER BECOMES REALITY

24 Swiss Writers Challenge the United States

An Anthology edited by

Cornelius Schnauber, Romey Sabalius,

and

Gene Stimpson

UNIVERSITY PRESS OF AMERICA

Lanham • New York • London

German Literature, Art & Thought

Copyright © 1995 by
University Press of America® Inc.
4720 Boston Way
Lanham, Maryland 20706

3 Henrietta Street
London WC2E 8LU England

Copublished by arrangement with
German Literature, Art, and Thought

Library of Congress Cataloging-in-Publication Data

The Dream never becomes reality : Twenty Four Swiss writers
challenge the United States : an anthology / edited by Cornelius
Schnauber, Romey Sabalius, and Gene Stimpson.
    p.   cm. — (German literature, art & thought)
    Includes bibliographical references.
1. Swiss literature.   2. United States in literature.   I. Schnauber,
Cornelius.   II. Sabalius, Romey.   III. Stimpson, Gene.
                    IV. Series.
PN849.S9D74   1994   809'.835—dc20   94–9392 CIP

ISBN 0–8191–9421–2 (cloth : alk. paper)
ISBN 0–8191–9422–0 (pbk. : alk. paper)

GERMAN LITERATURE, ART & THOUGHT

AN INTERNATIONAL FORUM FOR INTERDISCIPLINARY STUDIES

including THE McMASTER COLLOQUIUM ON GERMAN STUDIES

Edited by **Hans Schulte**

Published by University Press of America
(Lanham, London, New York)

ADVISORY BOARD

The editors will consider any high-quality manuscript, in English or German, with an interdisciplinary perspective appealing not only to specialists. Care is taken to ensure a high standard in the quality and appearance of volumes. With some pre-formatting and compatible software, production costs will be minimal.

Inquiries, submissions:

Prof. Hans Schulte
McMaster University, Modern Languages
Hamilton, Ontario, Canada L8S 4M2
Tel: (905) 525-9140 ext. 23454 or
FAX: Modern Languages (905) 527-0100

Table of Contents

INTRODUCTION

The reader of this anthology will be struck by the richness and diversity of contemporary Swiss literature, as well as by its apparent preoccuption with the United States. How can we account for this fascination? The most obvious explanation is the fact that "America" is the name of Switzerland's favorite modern utopia. For centuries now, the "American Dream" has evolved as a universal analogy of a "Swiss Dream" within the context of Europe: *one* people of different races and cultural origins asserting itself with an indomitable spirit of independence and civil liberty. But Switzerland was a small and locked-in state, with its citizenry succumbing to a small and locked-in state of mind — such, at least, has been the frustrated verdict of many Swiss cultural critics, especially in our century. It is no wonder these writers would look to the generous, giant brother for a model and shining example.

Accordingly, love of the American utopia was always a primal impetus of Swiss cultural self-critique, even when such love would hide behind poignant complaint or satire. Indeed this became the rule rather than the exception when writers experienced American *realities*, and lived American life and culture sometimes for many years. All of the texts in this anthology are based on such first-hand experience. Their occasional critical harshness should be taken with a grain of salt, since it is invariably based on that unacceptable truism that the American Dream, to quote one author and our own title, *Never Becomes Reality*.

However, there is another historical reason behind this dialogue of eager enthusiasm and critical melancholy. It is the antagonism

between a "modernist" admiration for progressive rationalism (represented by the United States) and passionate love for nature
and the irrational; an antagonism between the enthusiastic adop-
tion of modern civilization and the yearning "back to nature,"
between love of the purity of mountain life and the fascination
with the elegant comforts of the flatland and its cities. Above all,
it is the antagonism between a yearning for the world outside tiny,
locked-in Switzerland (quite often leading to emigration) and eternal homesickness for Switzerland as the secret center of the world,
the only world worth living in. *Le Milieu du Monde* (*The Center of
the World*) is the title of a novel by one of Switzerland's most
cosmopolitan authors, Daniel Odier (born 1945), and refers to a
small Swiss village.

All of these contradictions can be found in all four literary traditions: German, French, Italian, and Romansch, in spite of their
differences. The French, Italian, and Romansch-speaking cantons
became politically integrated into the Swiss federation relatively late
— Geneva, for instance, in 1815, Ticino (Tessin) and Grisons (Graubünden) in 1803. Accordingly, the authors of these cantons do not
associate themselves as readily with a Swiss national culture as the
German-speaking authors. This history of Swiss "minorities" informs
their literature, and it seems to strengthen rather than weaken their
"Swiss" orientation towards the United States.

The German part of Switzerland is its oldest and largest. Almost
two thirds of the population speak a Swiss-German dialect and write
in so-called High German. Therefore, it was possible for this community to develop a cultural identity, an identity which is also set apart
from that of the neighboring German-speaking countries, despite the
fact that German authors like Goethe and Schiller or, in our century,
Brecht and Böll had a powerful influence on Swiss-German literature, and that many Swiss authors publish in German publishing
houses. If one asked a German-speaking Swiss author today, what
his or her cultural identity was, the answer would certainly be: "I am
Swiss and so is our literature."

Most French-speaking authors would give a different. answer.
Nicolas Bouvier (born 1929), one of the most cosmopolitan Swiss
authors, answered: "First, I am a son of Geneva, second, I am an
author of the French language and only third, am I Swiss." An

extreme, seemingly anti-Swiss response by a French-Swiss writer was already given 70 years ago by Charles Ferdinand Ramuz (1878-1947), then one of the leading authors of Switzerland: "first, I write about the people of my home area, Vaud and Valais (French speaking cantons of Switzerland), second, the language and style of my work belong to French literature and only third, as a citizen, I have to call myself Swiss. But only because the mail boxes in which I put my letters are Swiss." A sarcastic response which pointedly contributes to the chorus of twentieth-century Swiss self-depreciation.

One finds a similar tendency in the literature of the Italian-speaking part of Switzerland. If Italian-speaking authors deal with Switzerland, they deal almost exclusively with their home canton Ticino — as the works of Plinio Martini (1923-1979) and Giovanni Orelli (born 1928) can testify. Their literary tradition depends on Italy rather than on their own cultural history, especially since they have never been able to produce powerful literary exports like the French-Swiss Jean-Jacques Rousseau (1712-1778), Rodolphe Töpffer (1799-1846), Germaine de Staël-Necker (1766-1817) and Blaise Cendrars (1887-1961).

The only Swiss literature which has been able to develop a complete harmony of language and homeland is Romansch literature, since the Romansch language is only spoken in Grisons (*Graubünden*). No other Swiss literature includes so many folkloristic motifs as the Romansch. But since only approximately 52,000 people speak one of the five Romansch dialects, most of their authors, such as Iso Camartin and Flurin Spescha, also write in German.

Yet, in spite of all these different cultural conditions and histories, a distinct "Swiss-ness" remains with all the authors of this volume, especially if we reconsider its Janus quality, that uniquely productive ambivalence mentioned above. To understand this quality, let uns briefly consider a few outstanding Swiss authors from several centuries.

The Renaissance philosopher, theologian and physician Paracelsus (Theophrastus Bombastus von Hohenheim, 1493-1541) already represented the tensions between the beginnings of rationalism in medicine and a certain magical view of nature. On the one hand he defended surgery — at that time still seen as unethical — and developed and used in his therapy the new knowledge of chemistry as a part of rational understanding of medicine. On the other hand, he combined his holistic, vitalistic view of the human body and nature with mysticism, magic beliefs and irrationalism. Treating the body, soul and spirit of the patient simultaneously became the fundamental principle of Paracelsus' practice and teaching.

Similarly, Albrecht von Haller (1708-1777), another great Swiss physician, combined the knowledge of rational, analytical medicine with a holistic view of the biological and physiological nature of the human body. This led him to a new understanding of the interdependence of somatic sensations, body functions, nerve reactions and even emotions. In his poetic masterpiece, *Die Alpen*, he develops the contrast between living "ideal nature," i.e., man's life in the world of the mountains, and the demoralized and decadent civilization in the cities.

Haller's *Alpen* made a decisive impression on Jean-Jacques Rousseau. He too was a typical proponent of that antagonism in Swiss culture. As a philosopher of state and government his aim was cosmopolitan, but his thinking was based on his experience in the still quite small city of Geneva. In the contradictions of his rationalism versus utopian "back to nature" we find not only the influence of Haller's *Die Alpen*, but also that of Johannes Calvin (1509-1564), that other powerful, rationally and ethically rigid Genevan. And of course we must not forget the inspiriation of an awesome Swiss mountain landscape. Moral rationalism and utopian irrationalism became the two facets of his philosophy which would influence literature, philosophy and politics in the centuries to come.

In such a context, it is not surprising that two Swiss scholars and *literati*, Johann Jakob Bodmer (1698-1783) and Johann Jakob Breitinger (1701-1776), spearheaded the coming "culture of feeling" in the midst of European Rationalism, reintroducing the magic and miraculous, subjective phantasy and poetic imagination to the creative consciousness of European literature. Again, Swiss cultural duality became productive, a sensitive and effective antidote against one-sidedness of thought. Characteristically, the two scholars remained equally adamant in upholding enlightenment principles; according to Bodmer, the full-fledged romanticism of Goethe's *Werther* was an abomination.

Swiss double visions of universal reason and individual 'soul' also inform the work of nineteenth-century authors like Keller, Gotthelf, and Meyer. Gottfried Keller (1819-1890), Switzerland's most famous author of the century, studied in Germany and shaped his "European" experiences in his novel *Der grüne Heinrich*. The universal humanity and society presented in this book are later applied with great and often humorous effect to the provincial narrowness and idiosyncracies of Zurich, i.e., the imaginary "Seldwyla." And Jeremias Gotthelf (1797-1854), one of the greatest European narrators, anchors his vision of a universal and religious ethic in the world of peasants and farmers in the remote valley of Emmenthal, in order to assert his faith in the moral strength of a country life overcoming the decadent civilization of the cities.

Only Conrad Ferdinand Meyer (1825-1898) breaks away from his early Swiss regionalism and takes refuge in the heroic landscapes of his masterful historical novel and especially in his novellas.

Meyer's example, of course, brings us back to the beginning of our historical reflections, namely, the tendency of Swiss authors to break away from their country's self-satisfied, less than "heroic" insularism. It is also one of the strongest motivating forces behind the twenty-four contemporary writers in the present anthology, as they look out, with their keen *engagement* and provocative critique, to the United States. The equation between the two societies, of Utopia gone awry, seems omnipresent, although with some of this social and cultural criticism — specifically of the leftist generation — frustrated love seems buried below the critical consciousness of systematic social evil. Some of the most radical criticism of capitalistic society, especially in the United States, has been put forward by these writers who had grown up in an extremely orderly and successfully capitalistic country. A social conscience driven to a high pitch within the confines of this failed paradise focused its critical aggression on the United States, especially during the Vietnam War and later during the period of the Reagan presidency. To them, the homeland of capitalism became the incarnation of evil, brutality, oppression, and war-hungry imperialism. The reader will find few such biased extremes among these contemporary texts, and aggressive critique is almost always tempered by a more or less hidden hope and trust (see Federspiel's *Best City of the Blind*.) But the reader *will* find, on occasion, a kind of crushing anger with the capitalistic establishment at home and abroad, which results in near anarchistic gestures. In Ueli Zingg's biography, which he himself distributes to his readers, we find these notes: "Beginning of life at 30. Step by step liberation from the notion of owing something to society. Withdrawal from the church, from the institution of marriage, from the norm of having a regular profession." Only one who has been satiated and ultimately frustrated by an all-too prosperous and sheltered world could develop this anarchic attitude. Once again, these authors respond to *their* loss of the American Dream with angrily sarcastic but deeply concerned aggression. They face, after all, the ultimate betrayal of their own, home-grown utopia.

This anthology includes excerpts from novels, short stories, essays and poems. Some of the texts have never been published before or were written especially for this book. The content of the texts includes personal life-stories, like the excerpts from Walter Vogt's *Altern* and Christoph Geiser's *Desert Passages*, encoded life-stories in Loetscher's excerpts from *Herbst in der Großen Orange* (here included in the text "From Coast to Coast"), historical episodes in excerpts from Eveline Hasler's *The Wax Winged Woman*, documentary style fiction as in the almost surrealistic excerpts from Daniel Odier's *Cannibal Kiss*, and, in various types of essays, reflections which reach from straight-forward observations, such as Adolf Muschg's "apocalyptic" collection of documents in "New Rights", to semi-fictitious essays, like Herbert Meier's "Terrence" or Iso Camartin's "Maxims for Los Angeles." The attitudes toward the United States range from Gomringer's friendly, though ironic "At Home with the Missionaries — Almost a Fairytale," to the dreams which created America but "never became reality" in Etienne Barilier's "The 'American Dream'" (the title of this anthology was taken from this text), to excerpts from Urs Jaeggi's novel *Brandeis*, which reflects both American brutality and the dreams and hopes during the student revolution of 1968 and the Vietnam War.

The original basis and inspiration for this anthology was the conference on *Cultural Unity and Diversity. Switzerland After 700 Years* at the Max Kade Institute for Austrian-German-Swiss Studies at the University of Southern California in March 1991. The authors Franco Beltrametti, Nicolas Bouvier, Iso Camartin, Hanno Helbling, Hugo Loetscher, Daniel Odier and Flurin Spescha read from their own work and discussed the subject, "How Contemporary Swiss Literature Views the United States."

Except for Nicolas Bouvier, whose work deals more with Eastern Europe and Asia, all the authors participating in the conference have become part of the anthology. After this "core" selection, other authors who have dealt with the United States in their work and have spent time in the US were also included. Many of them, Eugen Gomringer, Hanna Johansen, Hugo Loetscher, Herbert Meier, Adolf Muschg, Walter Vogt, Urs Widmer, Etienne Barilier, Daniel Odier, and Iso Camartin, were Swiss Writers-in-Residence for one semester between 1978 and 1993 at USC's Max Kade German Center (since 1984 Max Kade Institute). Eveline Hasler, Peter Bichsel, and again Hugo Loetscher, either taught at the City University of New York and at other academic institutions in the US, or simply lived in this country for an extended period of time.

Apart from its specific theme, this anthology wishes to display the rich imagination and critical thought of truly *contemporary* Swiss literature. Max Frisch (1911-1991) and Friedrich Dürrenmatt (1921-1990), the "modern classics," are therefore represented only indirectly, i.e., in critical retrospects. Another potential candidate for the anthology, which might not escape the literary connoisseur, was the poet Plinio Martini (1923-) with his late novel *Il fondo del sacco* (1970). In this novel, the poverty-stricken peasants of the author's home valley are forced to emigrate to the United States. California, appearing as the promised land, cannot fulfill their collective dream. This theme, close though it seems to that of our anthology, is presented through a kind of "peasant realism" which belongs to an older literary tradition. We decided on this basis not to include this text in our collection.

The layout of this anthology is alphabetical by author within their respective language groups. The German-speaking authors from Peter Bichsel to Ueli Zingg forms the first and largest group, followed by French-speaking authors from Etienne Barilier to Yves Velan, the Romansch authors Iso Camartin and Flurin Spescha, and finally the only representative of the Italian-speaking part of Switzerland, Franco Beltrametti. He is also the only poet represented with lyrical poetry, which is justified since the lyrical element in Italian-Swiss literature is clearly predominant. All the texts in the anthology are printed with special permission by the authors or their heirs. Previously published texts were reprinted by permission of the respective publishers, who also provided most of the photographs. We would like to thank the following publishing houses: Suhrkamp Verlag, Luchterhand Literaturverlag, Verlag Nagel & Kimche, Diogenes Verlag AG, Benziger Verlag AG, Huber Verlag, Zytglogge Verlag, Dimension, Random House, Editions Bestil Galland, Geiger, In de Knipscheer, Luxembourg, Grosseteste Books, Vehicle Editions, Cervo Volante, Coffee House Press, Coyote's Journal, and Poetics Journal.

If there is no translator mentioned at the end of the text, this indicates that the selection was originally written in English.

Cornelius Schnauber, Los Angeles
Hans Schulte (general editor)

Acknowledgements

This anthology was made possible through a generous grant by the cultural agency PRO HELVETIA, Switzerland. We also thank SwissAir, Los Angeles, for their support.

The United States in the Work of
Max Frisch

Romey Sabalius
Utah State University

S ome scholars have pointed out that no other contemporary German speaking writers have concerned themselves so intensively
with America as has Max Frisch.[1] Although this might be an exag-
geration and a claim hard to verify, there is no doubt that the United
States is an important motif in Frisch's work. But departing from his
frequent use of motifs as fixed patterns of recognition,[2] the image of
the United States undergoes a significant change. Frisch visited the
United States several times. In 1951/52, on the occasion of his first
trip as a recipient of a Rockefeller Grant for Drama, he stayed in
North America for an entire year. In 1956, he returned to the United
States and Mexico and this time also went to Cuba. In the early
1970s, he spent several winters in New York, and in the 1980s, he
even established temporary residency there. Frisch also travelled
extensively within the United States. He was not only very familiar
with New York, but also visited Chicago, California, Texas, Colorado,
the Midwest, and the Southwest. Therefore his depiction of the
United States is not limited to New York City, which, in the writings
of many German speaking authors, functions as *pars par toto*.[3]

Frisch's experiences on the other continent had a direct impact on
his literary work. *Stiller, Homo faber,* and *Montauk,* books in which
America plays an important role, were all completed after one of his
longer overseas stays. In each of these three narratives, the United
States is described in a different manner. Still, they share one common aspect. Critics agree that the depiction of America in these books
does not correspond to American reality or, for that matter, to the
view Frisch has of America.[4] The author merely uses descriptions of

the New World as a means to illustrate the process of self-realization of his protagonists.[5] Although the portrayal of the foreign society is often very detailed, seemingly object-oriented, and sometimes fairly accurate, its main function is to reveal the emotional state of the respective hero. Since much scholarly work has been done on Frisch's use of the image of America in his literary work, this article will provide only a brief overview of the different ways in which America is presented in the aforementioned books. It will then focus on an analysis of Frisch's essays and the *Tagebuch 1966-1971*, in which America is described per se and not in order to mirror the inner self of a literary figure. The study will conclude with a summary of Frisch's position as presented in his video-taped conversation *Gespräche im Alter*, which can be taken as his last word on the United States.

In *Stiller*, the episodes situated in America are quite lengthy. The imprisoned Stiller, alias White, reports on his experiences in the New World. Here, America clearly functions as the realm of escapism. Stiller tries to break away from Swiss society, which he experiences as narrowing his personal growth and freedom of development; there is a strong analogy between Switzerland and Stiller's prison cell. Most of all, he wants to free himself from the expectations of others and escape the image they have made of him.[6] America clearly functions as an antipode to Switzerland. There, Anatol Stiller, changing his name to James Larkin White, can develop his own personality free from society's restrictions and the predetermined expectations of his Swiss compatriots. Obviously, the picture of America presented by Stiller/White is as one-sided as his criticism of Switzerland. To him, the United States is literally the land of unlimited possibilities. Stiller/White narrates various stories in which he assumes the roles of a cowboy, a murderer, a playboy, and even associates himself with the characters of fictional stories such as Rip van Winkle. The United States seems in every way the opposite of the restrictive Swiss society: the country is immense in its geographic expanse and variety, the people are friendly and still possess a naive vitality — the latter becomes especially apparent in the author's depiction of African-Americans — and the protagonist is under no social obligations whatsoever.[7]

Although Stiller's stories often contain very realistic observations and descriptions of the American country and its people, they are always tailored to project his "inner landscape."[8] A well-known example is Stiller/White's discovery of the Carlsbad Caverns, convincingly interpreted as an analogy to the model of self-realization according to the psychology of Carl Gustav Jung.[9] It is not always apparent in the belletristic works themselves how the sometimes very authentically drawn picture of the New World differs from the real impressions the author has gained. A good case in point is the representation of Mexico. In the novel *Stiller*, Mexico seems to be an elysian land, largely untouched by civilization, and abounding with the wonders of nature. This idyllic depiction is only one side of the author's impression of that country. In his essay *Orchideen und Aasgeier: Ein Reisealbum aus Mexiko*, Frisch describes his ambivalent feelings, alternating between fascination and disgust — an ambivalence that is very well represented in the essay's title. One can conclude that the image of America in *Stiller*, although sometimes very realistic and often even resembling an authentic travel report, has a largely aesthetic function within the context of the literary work and is therefore very selective and one-sided. The projections of life in America have to be regarded as artistic means and cannot be taken as an attempt to accurately describe the other continent.[10]

In *Homo faber*, America again functions as an antipode. This time it is not opposed to Switzerland, but to Europe in general. Unlike Stiller, who tries to escape from a specific role in order to be true to himself, Walter Faber adopts a rigid behavioral pattern to establish his identity. To define his position in life, he chooses the role of a technician. An engineer by profession, he decides to acknowledge only those facts in life that are calculable, thereby creating the illusion that he is in control of his destiny. Faber, a Swiss by birth, subsequently settles in the United States, namely in New York, the epitome of hypercivilization. In contrast, Europe is perceived as the Old World: historical and mythological, which from Faber's point of view translates as archaic and irrational. While Faber is working for UNESCO, shaping the future of underdeveloped countries, his counterpart and ex-fiancée Hanna, an archeologist in Athens, is trying to preserve the past. These polarizations already indicate that, just as in *Stiller*, Frisch merely deals with models. Objectivity is not the author's goal in either the depiction of Europe or the "American Way of Life." Frisch's narrating protagonist describes only selected facets of his life which correspond to certain stereotypes that help expose the respective one-sidedness of his perceptions. In as much as Faber's perspective of the United States is very narrow — his life does not reach beyond the circles of the upper middle class in Manhattan — he only experiences a very limited part of Europe as well, thoughtfully selected by the author. The future-oriented Faber travels back in time on two different levels. With regard to civilization, his journey leads him from the United States via Paris (the Louvre), the south of France (the Papal palace and the Roman aqueduct), and ancient Rome (the Via Appia) back to Greece (the cradle of Western civilization).[11] On the personal level, his affair with the twenty year old Sabeth evokes the pleasures of his youth when he was with Hanna. To a degree, he also assumes the role of a parent toward her, without being aware that he is indeed her father; a responsibility he had tried to avoid at an earlier age. This journey is analogous to Faber's inner development. He evolves from the engineer living in New York who opposes concepts of predestined fate and superstitions into a man who is entangled in mythological concepts and who dies of stomach cancer in the Old World. Faber's perception of America reflects his change in attitude. His initial resentment of Central America and his arrogance toward its ancient civilization is later substituted by the likewise unreflective admiration of the vitality and naturalness of life in Cuba. There, he also expresses his strongest criticism of the "American Way of Life:"

> Their ugliness in comparison with people like these here, their pink sausage skin, horrible, they only live because there is penicillin, that's all, the fuss they make as though they were happy because they are Americans, because they have no inhibition, and yet they are only gawky and noisy — fellows like Dick, who I have taken as a model! — the way they stand around, their left hands in their trouser pockets, their shoulders leaning against the wall, their glass in the other hand, easy-going, the protectors of mankind, their back-slapping, their optimism until they are drunk and then hysterical weeping, sell-out of the White race, their vacuum between their loins. My anger with myself! (4: 176)[12]

Early critics of the book recognized a positive development in Faber,[13] who believes that in Cuba, he was able to open his eyes and see life as it is supposed to be. Later, however, scholars have pointed out that Faber only goes from one extreme to the other.[14] Just as his perceptions of the United States, Central America, and Europe were limited by one-sided stereotypes in the first place, at the end of the book, he has completed a 180 degree turn and is captured in equally dubious clichés. Neither his initial affirmative stance toward the United States as the promoter of progress and civilization, nor his harsh criticism of the "American Way of Life" later on, can be taken as a rational evaluation with a certain degree of objectivity.[15] Instead, Frisch clearly exposes and ridicules superficial judgements and stereotypical perceptions about America and Europe.

While *Stiller* and *Homo faber* were published only three years apart, *Montauk*, the next belletristic narrative in which the United States serves as the setting, was published in 1975, two decades after the earlier novels. Therefore it is not surprising that the depiction of the United States in this book differs substantially from the images in the previous novels, which resemble one another to a great extent. In *Montauk*, written after Frisch had already lived overseas for a longer period of time — as compared to the travels that preceded the work on his earlier two books — the United States seems to have lost all of its fascination and potential for adventure. Frisch's description of the American environment is rather subdued and nothing extraordinary happens.[16] With references in the work limited to New York City and Long Island, the United States serves as an appropriate background against which the main character Max, clearly an autobiographical figure, can develop a relationship with the young American woman Lynn.

Once again, America appears in contrast to the more romantic but memory-laden places in Europe, as that part of the world where the protagonist Max can free himself from restraining images. In the company of Lynn, who has never read anything about the world-famous author and therefore has no prefigured conceptions about him as a private person, he feels at ease and is able to behave without the pressure of confining himself to her expectations. He even tries to convey opinions contrary to those he has held earlier in his life: "Since Lynn has read none of my writings, I enjoy, for once, saying the exact opposite" (6: 635). He is relieved of the constantly felt pressure to play his role and able to enjoy the present, reminisce about his past, and act uninhibitedly. He enjoys full independence not only from his past, but also in regard to the future. His behavior will not have any lasting consequences, since it is understood that his relationship with Lynn is just a temporary one. Memories of her, unlike those of other women in the protagonist's life — Max's difficulties in his relationship with women are the major theme of his reflections on his past — will not be reminders of his guilt. Paradoxically, the communication barrier, introduced by Max's inability to make himself sufficiently understood in the foreign language, also benefits their relationship. It reduces the expectation of both partners of fully comprehending and completely understanding each other. Silence between the two is possible without pretext and awkwardness, and when communicating, Max has the feeling that he is saying everything for the first time. His expressions seem honest and unique, since he has not yet experienced stereotypical and prefigured speech in English. Furthermore, intensified reflection, a necessary part of communication in a foreign language, enables Max to arrange and select his thoughts more consciously.[17] Again, the America locale is a very important factor, because it provides the necessary framework for the inner development of the main character.

It can be concluded that in his literary work, Frisch artistically uses stereotypes of the United States to develop his story. Images of or attitudes toward America mirror the protagonist's inner self, or are at least used to establish the conditions for the protagonist's self-portrayal. They are functionalized within the context of the literary work and should not be taken as representations of America as such.[18]

Frisch has expressed his thoughts on the United States in non-belletristic writing as well. The essays *Unsere Arroganz gegenüber Amerika, Cum grano salis: Eine kleine Glosse zur schweizerischen Architektur*, and *Begegnung mit Negern: Eindrücke aus Amerika*, as well as large parts of his *Tagebuch 1966-1971*[19] deal with the author's experiences on the foreign continent. As in Frisch's literary work, a dichotomy of his American impressions is evident. Three articles appearing in rapid succession in the early 1950s stand in opposition to a lengthier examination of American problems within the broader context of his *Tagebuch 1966-1971*, which was published almost two decades later. His evaluations of the United States during these two different periods contrast strongly with each other.

His essay *Unsere Arroganz gegenüber Amerika* projects a total affirmation of the society he encountered there. In the beginning of his article, Frisch questions the judgments passed on this country with the argument that America (i.e., the United States) is too vast and too complex to be described in a few sentences:

> America is not a country in the European sense of the term, but a continent, not inhabited by one people, but by a migration of peoples that is far from being completed, and we dare to talk about America only within the first weeks. (3: 222)

He further points out that the more one gets to know this country, the more enigmatic and contradictory it seems to appear, indicating that he himself, who has spent as much as a year in North America, is fully aware of how difficult it is to pass valid judgements. Although, since World War II, people in Europe seem to know more about the United States than ever before, Frisch feels that the prejudices have not diminished at all, but instead have grown even sharper.[20] He assumes the Europeans' criticism of the United States is so intense due to the uneasiness of being dominated by the new world power. What frightens him in particular is the fact that this observation does not apply only to the average individual, but to intellectuals as well. "'You have spent a whole year in America?' ... 'How could you stand it?'" (3: 223) he quotes one of their standard phrases. Frisch further points out that since the United States has surpassed Europe in the economic and technical fields, the arrogance of the Europeans is focused solely on cultural aspects. But even there, he maintains, the American accomplishments are comparable and may even surpass those of the Europeans. He cites the excellent libraries, the lively museums, the contemporary literature, the scholarly activities and the devotion to music. The difference, he sums it up, is that in the United States the *"Bildungsspießertum"* (3: 224), the "petit bourgeois mentality in the cultural field," does not exist. There is no cultural middle class, which plays such an important role in European societies. Frisch follows up by questioning the legitimacy of measuring a nation's cultural achievements by the standard of its average citizen. At the same time, he enjoys the unpretentiousness of the Americans when dealing with culture. The often exaggerated respect for culture in Europe is not so pronounced in the New World, since it is the practical value of things that is held more highly. Frisch admits the anachronism of this phenomenon, originating in the lifestyle of the pioneers, which was governed by the exigencies of daily survival and left room for culture only in the form of entertainment. Yet he predicts that the next step of a developed United States, with its secure and established lifestyle, will be concentrated on "the conquest of leisure" (3: 227).

Frisch characterizes the relationship between the United States and Europe as being determined by a mutual inferiority complex. While Americans are envious of the European past, Europeans in turn see the United States shaping the present and the future. He compares the situation to a father-son-relationship with similarities in expectations as well as in disappointments and attitudes. But the son, in the meantime, has grown up, and the United States has surpassed the old continent in what Frisch calls "das Zivilisatorische" (3: 228), "the level of civilization," and he draws a second analogy:

> Americans are to Europe what Romans were to old Athens, a colony advancing to world power. Rome too had attained a high level of civilization, in the construction of roads and aqueducts, but Greece remained important — important in its intellectual assets, although they were undergoing change. It certainly was nearly impossible for the Greeks to recognize and acknowledge anything like a Roman culture. But it existed nevertheless. (3: 228)

Not specifically depicting North America, but clearly with impressions of Mexico and the United States in mind, Frisch wrote the article *Cum grano salis: Eine kleine Glosse zur schweizerischen Architektur*, published in the same year as the previous essay. Returning from his year-long stay overseas, he observes his hometown through the eyes of a stranger. Previously quite ordinary and unremarkable features, to which he never paid attention while living in Zürich, suddenly become the focus of his observations. He is astonished that everything seems to be much smaller and he notices the neatness, diligence, and seriousness in the design of the buildings, as evident in the care given to the very last decorative detail. Still, despite the superb quality of that architecture, Frisch, an architect himself, cannot generate enthusiasm for it. He complains about its restraint and unwillingness to take risks. He is disturbed by the mediocrity, which, he believes, is the result of the conservative Swiss mentality, and laments that striving for greatness is even regarded with suspicion and characterized as "un-Swiss" (3: 231).[22] Frisch goes on to diagnose the impotence of Swiss fantasy and he draws a comparison similar to his evaluation of culture on the two continents:

> Truly, our average is higher. But isn't the average, proclaimed as a goal, necessarily somewhat pitiful, stale, numb? (3: 235)

Switzerland does not plan for the future, but likes to indulge itself in its traditional past — "the Swiss desire to live in the 19th century," (3: 240) as Frisch calls it.[23] But tradition, says the author, also requires us to rise to the challenges of our time with the same courage as our ancestors did in their respective era: "Everything else is imitation. Or mummification" (3: 237). The aforementioned perfect finish of Swiss buildings and their elaboration in the detail is disregarded by Frisch as a "retreat into detail" (3: 232), functioning as a form of compensation for their lack of greatness. Switzerland, he concludes, is not a pioneer country but a country of watchmakers:

> Relatively soon, the home-comer longs again for the rougher, yet more generous and free, unsentimental and masculine-daring architecture of a pioneer country with all its mishaps. (3: 232)

This essay, as the title *Cum grano salis* suggests, should not be taken too literally. It is based on the same concept that Frisch has applied in his earlier novels: the exciting and progressive United States with its quest for grandeur is contrasted with the restrictiveness, pettiness, and the lack of enthusiasm in Switzerland. In Frisch's literary work, readers, who recognized the author's use of stereotypes to stress the different states of mind of his fictional heroes, were cautioned not to confuse poetic and empirical reality. In his essays, the author's enthusiasm and his fresh impressions of the New World certainly led him to exaggerated praise on the one hand and to harsh criticism on the other. Although they point out the differences in mentality very well, these essays reveal more about Frisch himself than about his objects of observation and therefore cannot be taken as adequate representations of the United States either.

In his essay *Begegnung mit Negern: Eindrücke aus Amerika* Frisch reports about problematic aspects of life in the United States. He describes the ghettos, the poverty of African Americans, and the ongoing discrimination. He tells the story of an African-American student, an athlete at a predominantly Caucasian university, who is aware that he functions as a token student to create the illusion of equal opportunity. After citing several examples of discrimination, Frisch laments "the scorn of justice on paper, the facade of democracy, the hypocrisy in not admitting what is being done and not to do what is repeatedly proclaimed as the ideal..." (3: 254). He describes African American pessimism, which is generated by the belief that change is not taking place. He further illustrates the vicious cycle of the ghetto. African Americans are being forced to live in the run-down parts of the cities for reasons of poverty or because other neighborhoods are inaccessible to them. According to Frisch, they will necessarily have to adjust to life in the gutter and will eventually start to believe that the gutter is appropriate for them. They will accept it as their destiny, thereby creating a self-fulfilling prophecy. The author tries hard to understand African Americans. He makes efforts to initiate personal contact and attends an all-African American religious service as well as a meeting of the African American revolutionary leader Paul Robeson. But despite all his attempts — he even, coincidentally or not, rented an apartment on the fringes of Harlem — a certain awkwardness remains:

> On the street itself, in the glimmer of city lights, I have never experi-
> enced abuse, despite being the only White all around, instead, plen-
> ty of friendly directions ... nevertheless, I don't deny that, one does
> walk somewhat faster than usual. (3: 245-46)

In addition to this inexplicable fear, a certainly well intended over-cautiousness in his social behavior toward African Americans makes him act differently than he would among Caucasians:

> I can only say: if I happen to be the only White, let's say, in a crowd
> in a small foyer, I notice that I consciously have to suppress an in-
> stinctive courtesy; if I picked up the dropped handkerchief of a Ne-
> gro lady — there wouldn't be any shooting, no, only looks; it would

be regarded as a reciprocal arrogance, as the master's condescension. (3: 246)

Apart from this awkwardness, more questionable prejudices surface in his perception of African Americans. Although Frisch tries to express his admiration for what he perceives as their vitality and ability to dance and move gracefully, his praise appears to be generated by a condescending stereotype. His repeated comparisons of African Americans to wild animals or naive children are disturbing.[24] He describes the aforementioned African-American religious service as follows:

... screams, such as in the jungle, howling, as one imagines the grace of cannibals, the shrieking of hundreds of voices going crazy, deafening, wild and savage like at a stock exchange. (3: 248)

Similar comparisons can be found in Faber's description of Cuba and in some passages in *Stiller*. But what seems to be legitimate in literature, within a given context loaded with symbolic meaning and, in particular, from the point of view of an unbalanced hero, appears to be rather problematic in a supposedly more objective essay. Equally questionable is Frisch's repeated assumption and regret that African Americans actually would like to deny their skin color and strive to be like Caucasians, both by means of make-up that lightens their skin and in the way they dress and behave. He concludes his observation of a garden party given by his African American neighbors as follows:

Nothing more actually happened — according to our understanding — the boring conventional, the caricature-like imitation of a White bourgeois atmosphere, which has not the faintest idea of Africa and immediate life, that especially was (I reckon) what they regarded as the event; in a more boring and conventional manner could it not have taken place in a White family either, that was what gave them such great satisfaction. (3: 252)

Obviously, the author expects a certain African American behavior, which is based on stereotypes and prejudices generated by his questionable, at best naive and romantic conception of Africa and his vague idea of a supposedly unalienated vitality.[25] Despite his certainly sincere attempts, a true encounter with African Americans — as the title promises (the German word *Begegnung* can imply understanding) — could not be achieved.

Frisch's essays were written in the early 1950s, when the United States enjoyed a period of wealth and success. The country's economy was expanding, Americans were setting the pace in technological progress for the rest of the Western world, and the nation was very self-confident. But the late 1960s and the beginning of the 1970s, the period covered by Frisch's *Tagebuch 1966-1971*, presented a society that had been completely changed. The Vietnam War was escalating, student protest was at its height, the civil rights movement seemed to become more militant after the assassination of Martin Luther King, and crime in the streets increased at a frightening rate. Consequently, Frisch's impressions are rather grim. He presumes the nation's collective guilt in the assassination of Martin Luther King and regards the Vietnam War not as an avoidable political mistake, but as a necessary consequence of the existing ideology. He refers to the war as genocide and reports about atrocities and war crimes, which were brought to the public's attention. To illustrate the social situation within the United States he cites the following example:

> In 1966, according to official reports, 14,000 babies and small children have been bitten by rats in America's slums. A proposal granting 40 million dollars in federal support in the war against rats was cut. One day of war in Vietnam costs 79.795 million dollars. (6: 124)[26]

These issues were, of course, common topics in public discussions in the United States as well as in Europe, and few German speaking intellectuals have not voiced their criticism.[27] But probably no one was able to gain as much immediate insight as Frisch did: into everyday life on the streets, the opinions among academics, and even into the power structure and the realms of the decision makers of the United States.

Unlike many other German-speaking authors, Frisch, with great modesty, strives to comprehend the viewpoint of the people responsible for the course of political action. But even a visit to the White House does not provide the desired understanding. His account of that event, which took place only two days after the invasion of Cambodia, shows his perplexity about the normality and unpretentiousness of the White House's interior as well as the casual behavior of its staff; a place, after all, where decisions about life and death, the destiny of entire nations, and the politics that influence the whole world are made on a daily basis. During his conversation with Henry Kissinger, Frisch contemplates how those decisions of the utmost importance are made and how the individual in charge is able to deal with the immense burden of responsibility. Two remarks by Kissinger can be quoted to summarize the answers to those questions, which Frisch actually never dared to voice: "Cynicals have never built a cathedral [sic]" (6: 276) and that "he rather endures responsibility than helplessness" (6: 284); explanations that do not help much in reducing Frisch's irritation and leave his quest for insight unsatisfied. This experience repeats itself during his visit at an executive meeting on Wall Street, the other pole of power and decision making in the United States. Frisch seems to realize his limitations in gaining a more comprehensive understanding. He refrains from criticizing the executives or Kissinger as individuals. He recognizes that a certain immunity is necessary on a level of such inflated responsibility:

> A person who makes decision or recommends decisions that affect millions of people cannot afford afterward to have doubts whether these decisions were right; the decision has been made, one has to wait and see what will follow. (6: 283)

The sentence "One could tell a joke right now, but I cannot think of any," which directly follows the previous reflection made during the conversation with Kissinger, clearly displays the author's uneasiness and his inability to appropriately deal with the situation in which he finds himself.

By the time Frisch's *Tagebuch 1966-1971* was published in 1972, he already had considerable knowledge of life in the United States. He had spent extended periods of time in the country not only as a visitor and traveller, but also many months as a temporary resident in New York. His fascination with and admiration for the United States, generated by the new and overwhelming impressions of his first encounter, had begun to fade and give way to a sense of the routine and the banality of everyday life. At this point, Frisch is able and willing to focus his attention increasingly on the problematic aspects of American society. The reader might be astonished by the contrast between Frisch's earlier and his later image of the United States. This change can certainly not be explained by the country's social and political development within these 15-20 years alone. After all, the early 1950s had been the time of the Korean War and McCarthyism. Despite his intense criticism, Frisch believes that the United States has changed for the better. He now finds a healthy self-criticism among Americans, as opposed to their complacency and self-righteousness in the 1950s. In his view, their skepticism about the direction in which their country is heading and the fact that they are starting to fear their own nation makes them more human and leaves him with hope for a better future.

But all positive aspects seem to have vanished by the 1980s. In a video-taped conversation entitled *Gespräche im Alter*,[28] Frisch laments that Americans, including most of the intellectuals, are largely apolitical. He perceives the Reagan era as a rebellion of the Californian farmer against East Coast intellectualism. The questionable over-simplification of this thesis aside, Frisch does not seem to realize that he now condemns what he had earlier so enthusiastically praised, namely the unpretentiousness and the practical attitude of the American pioneer spirit. In the increasing resentment toward the cultural dominance of New York, which is, according to Frisch, dominated by the American Jewry, he senses a latent anti-Semitism. Frisch further criticizes the willingness to fight a war (on foreign soil, of course) rather than deal with an economic recession. All these phenomena, combined with a rising nationalism, lead Frisch to talk of a "Californian fascism" and to repeatedly compare the course of politics in the United States with German National Socialism.[29] Still, he claims not to be anti-American, but to simply voice political criticism.

In conclusion, it can be stated that Frisch was overly affirmative in his judgement about American society in his earlier essays, while his later criticism often seems to be too harsh. The high hopes he had initially placed on the New World led to an equally intense disappointment and embitterment.[30] In this polarization, Frisch embodies the two elements that characterize the attitudes of post-war German literature toward the United States in general: the utopian and the dystopian, which are not often, as they are here, united in one and the same author.

NOTES

1. Cf. Sigrid Mayer, "Zur Funktion der Amerikakomponente im Erzählwerk Max Frischs," *Max Frisch: Aspekte des Prosawerks*, ed. Gerhard P. Knapp (Bern: Lang, 1971) 205. Also Anita Krätzer, *Studien zum Amerikabild in der neueren deutschen Literatur: Max Frisch - Uwe Johnson - Hans Magnus Enzensberger und das "Kursbuch"* (Frankfurt: Lang, 1982) 21.

2. Cf. Walter Schmitz, *Max Frisch: Das Werk (1931-1961): Studien zu Tradition und Traditionsverarbeitung* (Bern: Lang, 1985) 129.

3. Cf. Heinz D. Osterle, "The Lost Utopia: New Images of America in German Literature," *The German Quarterly* 4 (1981): 443. He points out that in the depiction of American society German authors "concentrated too much on New York to the exclusion of most other cities, not to mention the vast outlying areas where the majority of people live. New York has long been an irresistible magnet for visiting Europeans because there they could have enthusiastic visions of the future or, more recently, receive a profound shock over all the ills of society which are concentrated here." Osterle goes on to question the representativeness of New York for the United States as a whole.

4. Cf. Koepke's analysis of Frisch's ironic use of projection, image making, and stereotypes: Wulf Koepke, "Max Frisch's America: Between Dream and Reality," *Amerika! New Images in German Literature*, ed. Heinz D. Osterle (New York: Lang, 1989) 135-147.

5. Cf., among others, Walter Hinderer, "'Ein Gefühl der Fremde': Amerikaperspektiven bei Max Frisch," *Amerika in der deutschen Literatur: Neue Welt - Nordamerika - USA*, eds. Sigrid Bauschinger, Horst Denkler, and Wilfried Malsch (Stuttgart: Reclam, 1975) 358-359.

6. Since his *Tagebuch 1946-1949*, the secularized image taboo ("Du sollst Dir kein Bildnis machen") plays a predominant role in Frisch's work. The image, generally associated with inflexible expectations, limits people in their understanding of each other. It is the main reason for miscommunication between partners and leads to tragic results.

7. It is noteworthy that it is not only Stiller who seeks self-fulfillment in the United States. Also Sibylle, the wife of Stiller's prosecutor and friend Rolf, moves, or rather flees, to New York for the same reason. Unlike Stiller, she has been successful in her attempt to be self-reliant, to define her own identity, and to gain self-confidence. Not coincidentally, her experiences reflect everyday life in the United States more realistically.

8. Cf. Wulf Koepke, *Understanding Max Frisch* (Columbia, U of South Carolina Press, 1991) 133: "Frisch the writer is not much interested in designing landscapes. He does not show the views that his characters see. Landscape comes into focus in connection with human actions."

9. Cf. Gunda Lusser-Mertelsmann, "Die Höhlengeschichte als symbolische Darstellung der Wiedergeburt," *Materialien zu Max Frisch "Stiller"*, ed. Walter

Schmitz (Frankfurt: Suhrkamp, 1978) 165-172. Also Schmitz 250.

10. Cf. Hinderer 353: "Amerikabild und Amerikavorstellungen erweisen sich dergestalt immer wieder als Fiktionen, die mehr über die Urheber solcher Bilder und Vorstellungen aussagen als über das in Frage stehende Objekt." Also Krätzer 34. In his introduction, Ensberg strongly criticizes the attempt to read poetic reality against the backdrop of empirical reality: Peter Ensberg, *Das Bild New Yorks in der deutschsprachigen Gegenwartsliteratur* (Heidelberg: Winter, 1988) 1-7.

11. Cf. Gerd Müller, "Europa und Amerika im Werk Max Frischs: Eine Interpretation des 'Berichts Homo faber,'" *Moderna Sprak* 4 (1968): 397. During that trip, Faber, the man of modern technology, resorts to increasingly primitive modes of transportation: cf. Frederik A. Lubich, *Max Frisch: "Stiller", "Homo faber" und "Mein Name sei Gantenbein"* (München: Fink, 1990) 51.

12. All quotes have been translated by the author of this article and are taken from the following edition: Max Frisch, *Gesammelte Werke*, 6 vols. (Frankfurt: Suhrkamp, 1976).

13. Müller; also Günther Bicknese, "Zur Rolle Amerikas in Max Frischs 'Homo Faber,'" *The German Quarterly* 1 (1969): 52-64.

14. Lubich 50; Mayer 227; also Mona Knapp and Gerhard P. Knapp, *Max Frisch: Homo faber* (Frankfurt: Diesterweg, 1987) 74-75, and Walter Schmitz, *Max Frisch: "Homo faber": Materialien, Kommentar* (München: Hanser, 3rd ed., 1984) 60-61.

15. Paul Michael Lützeler, "Vom Wunschtraum zum Alptraum: Zum Bild der USA in der deutschsprachigen Gegenwartsliteratur," *Weimar am Pazifik: Literarische Wege zwischen den Kontinenten*, eds. Dieter Borchmeyer and Till Heimeran (Tübingen: 1985), p. 179: "Frisch setzt nicht einfach Europa gegen Amerika, Kultur gegen Technik, homo ludens gegen homo faber, sondern warnt vor der Verabsolutierung aller dieser Lebenshaltungen. Weder in der Überrationalisierung im System der Technik noch im Sichausliefern an das Unbewußte der Natur liegt für ihn die Lösung."

16. Mayer 232: "Auch die Manifestationen amerikanischen Lebens bieten offenbar nichts Bemerkenswertes mehr, bestenfalls Erinnerungen an frühere Besuche. Alles erscheint neutral, routinemäßig, kaum zur Teilnahme auffordernd. Kein ungewöhnliches Ereignis, das Beachtung verdiente, durchbricht den Alltagsbetrieb, der unter dem Zeichen gewohnheitsmäßiger Wiederholung steht."

17. Mayer: "... d.h. die Fremdsprache wird weniger als Kommunikationsmittel erfahren, denn als eine Art Widerstand, an dem die eigenen Gedankengänge sich klären; letztlich also als Mittel der Selbstanalyse." Cf. also Mayer's excellent summary of the significance of the foreign language situation (234-235).

18. Hinderer (354) has recommended that one should talk about perspec-

tives on America and not about an image of America in Frisch's work.

19. Within the context of this article, Frisch's *Tagebuch 1966-1971* is placed into the category of non-belletristic writings since the passages dealing with the United States are best characterized as reportage.

20. This is a phenomenon that scholars have observed among German authors as well. Cf. Gabriela Wettberg, *Das Amerika-Bild und seine negativen Konstanten in der deutschen Nachkriegsliteratur* (Heidelberg: Winter, 1987) 12-13: "... so eröffneten sich mit zunehmender Einsicht in die Fülle des Materials nicht etwa die erwarteten kaleidoskopischen Perspektiven, den amerikanischen Kontinent in seiner Weite und Vielschichtigkeit reflektierend, ja nicht einmal Ambivalenzgefühle, die sich aus den obrigen kontrastierenden Sichtrastern ergeben könnten, dominierten, sondern eine stark verengte Optik trat zutage. Zwar entspricht den vermehrten Kontakten deutschsprachiger Schriftsteller mit Amerika (den Vereinigten Staaten) eine Vielzahl einschlägiger Werke, aber der weitaus größte Anteil weist einseitige Überzeichnungen des Amerika-Bildes auf, die nicht als Teilperspektiven eines sogenannten ausgewogenen Ganzen eingeordnet werden dürfen." Also Wilfried Malsch, "Vom Vorbild zum Schreckbild: Politische USA-Vorstellungen deutscher Schriftsteller von Thomas Mann bis zu Reinhard Lettau," *Die USA und Deutschland: Wechselseitige Spiegelungen in der Literatur der Gegenwart*, ed. Wolfgang Paulsen (Bern: Francke, 1976) 29-51.

21. In his *Sätze aus Amerika*, Friedrich Dürrenmatt also compared the United States with ancient Rome, but, later than Frisch, in 1970, with the empire that had already reached its peak and got entangled in ever increasing problems: Friedrich Dürrenmatt, *Gesammelte Werke*, 7 vols. (Zürich: Diogenes, 1988) 6: 732.

22. The fact that not one building by Le Corbusier, the most innovative and celebrated Swiss architect, is located in Switzerland seems to underline Frisch's reproach.

23. Since the 1950s, Swiss society has been chastised repeatedly by its intellectuals for its regressive attitude; most intensely on the occasion of the *Landesausstellung* in 1964 and the 700-Year-Celebration in 1991.

24. Cf. Musgrave's critical analysis of Frisch's portrayal of African-Americans: Marian E. Musgrave, "Die Evolution der Figur des Negers in den Werken von Max Frisch," ed. Schmitz 201-207.

25. Musgrave (204) points out that Frisch reacts in a positive fashion only to the unfamiliar and exotic features in the lives of African-Americans and fails to recognize the normality of their class typical behavior.

26. For a more detailed summary of Frisch's criticism of the United States (on approximately 70 of the 400 pages within the *Tagebuch 1966-1971*) cf. Alfred L. Cobbs, *The Image of America in Postwar German Literature: Reflections and Perceptions* (Bern: Lang, 1982) 119-126.

27. Cf. Wettberg 17; also Osterle 442, who adds: "It must be remembered

that they were not only a response to the crisis of this country but also an expression of the partial radicalization of German literature during that time."

28. *Max Frisch: Gespräche im Alter*, videotape by Philippe Pilliod (Zürich: Ammann, 1987).

29. In twentieth-century German literature, the American system has often been accused of being fascist or, at least, of displaying fascist tendencies. Cf., among others, Malsch 32-33.

30. Cf. Heinz D. Osterle, ed., *Bilder von Amerika: Gespräche mit deutschen Schriftstellern* (Münster: Englisch Amerikanische Studien, 1987) 239.

The (Absence of the) United States in the Work of Friedrich Dürrenmatt

Gene O. Stimpson
Los Angeles

Spiritual enlightenment is inefficient
— if it is not political, too.
Friedrich Dürrenmatt (28: 122)[1]

L ike Max Frisch, Friedrich Dürrenmatt, too, visited the United States on a number of occasions. In May 1959, he came for the very first time and visited New York. Ten years later, in November 1969, he returned to the United States when Temple University in Philadelphia bestowed an honorary doctorate upon him. This time, he stayed for two months traveling from Philadelphia to Florida, Yucatan in Mexico, the Caribbean Islands, Jamaica, Puerto Rico, and New York. His third and final trip to the United States took him to Los Angeles where he spent four months as a Writer in Residence at the University of Southern California.

Unlike Max Frisch, however, Friedrich Dürrenmatt never gave the United States or her people a prominent part in either his prose or his dramatic works. The question is why, and the answer is obvious. At least, it was obvious to one of my students in London who once pointed out to me that Friedrich Dürrenmatt simply did not like the United States. At the time, we were discussing *The Visit*, probably Friedrich Dürrenmatt's most famous play. Claire Zachanassian, the protagonist in *The Visit* returns to her Swiss home village a rich lady, having left it years ago a poor girl. The people of Güllen expect her as a benefactor who has already donated a hospital, a kindergarten, and a church to other Swiss communities.

She, with all her money. She owns Armenian Oil, Western Railways,
the Northern Broadcasting Company and the red-light district in
Bangkok. (5: 15)

Güllen, her birth place, on the other hand is totally bankrupt, having
sold one of its last assets, her *Heimatmuseum*, to America three years
ago and it blames its fate on the Freemasons, the Jews, High Finance, and International Communism.

Since Claire Zachanassian only returns to have her former lover
assassinated, my student proclaimed that she had obviously adopted
her wickedness in the United States. My student simply assumed
the United States to be the country in which Claire had spent most
of her time over the past 40 years and where she had made her
billion-dollar-fortune, although Claire herself states:

Then you got married to Mathilde Blumhard and me to the old
Zachanassian with his billions from Armenia. He had found me in a
brothel in Hamburg. (5: 37)

So, her money is not American but Armenian. She or one of her
numerous late husbands seems to have invested capital in the United
States — Western Railways might give the impression— however,
they have obviously spread their wealth across a number of countries
and continents. There is a second referral to the United States: when
Claire arrives she is carried around by two sedan-bearers described
by Dürrenmatt as two chewing gum chewing monsters and by Claire
as :

Two crooks from Manhattan, awaiting the electric chair in Sing-
Sing. Due to my intercession released to bear my sedan-chair. Cost
me a million dollars each intercession. (5: 31)

She might have spent some time in the United States, but then she
might have been in Marrakech to get the black panther that travels
with her. As she says she has traveled extensively and lived in a
number of different places with a number of different husbands.
Nowhere in the play does it actually say that she spent most of her
days in the United States. There is, of course, that stereotype in the
Old World that the United States is the land of opportunity, the place
where Europeans are expected to go and make money; with this in
mind and with his presupposition that capitalism corrupts people,
my student simply read into the play what he had expected to read.

Dürrenmatt himself, however, wrote about Claire:

> Claire Zachanassian represents neither justice nor the Marshall plan nor even the apocalypse, she be only what she is, the richest woman on earth, her wealth putting her into a position to act like a heroine in a Greek tragedy, absolute, monstrous, somewhat like Medea. (5: 142)

Dürrenmatt expressively warns not to interpret her as an American (no Marshall plan!) but to take her as the classical Greek princess Medea. His other allusion to the States, the two gum chewing monsters from Sing-Sing, to me is only as much a common stereotype as are the brothel in Hamburg or the castle in Yorkshire. Throughout the play, these two characters never develop any identities of their own and can therefore be disregarded as representatives of their nation. It is highly unlikely that Friedrich Dürrenmatt meant to flatter England or to criticize the United States and Germany.

Cornelius Schnauber gives a very vivid account of Dürrenmatt talking to students at the Max-Kade-Institute about his inspiration for *The Visit*:

> The point of departure was not — as some students would like to have heard — a complex interpretation of the world and capitalism. No, it happened thus: Dürrenmatt took a train from Neuchâtel to Bern each day to visit his wife, who was spending time in the hospital. Along the route the train always stopped at the same deserted train stations of Ins and Kerzers, suggesting to Dürrenmatt the use of a desolate train station to illustrate the desolation and impoverishment of a town. The idea of a wealthy person returning to a destitute town already existed in the form of a short story *(Mondfinsternis)* ... The students became cognizant of the truth (which can be illustrated by other Dürrenmatt works as well) that often out of a simple, insignificant occurrence (here, the repeated stops at the lonely train stations of Ins and Kerzers) an author develops with simple but compelling logic, a story which is at first not some world-embracing idea but very concrete, developed out of the free play of fantasy; but then — and this is the secret of genius — is so devised, that this fable, like the ultimate monad of Leibniz, reflects within itself a universe of other thoughts and associations.[2]

Even in a highly political play like *The Physicists,* which is, to some extend, an analogy to the political situation of the then east-west confrontation, the United States is only alluded to by a vague representative of a western alliance who merely is the counterpart of the likewise vague protagonist of Russia, the eastern block, or communism in general. Romey Sabalius mentioned that

the same east-west confrontation or confrontation between communism and capitalism or an idealistic utopian but also totalitarian society on the one side and a profit oriented business world on the other is apparent in *The Marriage of Mr. Mississippi* and the radio play *Operation Vega*.[3]

Dürrenmatt keeps the true identity of his physicists vague as it really does not matter which secret service one or the other belongs to. It is any secret service's task to gather intelligence as, and this is the crucial point Dürrenmatt wants to make in this play, it is a very personal and moral responsibility that a scientist has towards his fellow human beings when he hits upon knowledge that could be of disastrous consequences for mankind.

Actually, there is one play that in its entirety plays in an American setting: *The Collaborator*. Had the author been Brecht as one might be led to believe when first seeing the play, a quick interpretation would spring to mind: The communist Brecht portrays America as a prototypically corrupt and evil society torn apart by power struggles and crime, and void of any moral values whatsoever. Dürrenmatt, however, again gives a rather different reason for the choice of his setting. Browsing through the volume *Der Mitmacher*, one will quickly notice that the 80-page-play is followed by 230 pages of Dürrenmatt's comments, which he opens with the rather ironical explanation:

Somebody once remarked that my epilogues grow longer and longer. I intend to write the longest I have ever written, not exactly to prove someone right but rather following the insight that it basically is impossible to come up with a half-way workable theater score. (14: 97)

In these short essays, Dürrenmatt deals with almost every conceivable aspect of this play, but only once does he refer to its setting:

In *The Collaborator*, the fictitious place of action lies underground. (14: 101)

He never expresses though that this setting is actually located somewhere in the United States. Spectators and readers, however, will assume this since all the names of the characters in this play sound

American rather than British or anything else.[4] Anyhow, Dürren-matt insists on placing his setting in no particular country.

In the epilogue to the epilogue, he explains how he first conceived the plot for this play. It happened on a hot afternoon on Manhattan Island in May 1959:

> I no longer remember the route exactly, only shadowy; I may confuse it to some extent with another walk through Manhattan; I am obsti-nately haunted by the memory of one sky-scraper which I tried to reach but kept missing only not to find it in the end .... I walked and walked; a police car drove next to me; the buildings suddenly were no longer especially tall or for some time had not been especially tall but it took me a while to realize the changes in the area; garbage piled up; sky-scrapers which I could have used for guidance were no longer visible, not even high buildings, only brick buildings as it seems to me today. The heat was atrocious; it was mid May; the street was boiling; one single endless run through bricks, concrete, and dust; the sky liquid lead; vapors rising from the manholes; one time I stepped over a drunk, then over a number of them; beer cans on the ground, bottles; again a police car drove next to me, a cop in his sweaty shirt had his arm hanging out. But everything is blurred, fuzzy, like a feverish dream; the story of Doc pushed in between my-self and Manhattan continuously obscuring reality. (14: 234)

Walking through this unpleasant environment, Dürrenmatt's fan-tasy takes over and the repulsive atmosphere, he tries to flee from, subconsciously evokes and nourishes a little tale about a man named J. G. Smith. Back in his hotel room, he wrote a 14-page-novella called *Smithy*. Fourteen years later he developed Smith into Doc and the novella into the play *The Collaborator*. For the sake of the play, he took various strains of Smith's personality and divided them up among a number of added characters so that the original Smith in his complexity is sort of a Leibniz' monad in which some of the other characters on stage are embodied. Dürrenmatt explains:

> A dialectic route leads from Smithy to Doc but no traceable route whatsoever from Doc to Smithy, other than one that would have been covered subsequently, for the play is not the dramatized story that I later reconstructed. Smithy is not Doc — Smithy is Doc, Boss, Cop in one... (14: 261-62)

And answering the question why he altered the novella to a play after such a long time, Dürrenmatt states:

> ... to confront myself as I am writing now with the one who once,

many years ago, found the story in impressions, associations and kept whistling it like a tune, and to find out why I then abandoned it, wrote different things, eight plays among others, and then suddenly took that story up again. When I found it, for the first time in the United States, for the first time on a different continent, impressions pounced upon me, the flight across the ocean, still in a propeller airplane, the icebergs, the vessels in-between like toys, the American land masses, deserted, the landing, the first days on Long Island, somewhere near a canal, the first trip to New York during sunset, the town monstrously towering into the darkening sky, the heat which suddenly appeared the following day and so on; the story was my answer but simultaneously an auxiliary device which I came up with to help me bear these impressions. I am not someone who writes diaries or mere descriptions, my answers to my impressions are indirect, by way of a detour, a story, and since it is my answer, since it was my way of coping with an impression, I had no need to write it down, it had been enough to think it, to write a couple of pages, to sometimes tell it — e.g., during one hot June night to Hans Arp —, to have whistled it like a tune. (14: 262-63)

Since *The Collaborator* was a product of his very conscious and practical analysis of the stage, the setting lost all references to the United States and became a very abstract place deep in the cellars. The protagonists received monosyllabic American names though some characters were deeply influenced by actual living people who were all Swiss.[5] Dürrenmatt nevertheless holds on to the American names as the very deep and diverse impressions his first trip overseas had made on him had been the inspiration of this work. Remembering his experiences fourteen years later, he no longer was totally captivated by the disquieting atmosphere of the poor Manhattan neighborhood, but also recalled the pleasant and exciting moments. His novella had merely been his way of dealing with an overwhelming reality, his flight into fantasy:

... when I conceived it (the story) it was not material I could use for the stage, it was nothing more than compressed atmosphere, only a pretext to get to grips with an experience, the experience of the megalopolis New York. (14: 325)

So when he wrote the play, he knew very well that his fantasizing was his way of coming to terms with an impression and as such he did not sever all the links between the play and its first inspiration. Like with *The Visit*, Dürrenmatt developed it from a concrete experience and that fable then again targets any kind of system or society that has lost its moral values.

Although Dürrenmatt said that he neither writes diaries nor mere descriptions, his essay *Sentences from America* comes very close to being a dairy of his second encounter with the United States, which took place in 1969. One has to remember that that period was characterized by a growing group of critical European intellectuals who uni sono castigated America for her role in Vietnam and her seemingly racist politics at home. The "hot summer months" in Paris 1968 and the European and American student revolts of the following year gave rise to a widespread criticism of the capitalist systems.[6] At first, Dürrenmatt's essay seems very much mainstream. Of his 91 paragraphs the third reads:

> In Philadelphia, Temple University is considered progressive. I imagined I would come to talk with Black students and professors but did not meet any. The university lies in the middle of the Blacks' neighborhood and is unpopular because it constantly grows and displaces the Blacks. And for other reasons, too, the Blacks withdraw further and further from the Whites. Rather than approaching each other, the two races polarize, whatever is the Whites' concern concerns the Whites and whatever is the Blacks' concern concerns the Blacks. My presence at Temple University was a concern of the Whites and was not taken notice of by the Blacks. (28: 77)

However, Dürrenmatt is obviously not prepared to lash out at the Americans as it was fashionable with so many of his colleagues. He openly writes of his expectations which he found proven wrong. He gives an accurate account of his first hand experiences and only once slips up on the role of the objective observer when commenting "rather than approaching each other, the two races polarize ...." This "rather" probably does not only imply his expectation but what he would have thought to be good and proper because Dürrenmatt is interested in the question of minorities. He asks questions about the fate of the native Indians; he listens, and then he draws his conclusions:

> So we belong to a race the Indians only deal with through their lawyers. (28: 78)

He considers the growing tension between the black and white American population a real danger for the American society, but he does not take sides. He tries to give each side its fair share of consideration:

> I think the error of Black Panther lies in the fact that they want to apply the tactics of the class struggle to their racial struggle. Through constant terror, a people can be prepared to accept Communism, but not even by constant terror can a white man be turned into a black man: The radicalism of Black Panther radicalizes the Whites. The feeling that a solution is impossible spreads among both, and both are armed. (28: 81)

Dürrenmatt is eager to learn on this trip and thus he takes note of every incident, even those that make him look the fool:

> In Jamaica, I came to talk with a Negro at the bar near the rainy swimming pool. He told me in his English that he had visited his old grandmother. Since my English was much poorer than his, I confused "meet" with "eat" and believed that he had eaten his old grandmother, where upon I was very happy to have met my first cannibal. When the error was resolved, the Negro had not become disagreeable to me, however, he had somewhat sunken in my esteem: I felt I was a match for him. (28: 88)

Here, his humor shows how lovingly open he is for every new encounter. He is in America to watch and learn. And it seems he does not miss a thing. He bestows all his appreciation for a good performance upon a group of students who performed one of his plays in his honor; he describes the incredible performances of dolphins in Florida; he describes how he mistook a lizard for an ancient stone carving. More and more often, however, he concentrates on the afterthoughts and conclusions he draws:

> Sin of omission: Arthur Miller sent me a telegram I should protest the way the Russian writers' federation had treated Solschenizyn. I protested. In Russia, the people are stultified by the Party, in the United States by television. This neither Arthur Miller nor I protested. (28: 83)

And he is highly aware and critical of the role the Europeans and his own fellow countrymen played in America's history:

> The second achievement we saw of a Swiss abroad was considerably more negative: the ruins of the Maya cities of Uxmal, Kabah, and Chichen-Itza in Yucatan. It was the Habsburgian Charles V who had the peninsular with its fifty settlements conquered, destroyed, and christianized. (28: 84)

Some of his paragraphs are short and witty, almost aphorisms:

> The unique hard luck of the United States is that there the capitalists have led capitalism to absurdity and the unions socialism. (28: 94)

Quoted out of context, some of these very short sentences could be misinterpreted since they float like icebergs with a tiny simple sentence as a visible tip and the vast majority of Dürrenmatt's beliefs and the actual reality that led him to this statement under the surface. Hence sentence number 52 is of utmost importance for the understanding of some of these remarks:

> The United States is a giant which I merely know superficially. I could compare it to Switzerland which I know better. But this would be a lame comparison. Less known would be compared to well known. It is therefore better to compare the giant USA with the giant Soviet Union since I know both only from visits. This comparison would indeed result in a superficial but for the very reason a more appropriate picture. (28: 99)

Thus we can say that Dürrenmatt does not believe in a dichotomous view of the world, he does not want to counterbalance or contrast the two different systems of capitalism and socialism by their national incarnations, the USA and the former USSR. Dürrenmatt understands the complexity of an entity like the United States to the degree that allows him to say that it is beyond the grasp of the human brain. The economy of thinking requires us to form stereotypes in order to come to conclusions. If each and every detail, every piece of information we could lay our hands on would have to be taken into consideration, we could never form a personal opinion. We therefore have to simplify matters of great complexity; we have to pick and choose from an endless flood of information; and we have to do our own comparison and contrasting. Only when preconceived ideas become the sole basis for opinions, when stereotype is turned into prejudice, is danger at hand.

Dürrenmatt seemingly crosses that fine line between stereotype and prejudice when writing catchy phrases like:

> The difference between Russia and the United States today basically is that in Russia everyone considers everyone an informer, and in the United States everyone considers everyone a gangster. (28: 94)

But sentences like these have to be taken with the grain of salt provided by Dürrenmatt himself:

The United States represents a uniquely more complicated entity than the Soviet Union but paradoxically thereby both empires become comparable. The factor of uncertainty that lies within the lack of information concerning a relatively simple entity is neutralized by the factor of uncertainty that a more complicated entity provokes by its more varied possibilities. (28: 100)

It is this awareness of the precariousness or ambiguity that makes all the difference. Dürrenmatt therefore stresses the impossibility of a diagnosis, let alone a prognosis:

A diagnosis is a conclusion that I draw from reality. It is of utmost importance for the diagnosis whether reality has been comprehended precisely or not. I dare not answer this question positively, neither with regards to the Soviet Union nor to the United States. I depended much too heavily on evidence which I only judge intuitively and which for lack of time and means I cannot scrutinize. My diagnoses therefore are impressions. This is even more so with my prognoses. A prognosis is a conclusion based on a diagnosis. The prognosis hints at a possible future development of the comprehended reality. The more vaguely reality has been comprehended, the more arbitrary the prognosis has to turn out. Most prognoses are shots we aim into the future without certainty whether we hit the bull's eye or not because we will only see the future once it has become our present. (28: 110-11)

Dürrenmatt, who disagreed with Brecht in that he does not believe a playwright could and therefore should educate his audience but must show the world as it is, in all its chaos and absurdity, is true to himself when he observes the grotesque reality he encounters without personal comment or evaluation:

Whoever volunteers to go to Vietnam only has to serve for one year; after a short training he is send directly into war. Whoever does not volunteer has to serve for a couple of years (depending on the branch of service and whether he is not send to Vietnam anyhow). Consequence: Intelligent boys who do not want to lose time for their studies are enticed into going to Vietnam even at the risk of losing their lives. Those, however, who take drugs will not be accepted by the army, thus young men are inspired to take drugs that are offered to them by the Mafia against which the state must pretend to be powerless because it is infiltrated by it, etc. (28: 105)

Dürrenmatt's critical intellect does not allow him to paint a simple black and white picture of this world. Still, his literary work is sometimes taken for its face value and hence misunderstood:

The difficulty is: today, there is no prevailing philosophy. Marxists had a school of thought. Brecht for the most was the poet of the leftist intellectuals but even they are split today. Like the Catholics. God and Satan, good and bad, capitalist and proletarian were commonly intelligible ciphers with which one could work. If you are neither good nor bad, neither left nor right, neither believe in God nor in Satan but cannot be categorized, like me, if you develop your own philosophy you face a public that has no idea of your way of thinking and thus your assumptions and their results. [7]

Walter Jens described Friedrich Dürrenmatt's way of thinking as he finds it expressed in his literary work as follows:

"I never was a Ptolemaist" is Friedrich Dürrenmatt's credo and that means: I have to depict people who, no matter whether they live in a province of the Alps, in Tibet, in the desert, in a Cretan labyrinth or in the small town of Güllen, are particles of the universe, inhabitants of a minute and extremely peripheral planet in the cosmos ... and this doubling based on the interaction between the intellectually known and the intuitively felt, or more precisely: based on the discrepancy between Copernican thinking and Ptolemaist feeling ... to describe this discrepancy that constitutes our condition is what after the great turn into the open has repeatedly fascinated Friedrich Dürrenmatt, who loves playing mind games and picture logics: to an extent where he had to invent a new language to measure up to the material that underlies all his later experiments ....
Unio poetica is Dürrenmatt's maxim: the design of models, allegories, illusions, notions and reflections that illustrate the incongruity of modern existence: that life-in-two-worlds with its split second breaks between scientifically veritable thought processing (which, however, is not achievable in daily routine) and faithful (but unrealistic) daily and hourly existence. [8]

The truth becomes all too obvious when one beholds Dürrenmatt's paintings which, even to the untrained eye, show far more clearly the intricate detail of the chaotic universe as Dürrenmatt sees it. However, he never painted a golden sunset or any other tranquil scenery; his pictures make him the Hieronymus Bosch of the twentieth century. Like the Dutch painter's, his worlds, too, reflect a deep, sometimes almost gruesome fantasy depicting individuals enjoying their lustful lives in the midst of a chaotic absurdity, but in contrast to the man from the Baroque, Dürrenmatt today does not see God as the easy answer to all our problems.

When we asked Dürrenmatt in 1985 for a motto which he would like to see on the cover of the Dürrenmatt issue of the *Londoner Lesehefte*, he asked us to print:

> The worst thing I can imagine is to walk past a book store and see a booklet in the window entitled "Take comfort from Friedrich Dürrenmatt."[9]

Dürrenmatt is very critical of what is going on in this world, especially in politics. But he is never one-sided, biased, neither anti-Communist nor anti-Capitalist. When he keeps referring to the USSR while writing his *Sentences from America* it sometimes seems antagonistic and yet, it is not, as it was not when he held his speech against the Russian invasion in the CSSR in 1968. Then he asked:

> Do we really live in an era of political crime, is this label not subjectively, theatrically, comically exaggerated? Doesn't it mean that it's always the others who are the criminals, for the United States the Vietcong and for the Vietcong the United States, for the Czechoslovakian the Russian and for the Russian the Czechoslovakian, and for the Chinese we all together? ... So when I call our times an era of political crime, I do this solely because I no longer believe in the pretenses of politics that it attributes to its actions .... Sartre is right when he calls the United States and the Soviet Union and their satellites war criminals .... The perspective offered by the satiated Switzerland is deceptive. The planet we live on is poorly organized, many areas are overpopulated, others reserved for a few, the capabilities of technology are only partly exploited, and most human beings suffer from starvation .... We, too, have to expand the idea of democracy because the democracy we practice in many ways bears similarly mythological features as the Soviet Communism, it is in many aspects as cultic. Let us merely think of the comedies of American party congresses, of the impertinence with which some parties call themselves Christian, of the illusions some people do not want to give up in order to further exploit them politically, of the support for dictatorships, of economic black-mail that is carried out under the pretense that some country has to be saved from Communism, and also of the fact that we, too, disregard people by manipulating them. (28: 36-41)

We, these are all the people in the free world, first and foremost the Swiss whom he addresses directly, then the Americans, and every citizen of any other free country. When criticizing the Russians, Dürrenmatt makes it a point to immediately say that not all is well in the West either, and vice versa, he shows the shortcomings of the communist systems whenever he criticizes the lack of freedom in the West. Dürrenmatt himself describes his political position as follows:

> ... in the Soviet Union when I am there I am an anti-Communist, in India or Chile, were I to find myself there, a Communist and so on. (14: 326)

In his play *Die Frist*, which to some extent depicts Poland in the days shortly before martial law was declared and the union Solidarity became illegal, America represents the country of freedom:

> HIS EXCELLENCY: Studying physics. You applied with the Ministry of Education for a grant for studies in the United States.
>
> STUDENT: I want to become a cosmologist.
>
> HIS EXCELLENCY: Change to philosophy.
>
> STUDENT: Cosmology is a science nowadays.
>
> HIS EXCELLENCY: That's news to me.
>
> STUDENT: It examines the structure and the limits of the universe.
>
> HIS EXCELLENCY: Hm. The origin, too?
>
> STUDENT: That, too.
>
> HIS EXCELLENCY: Pure speculation.
>
> STUDENT: Not at all. It infers facts that are not ascertainable from facts that are ascertainable.
>
> HIS EXCELLENCY: You conclude from theories to hypotheses. Very interesting. And why can't you conduct your cosmological research in our beautiful country?
>
> STUDENT: One does not conduct research in this country, Your Excellency. (15: 22)

Although the play *Achterloo* includes a Kissinger-like character and another one named Benjamin Franklin, the United States again does not play any prominent role. During all the stages of his writing and rewriting of this play and throughout the times of discussions, his wife, Charlotte Kerr, kept a kind of diary, an insight into Dürrenmatt's mind games and the making of this play. Here, too, the United States is never expressively mentioned. Ludwig Arnold provides some insight into why, commenting on Dürrenmatt's mania of rewriting plays over and over again:

The open form, the draftiness corresponds with the scientific way of thinking and experimenting: It allows for hypotheses from which the process of cognition is developed. Dürrenmatt calls this way of writing his "dramaturgy," this way of his thinking a "dramaturgical thinking."

Dürrenmatt's philosophy, if one may say so, is based upon Kantian dialectics, the play of chance and necessity, the concurrence of faith and doubt. One cannot distill aphorisms from such a prose; Dürren- matt mistrusts phrases that coagulate into maxims. He is not a moralist with a moral, he is a moralist by himself and in himself. ... Prose that is thus formulated does not hit upon popular formulas. It lives of its multilayered complex notions as Dürrenmatt is not con- cerned with humanity but with the human being, not with society but with the individual. He expressed a key phrase of his notion of the world in his book *Stoffe*: "Minotaur. By describing the world in which I lived as a labyrinth I tried to gain distance from it, to take a step back from it, to fix it with my eyes like a trainer a wild beast, but this image is inaccurate. I confronted the world that I experi- enced with a counter-world that I devised."[35]

Walter Jens concludes:

No doubt, solitude has grown dominant in Friedrich Dürrenmatt's world: the wild bustle in Balzac's work, the dazzling exuberance of the Comédie humaine is yielding to the monotony of snow- and de- sert landscapes, to the uniformity and humdrum of fictitious regions in which people hold colloquies that suddenly turn out to be mono- logues: intellectual mind games played with oneself within a world that is a maze because it holds the supplies of knowledge, experi- ence, and thought of all times: gigantic arsenals and depots, the res- ervoirs of which are all equally important, that is, in their sum absurd.[11]

Dürrenmatt did, however, continuously make political speeches in which he more than once referred to the role of the United States. In his laudatio for Václav Havel in November 1990, he chose to entitle his speech "Switzerland — a prison," he opened by reminding his audience of the 1968 meeting at the Basel Stadttheater at which he had protested the Soviet invasion of the CSSR. Meanwhile the world had changed considerably, Dürrenmatt thus said:

More than twenty years have since passed. The United States did not only lose the war in Vietnam but also her honor. The power of dogmatists in Eastern Europe has crumbled; the heavily armed mili- tary blocks on both sides have become useless; their respective ene- mies have vanished; both the superpowers are increasingly confronted by themselves rather than each other.[12]

Friedrich Dürrenmatt reminded his audience of Václav Havel's essay *"Attempting to Live Within the Truth"* in which he had expressed his ideas on democracy too readily forgotten by some:

> It does not look as if traditional parliamentary democracies had anything to offer concerning how to resist on principle the "automotion" of technical civilization, industry, and a society of consumers. They, too, are taken in tow and find themselves perplexed. Only the way they manipulate people is so much more sophisticated and subtle than the brutal way of post totalitarian systems. However, this entire static complex of paralyzed mass parties, void of concepts and politically solely active to suit their purposes, run by a professional party machine and dispensing its citizen from any concrete and personal responsibility whatsoever, this omnipresent dictate of consumption, production, advertising, commerce, consumer culture, this entire flood of information — all this already so often analyzed and described can indeed hardly be seen as a perspective, as a way in which man will find back to himself.[13]

In his laudatio entitled *"The Hope of Pulling Oneself by One's Own Hair Out of the Fall"* which he held for Michail Gorbachev on November 25, 1990 in Berlin, Friedrich Dürrenmatt said:

> To him (Gorbachev), two super powers were facing each other interlocked in a deadly arms race, especially, since the United States had decided to spend hundreds of billions on installing a safety umbrella to secure her territory against nuclear attacks and thus forcing the Soviet Union to develop new arms capable of penetrating this umbrella to resurrect the balance of power. Today, we know that this nuclear arms race has weakened both superpowers economically.[14]

And on the most recent world situation and the war against Iraq, Friedrich Dürrenmatt said:

> We are building a technical and ecological world of catastrophes for ourselves. A galaxy of poverty threatens to penetrate our galaxy of prosperity, the free market economy conjures up crises, the boom does not last for ever, like a black hole it absorbs the resources of the Third World. Old nations promote new independent states, others are threatened by demise. Never before were hunger, misery, and oppression so great, and already there is a war looming in the Persian Gulf in which men will not die for an ideal but for oil.[15]

In one of his discussions with his wife, Charlotte Kerr, Friedrich

Dürrenmatt explained the role of the critical writer in today's world as he sees it:

> How do you grasp present times; how do you comprehend present times? It is a paradox. You are better informed than ever by newspapers, radio, TV, you are buried under an avalanche of news and pictures, but underneath this avalanche you no longer see the times you are living in. You try to fight your way back to the surface but the avalanche keeps rolling over you: morning news, midday news, evening news; all you are left with is a minute space so that you do not suffocate. You must strive to come up with your own notion, you must try to understand the world from within yourself, and then you have to scream. Maybe someone will hear you. To write is to scream. Who in the world has not screamed? Sartre tried to combine the notion of reality he had created for himself, i.e., existentialism, with Marxism, and then Marxism took a different path, past Sartre, and his screaming was no longer heard. Becket screams but knows that it is absurd to scream. — And you? — As a warning. There is only one way to escape the avalanche, not to get into it: do not engage yourself too much in the news of the world and about the world but in contemplation.[16]

As this anthology will show, the United States is a country that a number of Swiss authors have written about for various reasons. Max Frisch was fascinated by the States, her freedom, her vastness, her modernity which he repeatedly contrasted with the narrowness and reactionary attitude and atmosphere of his native Switzerland. Others like Federspiel and Jaeggi were deeply but negatively impressed by the anti-social side of American capitalism, by the extremes of wealth and poverty, friendliness and crime. Velan mistrusted the hype and power of the media, especially television; and Loetscher, Vogt, and Geiser used the west of the United States as a backdrop for their own personal experiences. All three describe a mid-life crisis of some sort.[17] Bichsel is probably the one author closest to Dürrenmatt in that he continuously questions the stereotypes Europeans have about the United States: "And why is it that only one in one hundred American women is typically American?"[18]

Widmer, on the other hand, openly plays with these images.

Dürrenmatt, however, is the one author who, one might say, avoided using the United States to a great degree in his work. His reasons are obvious: This world and all of its societies are too complex and too complicated to be dealt with analytically. If one uses a nation like the United States or a society like the American, one cannot be truthful. On the one hand there are the stereotypes and prejudices the reader holds on to which are to the author to some extent unknown as are his to his readers; on the other hand, using the United States as a negative example of anything would be unfair and untrue as she has so many great virtues but using her as a positive example would be an equally false simplification since there are so many shortcomings, too. Dürrenmatt hence uses the United States mostly to clarify certain aspects by contrasting her with other nations such as the former USSR. His prime concern, however, is not a nation, neither the United States nor the Soviet Union as it was nor Switzerland; his prime concern was and has always been the individual rather than society and the human being rather than mankind. In a world of absurd masses of information, speculation, and conceit, Dürrenmatt reminds us that this world is but one planet somewhere at the periphery of one galaxy among billions and that the only way of survival in this endlessly chaotic labyrinth is to find oneself against all the odds. It is not a question of being Swiss, Russian, or American; it is a question of being human.

NOTES

1. All quotations of texts first published in German have been translated by the author of this article, and those by Dürrenmatt are taken from: Friedrich Dürrenmatt, *Werkausgabe in dreißig Bänden*, 30 vols. (Zürich: Diogenes, 1980-1986), unless stated differently.

2. Cornelius Schnauber, "Friedrich Dürrenmatt in Los Angeles: Foreword." *Play Dürrenmatt*, ed. Moshe Lazar (Malibu: Undena, 1983), 2-5.

3. Romey Sabalius, "The United States in the Work of Max Frisch and Friedrich Dürrenmatt," opening lecture at the conference "How Contemporary Swiss Literature Views the United States", Max Kade Institute, University of Southern California, Los Angeles, March 6, 1991.

4. Doc in those days was a well-known character, a doctor, in American cowboy films shown on German TV.

5. Cf. 14: 171-72.

6. Cf. Gabriela Wettberg, *Das Amerika-Bild und seine negativen Konstanten in der deutschen Nachkriegsliteratur* (Heidelberg: Winter, 1987), 13.

7. Friedrich Dürrenmatt, Charlotte Kerr, *Rollenspiele: Protokoll einer fiktiven Inszenierung und Achterloo III* (Zürich: Diogenes, 1986), 13.

8. Walter Jens, "Zu Hause im Emmental und unter den Sternen. Würdigung Friedrich Dürrenmatts anläßlich der Gedenkfeier am 1.. Januar 1991 im Berner Münster." In *Kants Hoffnung: Zwei politische Reden, Zwei Gedichte aus dem Nachlaß, Mit einem Essay von Walter Jens* (Zürich: Diogenes, 1991), 57-58.

9. Friedrich Denk, Gene O. Stimpson et al., eds., *Friedrich Dürrenmatt: Dramenanfänge*, Londoner Lesehefte 6 (London: n.p., 1985)

10. Heinz Ludwig Arnold, "Das Spiel von Zufall und Notwendigkeit," In: *Herkules und Atlas, Lobreden und andere Versuche über Friedrich Dürrenmatt zum siebzigsten Geburtstag*, ed. Daniel Keel (Zürich: Diogenes, 1990), 13-14.

11. Walter Jens, 60-61.

12. Friedrich Dürrenmatt, *Kants Hoffnung*, 9-10.

13. Friedrich Dürrenmatt, *Kants Hoffnung*, 19-20.

14. Friedrich Dürrenmatt, *Kants Hoffnung*, 31.

15. Friedrich Dürrenmatt, *Kants Hoffnung*, 48.

16. Friedrich Dürrenmatt, Charlotte Kerr, *Rollenspiele*, 45-46.

17. Cf. Romey Sabalius, "Das Bild der USA in der zeitgenössischen Literatur der deutschsprachigen Schweiz." Presentation at the Annual Conference of the German Studies Association, Minneapolis, October 1, 1992.

18. Peter Bichsel, *Im Gegenteil: Kolumnen 1986-1990* (Frankfurt: Luchterhand, 1990), 125.

PETER BICHSEL

Peter Bichsel

Born March 24, 1935 in Lucerne. Studied pedagogy. Taught school for many years. Lecturer positions at various colleges and universities in the US and Europe. 1974-1981 advisor to federal minister and president of Switzerland, Willi Ritchard. 1981/82 "Stadtschreiber" of the city of Bergen/Enkheim/Frankfurt. Member of literary academies in Germany. Member of PEN. Received several literary awards. Lives in Solothurn. Short stories, novels, essays: *Eigentlich möchte Frau Blum den Milchmann kennenlernen,* 1964; *Die Jahreszeiten,* 1967; *Kindergeschichten,* 1694; *Geschichten zur falschen Zeit,* 1979; *Schulmeistereien,* 1985; *Der Busant,* 1985; *Im Gegenteil,* 1990; *Zur Stadt Paris,* 1993.

America Doesn't Exist

I got this story from a man who tells stories. I have told him many times that I do not believe his story.

"You're lying," I said, "you're fabricating, you're dreaming, you're deceiving."

It did not impress him. He quietly continued to tell his story, and when I yelled, "You liar, you fabricator, you dreamer, you deceiver!", he looked at me for a long time, shook his head, smiled sadly, and then said so quietly that I was almost ashamed, "America doesn't exist."

To console him, I promised to write down his story:

It began five hundred years ago, at the court of a King, the King of Spain. A palace, silk and velvet, gold, silver, beards, crowns, candles, servants and ladies-in-waiting; courtiers running swords through each other's bellies in the gray light of dawn who, the night before, had thrown gauntlets at each other's feet. On the tower, fanfare-blowing watchmen. And messengers who leap from horses, and messengers who leap into saddles, friends of the King and false friends, women, beautiful and dangerous, and wine, and outside, all around the palace, people who knew nothing except paying for it all.

But the King also knew nothing except living that way, and also that no matter how one lives, whether up to the hilt or in poverty, whether in Madrid, Barcelona, or somewhere, in the end, it is the same thing every day, and one gets bored. Thus, the people who live someplace think Barcelona must be great, and the people in Barcelona want to go to someplace.

The poor people think it must be great to live like the King and are suffering because the King thinks being poor is right for the poor people.

The King gets up in the morning and goes to bed at night, and during the day he bores himself with his problems, with his servants, his gold, silver, silk, his velvet, bores himself with his candles. His bed is splendid, but one cannot do much more than sleep in it.

In the morning, the servants bow deeply, every morning just as deeply, the King is used to it and does not even pay attention. Someone hands him his fork, someone hands him his knife, someone places his chair behind him, and the people who talk to him say Majesty and many other fine words and otherwise nothing.

No one ever says to him, "You fool, you birdbrain," and everything that they say to him today, they have already said to him yesterday.

That is how it is.

And that is why Kings have court jesters.

They can do anything they want and say anything they want to make the King laugh, and when the King cannot laugh at them anymore, he kills them or something like that.

For instance, at one time he had a jester who would mix up words. The King thought it was funny. He would say "stajesmy" instead of "majesty," he would say "lapace" instead of "palace," and "dood gay" instead of "good day."

I thought it was stupid, the King thought it was funny. For a whole half-year he thought it was funny, until the 7th of July, and on the 8th, when he got up and the jester came and said "dood gay, stajesmy," the King said, "get this jester off my back!"

Another jester, a small fat one, his name was Pepe, amused the King for only four days, he made the King laugh by spreading honey on the chairs of the ladies and gentlemen, the princes, dukes, freemen and knights. On the fourth day, he spread honey on the King's chair, and the King did not need to laugh anymore, and Pepe was not a jester anymore.

Then the King bought the most terrible jester in the world. He was ugly, fat and thin at the same time, tall and short at the same time, and his left leg was deformed. Nobody knew if he was able to speak and was purposely not speaking, or if he was mute. His face was sullen, his glances were angry; the only thing charming about him was his name: he was called Johnny.

The most hideous thing, though, was his laugh.

It would start real small and glassy deep in his stomach, would gurgle upward, turn slowly into a belching, would turn Johnny's face red, almost choke him to death, until he would burst forth, explode, roar, scream; then he would stamp his feet and dance and laugh; and only the King got enjoyment out of it, the others would turn pale, begin to shiver and were afraid. And when the people around the castle would hear this laughing, they would lock their windows and doors, close their shops, put their children to bed, and stuff their ears with wax.

Johnny's laugh was the most terrible thing there was.

The King could say whatever he wanted to, Johnny would laugh.

The King would say things that no one could laugh at, but Johnny would laugh.

And one day, the King said, "Johnny, I am going to hang you."

And Johnny laughed, roared, laughed like he never had before.

So the King decided that Johnny would be hanged in the morning. He ordered a gallows built, and he was serious in his decision, he wanted to hear Johnny laugh before the gallows. Then he ordered all the people to watch the cruel show. But the people hid themselves and bolted their doors, and in the morning the King was alone with his hangman, with his servants, and with laughing Johnny.

And he shouted at his servants, "Bring me the people!" The servants searched all over the town and found nobody, and the King was angry, and Johnny laughed.

Then finally the servants found a boy and dragged him before the King. The boy was small, pale, and timid, and the King pointed at the gallows and ordered him to watch.

The boy looked at the gallows, smiled, clapped his hands, looked surprised and then said, "You must be a good King to build a little bench for the doves; look, two of them have already sat on it."

"You are a fool," said the King, "what is your name?"

"I'm a fool, Mr. King, and my name is Colombo, my mother calls me Colombin."

"You fool," said the King, "someone is going to be hanged here."

"What's his name?", asked Colombin, and when he heard the name, he said, "A nice name, so he's called Johnny. How can you hang a man who has such a nice name?"

"He laughs so hideously," said the King, and he ordered Johnny to laugh, and Johnny laughed twice as hideously as the day before.

Colombin was astonished, then he said, "Mr. King, you think that's hideous?" The King was surprised and could not answer, and Colombin continued, "I don't much care for his laughing, but the doves are still sitting on the gallows; it didn't scare them, they don't think his laughing is hideous. Doves have a delicate ear. You have to let Johnny go."

The King thought about it and then said, "Johnny, go to hell."

And Johnny spoke a word for the first time. He said to Colombin, "Thank you," and smiled a beautiful, warm smile, and left.

The King had no jester anymore.

"Come," he said to Colombin.

The King's servants and ladies-in-waiting, the countesses, and everyone, though, thought that Colombin was the new court jester.

But Colombin was not funny. He stood there and stared, hardly said a word and never laughed, he only smiled and could not make anyone else laugh.

"He isn't a jester, he's a fool," the people said, and Colombin would say, "I'm not a jester, I'm a fool."

And the people laughed at him.

If the King had known about that, it would have made him angry, but Colombin told him nothing about it since he did not mind being laughed at.

At the court were strong people and decisive people, the King was a King, the ladies were beautiful and the men brave, the priest was pious and the kitchen maid industrious — only Colombin, Colombin was nothing.

Whenever someone said, "Come on Colombin, fight me," Colombin said, "I'm weaker than you."

Whenever someone said, "How much is two times seven?" Colombin said, "I'm dumber than you."

Whenever someone said, "Dare you think you can jump over the brook?" Colombin said, "No, I don't dare."

And when the King asked, "Colombin, what do you want to be?", Colombin said, "I don't want to be anything, I'm already something, I'm Colombin."

The King said, "But you must become something," and Colombin asked, "What can one become?"

Then the King said, "That man there with the beard, with the brown, leathery face, that is a seaman. He wanted to be a seaman and he became a seaman, he sails across the oceans and discovers lands for his King."

"If it's what you want, my King," said Colombin, "I will become a seaman."

There the whole court laughed.

And Colombin ran away, out of the hall, and shouted, "I will discover a land, I will discover a land!"

The people looked at each other and shook their heads, and Colombin ran out of the castle, through the town and across the fields, and yelled to the farmers who stood in the fields and looked at him, "I will discover a land, I will discover a land!"

And he came to the forest and hid for weeks in the bushes, and for weeks no one heard anything from Colombin, and the King was sad and blamed himself, and the people of the court were ashamed because they had laughed at Colombin.

And they were happy when, weeks later, the watchman on the tower blew the fanfare and Colombin came across the fields, came through the town, came through the gate, stood before the King and said, "My King, Colombin has discovered a land!"

And since the people of the court did not want to laugh at Colombin anymore, they made serious faces and asked, "What is it called then, and where does it lie?"

"It's not called anything yet because I've just discovered it, and it lies far away, out in the ocean."

Then the bearded seaman stood up and said, "Good, Colombin, I, Amerigo Vespucci, will go find the land. Tell me where it lies."

"You get onto the ocean and then head straight, and you must keep going straight until you get to the land, and you mustn't give up," said Colombin, and he was terribly afraid because he was a liar and knew that the land did not exist, and he was not able to sleep anymore.

But Amerigo Vespucci began the search.

Nobody knows where he went.

Maybe he, too, hid in the forest.

Then the fanfares were sounded, and Amerigo came back.

Colombin went red in the face and did not dare look at the great seaman. Vespucci stood before the King, winked at Colombin, took a deep breath, winked at Colombin again, and said loud and clear, so that everyone could hear, "My King," he said, "My King, the land exists."

Colombin was so happy that Vespucci had not given him away, that he ran towards him, threw his arms around him, and shouted, "Amerigo, my dear Amerigo!"

And the people thought that that was the name of the land, and they called the land that does not exist "America."

"You are now a man," said the King to Colombin, "from now on you will be called Columbus."

And Columbus became famous, and everyone admired him and would whisper to each other: "He discovered America."

And everyone believed that America existed, only Columbus was not sure, he doubted it his whole life, and never dared ask the seaman the truth.

Soon, however, some others went to America, and soon many others; and those who came back claimed, "America exists!"

"I," said the man from whom I have this story, "I have never been to America. I don't know if America exists. Maybe the people only act that way in order not to disappoint Columbin. And when two people talk about America, they still wink at each other today, and they almost never say America, they usually say something indefinite about 'the States' or 'over there' or something like that."

Maybe, on the boat or on the plane, someone tells the people who want to go to America the story of Colombin, and then they hide somewhere and come back later and tell of cowboys and of skyscrapers, of the Niagara Falls and of the Mississippi, of New York and of San Francisco.

In any case, they all tell of the same things, and they all tell of things that they knew about before their trip; and that is very suspicious.

But still the people argue over who Columbus really was.

I know.

(Translated by Tom Schnauber)

Waiting in America

American films do not give a true picture of the way Americans drive. Although it is, of course, well known in Europe that American films rarely depict American life as it is lived by Americans, Europeans are only too eager to emulate the America of the movies when they drive their automobiles. They speed, turn clever tricks, take heroic chances.

In America, driving is an almost leisurely thing. Missing a green light does not brand the driver an unredeemable fool. The drivers around him just take their time and wait. No one taps his forehead to characterize the delinquent a bone head. No one yells at him. If one makes an unlawful turn, well, that is just that, a mistake. To be sure, there are horrific automobile races with arranged collisions on television. And there is plenty of violence on television. Yet, in the streets, such scenes are rarely seen. Only in American films do we see two automobile drivers call each other vile names and come to blows.

We consider Americans naive — simpletons. Yet, in accepting American films as American reality, we are the true simpletons.

I do not really know why driving in America is so devoid of aggression, to the point of being an almost leisurely pursuit. Perhaps it just happens to be that way — one of those things. Perhaps it is simply a matter of ordinary decency or friendliness.

Or, perhaps, the Americans are not as soft in their heads as we like to believe. There is one thing that particularly astounds me, because I have noticed it again and again, not only about driving, but in any type of personal relations. When someone seems to miss the point, does not conform to current fashion in his dress, speaks louder than those around him, or not as loud, or does not promptly step on the gas when the light turns green, people simply assume that he has some good reason for it, or that there is some more or less good explanation for it. People seem to understand that human conduct is determined by many circumstances and that a person who fails to conform to what seems to be the norm is not necessarily a certifiable moron.

When I first visited the United States some 15 years ago, I did not notice these things. Now I do. Could it be that we in Switzerland have become less friendly and more aggressive in the interim?

All American team sports are aggressive. We accept this statement as an article of faith. Yet, it reflects prejudice. Take baseball. It is a kind of stick ball. I cannot warm to it, not even after I finally broke down and had someone explain the rules to me. It is a slow game, with many pauses. The players are almost never in a hurry, sauntering along the marked pathways. The most interesting actor on the field is the fellow who throws the ball. One just has to be an expert to appreciate the finer points of the game.

I suspect that my flagging enthusiasm is not explained by the fact that I have not grown up with the game, but rather because I am simply not an American. I am not patient enough. The same holds for long lines at the check-out stands in shopping centers. I am the only one who gets impatient, or nervous, when the checker seems to be too slow. Stress creeps up on me when I have to wait and also when I cause others to wait. I am the only one who is so afflicted. All others seem to be satisfied that there is good reason for my sluggishness.

(Translated by Sandra & Ewald Schlachter)

Typically American

For the past two months, I have been living once more among Americans. They, as people everywhere, are as different one from the other, as people in Switzerland, perhaps even a bit more different. Nevertheless, it does not suffice for me to simply take note of the broad range of American attributes. In fact, I keep a sharp lookout to spot among the people I meet those who conform to my expectations of what "typical" Americans are like.

So far, I have met only one woman whom I recognized as a "typical American woman." Do I have to tell you that I do not like this woman? To call someone a "typical American Woman" implies a negative judgment in the same way in which the terms "typical German," "typical Belgian" or "typical Swiss" imply negative judgments. How do I know what makes a person "typically American?" And how can it be that among roughly one hundred American women only one qualifies as a "typical American woman?" Doesn't that sound odd? When one percent is "typical," what about the ninety-nine percent who are not?

I call an American woman "typical" when she conforms to my preconceived notions about American women. I knew that long in advance of coming to America. And then I have to conclude that most American women are not "typical" at all. Does that perhaps induce me to change my preconceived notions? Not at all. This inconsistency has nothing to do with my actual observations. I simply expect that, for example, a German behaves in a disagreeable manner. When I meet one who does not conform, I simply reclassify him as not a typically German person. That is the way it works.

Again and again, I am dismayed how difficult it is to resist this temptation. In every instance, I struggle mightily with myself before I give in to the prejudice. I have been often in America. I like it here. And nowhere else in the world do I have so many occasions to notice how much I depend upon my preconceived notions. It is now twenty years since I first visited here. Much is different now from what I encountered then, but I barely notice the differences, because they are not typical of the country as I envision it.

When I arrived twenty years ago, I expected to find a country with few laws and few prohibitions. In any event, I expected fewer signs telling me what I was not allowed to do than in my own country. The general appearance of the country has not changed much in that respect since then. But when I open a newspaper, turn on the radio or television, I am awed by the many references to the Supreme Court. Everyone and everything is, or is to be, regulated in every aspect by the law. Congress and government seem to be preoccupied, to the exclusion of broadly based politics, with the promotion of narrow objectives by means of more new laws.

It has always greatly amazed me to observe how the handicapped are treated at American universities. Special accommodations for the blind, the deaf, for people in wheelchairs, are the rule, as are special considerations by students in dealing with handicapped fellow students. And when I mention to Americans how extraordinary this seems to me, what do I hear? "That is the law." And there go my positive preconceived notions about the country. That matter of fact answer hurts. Similarly, here at the College, alcoholic beverages are no longer served at festive occasions. Why not? Perhaps because of moral considerations? Not at all. The reason is that deans and professors might become personally liable if a festive participant drove off and, perhaps hours later, injured someone. Such liability suits always go into the millions of dollars. They have become a popular preoccupation. Attorneys advertise in the media to make sure that no one who might have a reason to sue someone for some reason remains ignorant about his chance to become an instant millionaire.

I concede that I am arguing in this case for "more individual freedom and less government interference," but my political opponents in Switzerland had better be careful about their glee. This lack of personal freedom in the United States, translates itself, by means of negative restriction on possibly irresponsible conduct, into a desire for positive protection for all from possible consequences, a form of wealth to which every person is entitled. Sickness and injury can impoverish anyone, rich or poor. Societal protection, protecting all against poverty resulting from any cause, is utterly inadequate. Therefore, such liability suits afford the only adequate insurance available to everyone, a kind of economic self-defense. When I consider, from this perspective, what is going on in Switzerland, I catch glimpses, here and there, of "typically American" arrangements. There are these slogans calling for "more freedom — less government." They appear to me like thinly veiled attempts to undercut our system of institutions which insure social security to all under all circumstances with the American way, but without the unsightly spectacle of the liability suits.

(Translated by Sandra & Ewald Schlachter)

The Despair of the Peaceful

I was always peaceful, I was quiet and calm, it was tough and I didn't scream — and one day, I got awfully angry and I destroyed everything around me, I set fire to my own house, I screamed out 'cause I wanted to be heard — and now they come, the Whites, and the only thing that they can think of to tell me is: "Be peaceful!" But that's exactly what I always was, even before, my whole life long.

This is what a black man told an American reporter after the riots in Los Angeles. I think I know this — in smaller dimensions — it is my own plate I break when I am enraged, not my neighbor's, and I don't experience my rage as rage but as despair.

I get asked whether I lived through the unrest in New York. There must have been corresponding pictures on TV — but I didn't see anything, only a small demonstration in which two cars were destroyed right around the corner — but that, too, I only know from the newspaper. No, New York was quiet — a monstrous phrase as everyone knows that it is not true, and angst spreads, the angst that someday really everything could go up in flames — and not just two cars that maybe, who knows, to their owners, were almost everything they had.

But for the time being it is still a lottery with few chances, it affects someone, but it does not affect everyone, it does not affect me, it has not affected me so far. Maybe it will affect me only when it affects everyone and maybe our angst is nothing but our realization that there are millions in this world who "were always peaceful, calm and quiet, for whom it was tough and they didn't scream — and one day, they got so extremely angry" like that black man in Los Angeles said.

Question: How much would they have given in advance to those who took everything from them so that they would not take anything and leave them with a good deal — half, a quarter, ten percent?

The question — unfortunately — cannot be answered easily: I won't give them anything because they cannot claim it legally. And if I gave one, another one would come — and besides, everything I have belongs to me and I believe I earned it through ardor and fervor — or at least my fathers or my Switzerland did. I feel — I believe rightly so — innocent of their misery, of their poverty. And if nobody is to blame, then they themselves remain as the guilty, then it is all their own fault.

Only, in reality, we have all long known what the black man in Los Angeles expressed and we all cannot think of anything else except saying what embittered him: "All my life I was peaceful — and now they cannot come up with anything but telling me: Be peaceful."

Up to now the violent have been destroying their own property, the Yugoslavs their beloved Yugoslavia, the hooligans their beloved soccer, the Blacks their own huts.

We, however, do not suffer with the Yugoslavs — we only fear that one day it could be our huts or our countries. And there are even people who believe that something like this could be prevented by our refusal to belong to Europe; because our world is basically — as it always was — in order. We would only need "stability" and "peace," and we call out to others: "Be peaceful!" and we believe we have made a humane and Christian proposal — only, we thereby do not mean their peace but ours.

They would have to accomplish something — to be peaceful — so that we can enjoy our peace. And they accomplish it and accomplish it and accomplish it, until they despair and we do not realize that it would be our task to find peace and to invent peace so that the others not only have to be peaceful but could also enjoy their peace. I cannot help it, I believe in a possible peaceful world. Only, I do not do anything for its realization although I know it won't be given to us — especially not from others.

(Translated by Gene O. Stimpson)

He talks to me

The path to my apartment here in New York leads through the bedroom of another man. Normally, he is already asleep when I come home. He goes to bed early, between nine and ten, and he often reads a book before dropping off. I tiptoe when I pass him at eleven, and when the night is not too cold I see his face totally relaxed like the face of a child, the book lies still open besides him, it has slipped from his hands, a bottle of orange juice stands next to his bed. It is indeed a little embarrassing to have to walk every night through his bedroom on tiptoes. Even though, when he is still awake, he greets me friendly, wishes me a good night and I return his wishes. He is my neighbor and we know each other without me knowing his name or his background. But if I met him somewhere in a station I would recognize him, would approach him and say, remember, we used to live in the same street in New York. Maybe he would recognize me, too, because from time to time I give him a couple of bucks or put them next to his bed. Somehow I find this, too, embarrassing but he thanks me obligingly and wishes me well.

In front of my building there is a homeless person who sleeps here in any kind of weather, freezing temperatures or rain, and he is my neighbor. What I find so fascinating about him is that he lives so tidily. I myself find it hard to keep my good and proper apartment up here as tidy, my bourgeois existence always has an air of decay — he defends his life on the brink with tidiness, he has to survive and he has to do it day after day, night after night.

"Not so bad," he says when I talk to him about the bitter cold and I ashamedly sneak upstairs into my warm apartment. He probably only says "Not so bad" to comfort me as if he felt it was hard on me. "Not so bad" means something like "Don't worry!"

Well, perhaps my homeless neighbor is an exception. For example, he does not seem to be an alcoholic, he does not seem to have given up on himself yet, he still reads books and the newspaper.

And when I describe him I do him wrong since anything one describes gets a touch of romanticism — the romantic vagrant, vagabond, tramp, hobo. At least these romantic names have disappeared — now they are only called homeless.

And what impresses me is that he talks to me. He does not even ask where I'm from, where I got my accent from and he does not resent me for walking daily through his bedroom on my way to my warm bed — because I am the twofold stranger for him: I am — my accent gives me away — a tourist, a rich one, too, and I am someone with a warm bed, someone privileged.

I don't know whether it would be so easy if someone were to set up his "bedroom" in front of my house in Switzerland.

Well now, that does not happen in Switzerland or at least not so often. But anyway, I ask myself what would happen if it happened.

Would we talk to him, would he talk to us, and would we become neighbors?

But, as I said, the situation does not exist in Switzerland.

Or does it? Is there possibly something similar, comparable in Switzerland? And we just don't want to see it and we do not want any such neighbors. And we do not want them to talk to us. I for one am grateful that my "neighbor" tolerates my bad English.

He talks to me — perhaps to comfort me — and I may be his neighbor. He does not hate me.

(Translated by Gene O. Stimpson)

The Privatization of Life

New York is a city that leaves you alone and I enjoy that — to be alone among many people, friendly people, too. A city for long walks, a city for amazement.

"Where do you come from?" I ask the cab driver. From Afghanistan, from Russia, from India, from Senegal. Many hardly speak English. Almost all the drivers are emigrants. Driving a cab is their first — poorly paid — job. "How long have you been living here? How do you like New York?"

No, he doesn't like it at all. His life here is miserable and the question whether he would like to go back to Pakistan raises an emphatic "Yes."

He fled from the poverty among people to the poverty without people, to the poverty in solitude and I start to feel ashamed for my enthusiasm for New York. Whoever is a nobody here, whoever has no money, does not belong with anyone here.

The American society is ghettoed. If anything, you live here with a minute circle of friends. You don't meet them here in bars but at parties: family, friends, business partners, like-minded, equals, possibly even of identical denomination.

You don't even meet others in the bar, the poor, the every-day-people, the alcoholics — because the bar is too expensive and whoever sits there has money. And whoever has a lot of money does not go to bars but to restaurants with the same friends over and over again. And New York is still the one big exception in America. Here, the cozy bar is still in existence.

Outside New York, — in America — there is nothing left but private circles.

That once had its good reason and again and again was a reason for emigrating. Our Swiss Anabaptists emigrated to America because they could live there among themselves in peace and they still can. Homosexuals can live here among themselves, alternative people, sects, weirdoes. That is good and nice, that has always impressed me, and it took me a long time, some years, before I realized that I could not live here for good. You don't meet in this country. I miss the pub here, the local pub where I meet those who are different from me and where I meet everyone, those, too, that I don't like.

There is much discussion going on here about the riots in Los Angeles — what should be done to socially improve and integrate the Blacks. And whatever is suggested, there is no money for its implementation, be it education, social programs, or information.

However, what is really missing in this country is the place, are the places where you meet. The one Black will succeed, he will rise into the partying society, into a circle of professors or business people or Catholics or Protestants.

Whatever is happening here has to do with racism — but only marginally, only marginally. But even without hate — and hate is here rather rare, Americans don't have much talent for hate — even later, when everything was fine, education and social programs for example, the basic problem would still be the same: You don't meet in this society, the private party is no substitute for public life. Not only the poor live here in ghettoes but everyone. The holy credo of privatization is here not only an economical credo — it has taken over every aspect of life — there no longer is any public life.

I will soon return to Switzerland — not wholeheartedly, I love New York — and I have already dreamt that my pubs in Solothurn have been closed in the meantime. Many have over the past years.

Once they have all closed — and there won't be any but nice restaurants — then we, too, will become an American society that does not meet. We are already on our way.

(Translated by Gene O. Stimpson)

JÜRG FEDERSPIEL

Jürg Federspiel

Born June 28, 1931 in Kempthal. Lived in Berlin, Paris, Basle. Journalist and critic for several newspapers. Received numerous literary and cultural awards. 1979 "Werkjahr" of the city of Zurich. Lives in New York and Zurich. Short stories, novels, reports, radio plays, stage plays, film scripts, poems: *Orangen und Tode*, 1961; *Massaker im Mond*, 1963; *Tod eines Fohlens*, 1964; *Museum des Hasses*, 1969; *Die Märchentante*, 1971; *Träume aus Plastic*, 1972; *Brüderlichkeit*, 1977; *Die beste Stadt für Blinde und andere Berichte*, 1980; *Die Ballade von der Typhoid Mary*, 1982; *Wahn und Müll*, 1983; *Kilroy: Stimmen in der Subway*, 1988; *Geographie der Lust*, 1989; *Eine Halbtagsstelle in Pompeji*, 1993.

The Best City for the Blind

In March of this year, at 4:30 p.m. on Long Island, a 41 year old blind man was thrown from the platform of the IND subway station, and the assailant, a young man, left the scene in no particular hurry; only as he began to realize that he was being watched did he start to run. Intention to rob the victim could not be established. He had simply pushed a blind person off the platform; the blind man remained lying, unconscious.

That was on the 14th of March. Four days later, in the subway, 23 year old James Pacheco (also known as Mudo), deaf and mute, had his throat cut, and the assailant was an old man, a vagabond and homeless, a 60-year-old. He let himself be arrested without a struggle. The victim, the deaf-mute, belonged to the Gang of Crazy Homicides, who want to call attention to their rights as a minority, as well as to the injustices (intentional or unintentional) inflicted upon them by the rest of the millions of "normal" people, and for their "rights" and their "recognition," no knife is too sharp, no blow too heavy. James Pacheco, killed in the subway, had been sentenced in 1975 to eight years in prison for raping two adolescent girls in a subway car. In the fall of 1977 he had been released on parole.

There is no connection between the act against the blind man and the act against the deaf-mute.

To the Light House on 57th Street in Manhattan, a school and place of contact for the blind, come many complaints, by way of telephone or mail, such as: the blind get in the way of the pedestrian traffic; others complain that the sight of blind people depresses them, and then still others would want to know that "certain" blind beggars do not pay taxes on their begged income or that too much tax money was going to the blind and other physically handicapped. Of course, these are exceptions, and as exceptions not *particularly* meaningful. Despite that, they are meaningful. In the metropolitan area there live more than two million invalids: those who are actually physically handicapped, then the deaf-mutes, who are usually incorrectly categorized (there are many more deaf people, i.e., without hearing, than mute people), and then the blind; and all these blind people are, in their numbers, a political force. Over 36 million people in the country are handicapped. In New York state alone, 100,000 handicapped people voted for President Carter, and if he is to keep his promises, the government will have to spend billions on them. Special access ways or bridges to trains and boats, subways and busses; mechanical stair aids or elevators and so on (*and so on?*). The physically handicapped belong to those minorities (*minorities?*) who have been affected by the growing unemployment rate.

Julius Shaw, head of the office for the physically handicapped, says according to the Daily News, "The needs and demands of the handicapped are growing rapidly."

Between 500 and 1,000 calls daily, asking for help, but it all points to the downfall of humility. If necessary, the cripples will block the traffic with their wheelchairs, as in the recent occurrence in San Francisco: "We have learned from the women and the blacks how to fight for ourselves. We must either ask for sympathy or demand equality ..." If necessary, the cripples will even use their crutches in violence. And in the schools, the parents threaten and complain that the niveau of their children is being lowered to the level of the cripple. The Crazy Homicides are determined as a gang to always use violence whenever a deaf-mute is insulted or discriminated against. They also demand that every television program provides subtitles or sign language for the hearing impaired — at least that is what the opponents of the so-called "Wheelchair Lobby" claim, that lobby which, in fact, represents the interests of 36 millions in the country ....

The revolt has begun, and it is more than a revolt: it is an uprise against Creation, and who would not want to take part in the downfall of its absurdity? One person becomes a left-winger because he lost his left arm in an accident; he would have preferred it to have been the right one. The epileptics will not stand for it anymore, and that is final. The asthmatics join together in thousands because there is no air that is tolerable for them, nowhere, not before and certainly not now. Those with kidney disease have had enough of the complaints from those with liver disease for a long time, — where are the rights of those with liver disease? Which law helps women who hate their mothers? None. And who raised the level of cholesterol in pork? Probably the Jews. Who colored the skin of the Negroes black? Is the sun responsible for their pigmentation, or is it a God? Which party of asses invented rheumatism and brought it among mankind? The Temperence people want to abolish the grape, once and for all, otherwise the drunks will get drunker. He who eats only carrots will die of malnutrition: down with the carrots! Hemorrhoids are a social disease — man has to sit too much. Burn the chairs! Every girl is in danger of incest. (Just take a look at her father's face, mm?) Teachers are masochists, students have become sadists. Before we finally run out of things to eat: down with the dentists and out with the teeth! The lawyers fear the downfall of injustice and demand: more injustice! And as for the shortage of housing and living space: should the churches be allowed to remain empty? The car owners ask: is that not a waste of parking space? In India they are starving and their religion even forbids cannibalism.

Rats are invading mankind: death to those who oppose vivisection. Woe is me, I am melting, screams the ice. Down with the sun. I'll only shine for another few billions years, screams the sun. Down with Time — long live justice ....

What a Creation! Something went wrong with it. What? When? Down with humility!

"I'm Thora. Pleased to meet you. How are you today?" Thora, gentle, and with a radiance that reveals her innermost self, is a stout woman in her late thirties; she works at the Light House and helps primarily old people, most of whom have been blinded by diabetes: how to handle a watch designed for the blind and how to set the alarm; how to put lids over pans without burning yourself, or how to use the telephone. (Try to call somebody up with your eyes closed sometime ...) She helps the blind to see without their eyes. Thora comes from the South, from Alabama. Her father was murdered while she was still a small child.

"One of those stories from the southern states," she says casually. The screams, the shots, and again the screaming — those belonged to her first memories. Thora ran out of the house and hid behind a tree trunk. Already that morning her father had said that something would "happen"; it happened. It took years before she could even touch a gun. That is something that now she has learned, gotten over. She can touch a gun without being consumed by fear.

She had lived in the country, and her doctor had said that blindness, or in any case eye diseases, were abundant in areas near cow pastures; during pregnancy, Thora's mother had been infected, indeed, during all her pregnancies. Thanks to timely medical aid, the eyesight of Thora's siblings was able to be partially salvaged. Only Thora became blind; she "sees" shadows and colors. After the murder of her father, she was raised by her grandparents. The Lions Club of Alabama had put up money for an operation; nothing could be saved. Nevertheless — she was the first black *and* blind female ever to successfully graduate from high school and college. In 1959 she came to New York and was hired as a teacher by the Light House.

"Life's objective," she says, and I, of course, do not understand the phrase. She laughs. She always laughs, as if she sees something that others cannot.

On Friday, she is going to visit her wards in Harlem, and we make a plan to meet at the Light House; a young black boy (he is dumb as a post and unwitting — does he even know what his job is?) is already waiting for us.

"I have to escort people," he says sweetly, "blind people, you know." He leafs through the telephone book for hours and moves his lips along with it.

Thora wanted him to come with us. She does not let him take her arm, she simply holds his elbow in her left hand. "Harlem can be dangerous," she says, and smiles. Some of the apartments near

140th St. have been burned down; the jobless people are loitering about: total poverty is static and apathetic. Thora says from above the area looks like Hamburg after the war. How does she know that? Friends have described it to her. We take the elevator to the 15th floor. A dark-skinned black woman opens the door; the waiting student, the blind one, is her sister, 62 years old; she sits there, smiling, stretches her hand into the unknown which used to be familiar. She and her sister are Jehovah's Witnesses; in the neighboring room lies their 85-year-old mother and waits for death. It smells like bedroom.

The lesson with Thora begins. Everyone laughs, friendly laughter, like children playing Blind Man's Bluff — Thora's new patient is full of desire to learn. She will soon be able to thread a needle with a very large eye. "You must always try, as it was when you could still see," Thora informs her patient. "Everything has stayed the same, except you just can't see it anymore. But it'll work out."

"Yes," says the old lady, attentively. She smiles. Thora also smiles. A sort of triumph of patience, I think. (The Jehovah's Witness's apartment is unbearable — forgive my arrogance), Jesus is hanging everywhere, between the photographs of children and fathers and relatives, and once Jesus is even drawn in front of the Matterhorn, *the Matterhorn!* Did he have a souvenir shop there? The sofa is covered with a clear plastic sheet to preserve the original material.

Thora opens the little cover of her wrist watch and feels the clock face. The lesson is over.

We all thank each other profusely. "It was beautiful."

It is raining outside. Gloomy.

On the ground floor there is a school that bears the name of Langston Hughes, the black lyricist who died in the mid sixties: "Night coming tenderly. Black like me."

[...]

"Life is easier for those who were born blind," a man who could at one time see with his eyes tells us. "Those who were born blind need no readjustment. They probably (*probably*) have no need to know what an object's form or color is since the mind-set that was originally created for it is not available to them."

How does a blind person imagine (see?) color: When he smells freshly cut grass and someone says: that is green, he will always associate the color with the smell of freshly cut grass.

(How little *any of us* know about each other.)

A young girl in the lobby of the Light House listens attentively, her stare fixed in the direction of *our* nothingness, and smiles. (Always this smiling.) She still remembers when she had the ability to see, and is convinced that blind people who have *never* seen before can *see* clearly in their dreams — faces, animals, landscapes, moons, seas, and grimaces.

I do not dare to ask:

The dreams of the blind who have never been able to see ...

Do we remember (Platon's *Phaidon*) — in the prisons of our bodies — past lives? Does learning mean: to remember? Life in general: to remember? "They get their things together," the girl adds, "by listening, smelling, feeling, and touching."

"New York is the best city for the blind," says Paul, a young teacher, "I was only 22 when I began to lose my eyesight. Was pretty tough, wow!" He laughs. "For two months I was in complete despair, I hung around in the apartment and didn't do anything. Then I pulled myself together, afterall, I had my job, I was a math teacher and still am. I've always had good luck. I learned Braille and all that stuff, learned to get around and bought a dog, didn't want a walking stick. I didn't want people to help me all the time. It's too degrading. I live with my parents. What I do at night, you ask?"

He laughed again.

"I like people, see? There's a couple of dives I go to a lot and sometimes I meet friends there. Yeah, and girls. I also like girls, of course. Sometimes I go to a movie, too. It's too bad that the love scenes are usually silent. The last movie I saw was a movie about Switzerland and an Italian. It was called "Bread and Chocolate"; all my friends talked about it, but they forgot I couldn't see anything, and I don't know from German or Italian. I walked out after fifteen minutes. When you're blind, you've got to keep doing things, you've got to stay active." He knows New York very well. No, he doesn't read much, no novels in any case, more along the lines of scientific material, and once a week the weekly Braille edition of The New York Times. The school at which Paul teaches, Uptown Brooklyn, is a school for those who were thrown out of high school for one reason or another, and who now want to make it up. Most of them are 18, 19, or 20; they cannot attend every period since most of them have to support themselves, and sometimes they already have a wife and children.

The schoolhouse — shabby and dilapidated — is reminiscent of the school in the movie from the fifties *Blackboard Jungle,* and the students, mostly colored, seem at times as if they had been tamed or are under the influence of tranquilizers. Kindergartners, six foot one tall; certainly few of them had had any childhood in the sense that a European would understand it.

"Paul is terrific," says one student, and others agree: "He's absolutely fantastic!"

"Man, he's the best man I know," says another, blowing a bubble and letting it pop.

"Okay folks," yells Paul, "let's start!"

He must explain the European decimal system to them, and asks how many ounces of marijuana someone can be carrying if caught by the police; that is, the allowable weight. Laughter.

"Okay," says Paul, and quickly writes the rounded-off numbers (not the exact ones, he does not want to complicate anything) on the drawing board.

The students, adults actually, are sitting around the room however they please; they laugh, not because of the example, but because some numbers and sentences from the previous class were left on the board. Someone quickly goes up and wipes the writing away with a cloth.

The charisma of the young teacher is fascinating. His eyes stare into emptiness, yet he knows exactly where every student is. He also knows who is not there, who is ditching.

"Sometimes," Paul says later, "they try to trick me, but I know all their voices. I can also hear if someone is turning the pages of a comic book or of a text book."

A couple of the students hang around him after school; questions, which courses they should take next semester, what is worth it and what is not. Paul answers (it is not necessary for the person who is asking to give his name), and they are not only questions about school, they are questions about life. He knows what concerns each one, what problems lie in each one's way.

The following day we go out to eat together; we have planned to meet in the lobby of the hotel. The dog pulls him — he has become uncertain — towards the hotel desk.

"He wants to sign in," says Paul, "he seems to like the place."

I advise against it. Sometimes I find cockroaches sitting on the bristles of my toothbrush.

"He wouldn't mind," says Paul, "he never brushes his teeth. Right, Hal?" The dog wags his tail.

After Paul became blind and realized that he would never see again and had everything under his belt that a blind man needs to learn, he began to look for a position. Naturally, he was never simply rejected; there were excuses that really were not: a surplus of teachers.

Finally, he introduced himself to the principal of *this* school, and something happened that left him almost desperate: the principal asked what the name of the dog was. He answered, and the principal laughed: "That's my first name, too." The principal asked him to come back the next day; he had to ask the rest of the faculty if they would agree to work with a blind teacher. Out of 20 teachers, 18 agreed.

"The kids don't have many chances later on. They've missed too much, the competition is too big and the unemployment — you know."

When we want to sit down at a table in a Chinese restaurant (I am a bit at a loss, my companion less so since she is a woman), I throw my hands up in the air. I do not know *how* Paul wants to sit or *where* he wants his dog. He is a mathematician through and through, he feels all the chairs, thinks about it, sizes up the situation, lifts a chair up over the table and hands it to me, and shoves the dog into the empty space.

The waiter brings the menu, hesitates, and then hands it to me. Should I read it out loud?

Not necessary. Preferably shrimp. And soda, a Tab. Do I have any specific questions?

The night before, I had scribbled some questions on a piece of paper, and now, suddenly, they seem awkward to me and as if written by someone who was planning to interview a particularly unhappy individual. Paul is not unhappy, on the contrary. He does *not* know self-pity anymore, and I had thought up questions that were supposed to *avoid* self-pity.

"Are my shrimp here already?" askes Paul and feels the table-top. Nothing has been served except tea and Tab.

When Paul had completed his studies, becoming a math teacher, he had to forget his newest and oldest wish: to see Europe. "I would have loved it," he says, and smiles. (It is embarrassing for the author to always be mentioning laughing and smiling — one must tell *the things*, said Goethe, not what one *feels about* the things, a sign of dilettantism ... although when *dealing with* the blind, everyone is a dilettante.) Paul is always active. This morning he taught and advised at a hospital for veterans (most of them from the long-forgotten Vietnam war).

"Poor devils," he says, "the veterans of World War II are still hailed as heroes today. The crippled veterans of the Vietnam war are for many something like criminals who lost the war. Most of them aren't yet thirty. What caused their blindness I don't know. Partially diabetes, others somehow slowly became victims of their injuries, I'm not a doctor."

Tomorrow Paul will be training seeing-eye dogs, he has also learned how to do that.

With no real connection, I tell him about a twenty-year reunion of the elementary school in the village of Davos.

"How was it?", he asks, interested.

"Terrible at first. We had all become old, or something like that, and needed hours at first just to rediscover the 'schoolboy' of days gone by," I said, clearing my throat. The waiter had brought his shrimp.

Blindness is not hereditary, Paul says later, only diabetes is. Both grandfathers, maternal and paternal, were diabetics and had gone blind in their old age. Paul's siblings and cousins and relatives have not as of yet suffered from this disease or its consequences. "Well," says Paul delightfully, "but *I* got the ticket."

Paul is looking forward to summer. He has a light and agile body, is a good swimmer, and he loves sensing the girls around him. There is no showing off — he is manly and proud and strong, and for a woman he needs no seeing-eye dog, something that distinguishes him above countless sighted men. His sexuality has dignity, his skills at life and at love are recognizable.

He eats the shrimp and the rice down to the last kernel. Paul gets back to my class reunion: "I see everything just as it was until the moment of my blindness. My siblings have not gotten any older to me. When they talk to me, I see them just as I did in those days since I've lost my sight. My parents tell me they've grown old and gray, but in my mind they are still youthful people. Only through their voices have I begun to tell that they have gotten old, shaky."

For Paul, everything stays as young as he had once seen it. No aging or rotting spoil the memory of his sight. The world behind his eyes stays young. Without sadness, I go back to my hotel after this second meeting, but when I awake two hours later, my face in the mirror looks as if I had been crying, aged, as if I had met myself again at a class reunion.

The last person I want to talk about is Bernie L. He looks a bit like the actor Walter Matthau (his virility has left his body), but milder, kinder. He comes from a good household, money was always there, his mother spoiled him rotten. As a four year old, he had had a brain tumor and could see everything. But he can no longer remember his sight. The tumor was removed, his visual nerves were damaged in the process. When he awoke, he was blind. Blind?

He played with the neighborhood kids, was teased and made fun of at first, he kept his cheerfulness, even when a ball would hit him in the middle of the face.

Once the teasing and the making fun of got to him more than usual, and in his childishness he asked, "Why do you treat me like this? Am I different than you?"

The children laughed and said nothing. They just laughed.

Bernie went home. He knew the way.

"Am I different than the others?" he asked.

"Why do you ask?", said his mother.

"Am I different than Joey?", asked Bernie.

His mother began to cry, at least, he thought he heard her crying.

"You are blind," she said finally.

"Blind? What's that?"

"You cannot *see*. You are *blind*."

That is how he discovered something that for a long time he still was not able to understand.

"I was just too little," said Bernie. "Later, I began to understand, I mean, that I'm blind and all that, you know."

You get used to it. You also get used to giving or not giving, beggars are a whim, just as their own moods or the attitudes they decide to project, attitudes of the misfortunate, vericose veins of poverty colored black, purple, or sky-blue. The class-conscious beggar with one clean and shiny black shoe, the other foot is bare, dirty; the distinguished beggar who lapses into a humble mannerism when approaching, and whose folded hands, when given nothing turn immediately into lashing, snapping, aristocratic fingers; the half-naked beggar, even in winter, bearded, tough, who kindly, lovingly, lets his dog rest on a small rug — a silver ashtray at the animal's nose, that beggar, who tells his tale of legal tragedy, housing tragedy or so, handwritten on two cardboard placards, takes dollars only — *underlined* —, green paper, because lawyers and justice are expensive (so that the money will not be blown away, he has placed a loudly ticking alarm clock on the three or four bank notes); the beggar who always whines like a small child (he whines so miserably that some people have already threatened to beat him up) — he gets on your nerves, the poor guy; that beggar with the shriveled balloon that hovers shakily above his hand:

Parkinson the First; that one also with the bandaged knee who for months has been begging for a contribution, he wants to go back to Philadelphia to die, a little while ago it was San Francisco — How much patience it takes, how much courage, how much imagination and endurance, false and true humility. The God of Beggars has invented tricks for humility. Woe to the beggar with whom he cannot put up. He is the lazy one.

A few blocks away, on Madison Avenue, stands another one with a German shepherd. He holds a tin can in his hand, rattling the coins busily and monotonously. His eyes have no pupils, smashed egg whites, nothing else. He shakes the change and mutters thanks.

With this description thrown to the reader like stinking meat comes sympathy, a cheap and bad conscience, a vague fear of blindness, very unpleasant in an optical era without any vision; thumb and forefinger search through the pocket for the quarter that the ketchup-fingered bartender had just tossed on the counter as change.

Noon, and the blind man stands firmly in the blazing sun. He is a power. And he knows it. Whoever cannot become quickly involved in a conversation, deeply involved, God knows he must look at him, the blind Negro.

Maybe, why not, he lost his sight attacking a store owner; a bad kid? Nobody would deny him a nickel, on the contrary, but one would have to be able to *say* more about him. What good is a description to the reader? Maybe he is a victim of toxoplasmosis, maybe he fell into the spikes of a garden fence — whatever, he is a power, and, as is often the case, he is a power without proof or argument.

Yesterday — or is it tomorrow? — I walk past him. The street is empty. He hears me coming, I know it.

"Hey, mister," he yells.

I stop.

"How about a dollar?"

The dog on the leash barks and bites into the air. "I could, say, let the dog loose a little, mister," he yells. "Ya hear? Seeing-eye dogs are loyal and sharp, how about that dollar! Let's say two dollars. Yeah, two! What would it look like, mister, if a seeing-eye dog attacked you? You'd have to think up a pretty good excuse. Imagine the police when you tell them, 'The blind man's dog on Madison Avenue attacked me!'" The blind man laughs.

"I said two dollars. Two. And don't ever try to describe me again, mister, never again!" Nearby, a trash can blazes. They burn often in the summer, the trash cans.

It just takes the burning end of a cigarette.

(Translated by Tom Schnauber)

CHRISTOPH GEISER

Christoph Geiser

Born August 3, 1949, in Basle. Journalist. Co-founder of the literary magazine "drehpunkt." 1980 lecturer at Oberlin College, Ohio. Lived in Berlin, London, Paris. Lecture tours in Australia and the United States. Received several fellowship awards. Lives in Bern. Poems, short stories, novels: *Bessere Zeiten*, 1968; *Mitteilung an Mitgefangene*, 1971; *Grünsee*, 1978; *Brachland*, 1980; *Disziplinen*, 1982; *Wüstenfahrt*, 1984; *Das geheime Fieber*, 1987; *Das Gefängnis der Wünsche*, 1992.

Desert Passage

It was as if all the inhabitants of the desert wanted to quickly show themselves to us again before it turned totally dark.

Look, it tried to grow outside the reservation — a stunted Organ Pipe whose sparse thorns never hurt anybody; just before the entrance to the park, right next to the sign that marks the protected area: "Organ Pipe National Monument."

The symbol — a typical case of wild growth, you said, almost moved, as you are by everything that flips out and grows a bit over the allotted boundary.

A border crossing, but it hasn't done it any particular good.

We stood around for a while in the parking lot of the Visitor's Center, which had already closed, and waited — until, as a prelude, a vulture actually appeared. Gliding away low and slowly above us, he presented himself, circling, to give us time to quietly recognize him — the faithful companion of our travels.

At best, I had known of vultures through books and zoological gardens of my childhood; dilapidated, with truncated wings, sadly hobbling about: caricatures of this mythic bird that for me did not exist in the wild — until all of a sudden the cloud appeared in the sky over the black stone desert at the edge of the Sahara. Egyptian vultures, you called them — somewhere an animal has died. Since then, they have been following us, and you have recognized them every time. At first most of them were only misleading shadows — the large, hazy shadows on the yellow cliff walls of the Greek mountains — until we made the birds out in the glare with the binoculars, perfectly camouflaged, sailing just under the bright background. Griffon vultures, you were certain. If they had not cast shadows, we would have missed them.

Yet we did not find the carcass over which they were circling, neither at the edge of the Sahara nor at the foot of the Greek mountains.

We were actually still waiting to be met by a condor, the largest of them all; we would have deserved it. But you did not want to drive to the particular reservation in Northern California where the various conservation groups were arguing over the last two hatchlings — miles away, only to quite possibly not see the condor anyway.

He was supposed to have met us by chance, like the signs over the Sahara, the shadows over the cliff walls, like the small turkey buzzard that gradually rose in the last glimmers, after we had recognized it, until it was lost in the twilight.

It is always a little startling — the impatience with adjusting the focus to our different eyesights. I let you, the expert, have the first look, then we passed the binoculars back and forth for a while.

Naturally, it is always a revelation when something that does not exist suddenly appears. After all, the roadrunner is a cartoon character from California television: as if he had only been waiting for the departure of the turkey buzzard, he flitted out from the shadows of the Jumping Chollas, brushed back and forth across the parking lot, stopped suddenly, head lifted, hopped on to one of the picnic benches, from there, after a sideways glance towards us, hopped up onto the table upon which a sloppy tourist had left a half-empty cup of coffee, stuck his beak in, rejected the coffee, danced an encore for us, and finally, after the show was over, sprinted up into the Smoke Trees.

You first missed his pursuer from the television series. You were studying the pinned up information sheets in front of the Visitor's Center bungalow with your back to me and were, for the moment, out of the line of sight — I stood alone in the growing twilight at the edge of the parking lot, where, in red, handwritten letters, a wooden sign warned to beware of rabies.

At first I took him for a wild dog, a sort of wolf, longlegged, with ochre-yellow fur, in amongst the loose shrubbery. He stared up at me, I stared at him and did not move — both of us motionless for a while, watching distrustfully.

Slowly and carefully, without letting him out of my sight, I backed up to our car, ready to bolt. Possibly a predator, I was not sure.

By the time you appeared again, he was already gone — without a sound, without a trace, I had not seen him run away, in amongst the shrubbery, in the growing twilight.

But it had not been a wild dog — *you* were certain. I had stopped abruptly by the side of the road, and you had come much closer to him than I had. As I stayed behind in the car, you approached him slowly, quietly, and upright, across the open terrain, in the already murky, gray light of the approaching night, until he gradually veered off sideways, hesitantly, slouching, with his tail tucked under.

Suddenly he disappeared in the murky light, so that we would not have been able to see how he fled. He did not flee; he looked at you nearsightedly, then he, the meeker one, went on his way.

He stole away, peacefully and cowardly, no threat to people, seeking civilization, you said.

Like our little desert fox — content and accommodating, a silent companion?

Actually, we had wanted to hear the coyotes howl ....

Foxes bark, right — but that is not exactly true. Your unfitting zoological comparisons and the characterizations in the cartoon series on California television confused me; if I had already known at the edge of the parking lot, next to the red sign, that the coyote belongs to the family of wolves, my fear would have been even greater — and just as uncalled for, of course.

But his flight behavior is the same: suddenly gone, like Stevy.

No howling came from the prairie wolves. We waited at a trailhead, windows down, motor turned off, headlights dark, until the outlines of the giant cacti gradually appeared in the moonless night, and our eyes began to adjust. But only the muffled rumbling of the cars from the highway was to be heard.

We had still wanted to drive around in the night a little, just cruising you said, like pilots when they are unable to land and have to circle the stopped-up American airports; but on the highway, I was forced to break every tolerated speed limit. Was there an RV rally going on here? You were also irritated: nothing but oversized RVs, tailgating with their brights on, passing me only at the last second, until I couldn't see anything anymore and had to blindly save myself in a turn out. We climbed out and fled into the night, into the stillness.

It had become comfortably cool, a light evening breeze blew, the ground rustled under our steps — parched, invisible stuff.

Be careful, you'll set the prairie on fire —

I was startled, it hadn't even occurred to me, a stupid western European city dweller from a rainy country. With a bad conscience, I trampled the lit cigarette out immediately, angry with myself, until nothing was left glowing in the darkness.

You hadn't meant it *that* seriously — actually, for a real brush fire, you comforted me, there needs to be a consistent groundbed of grass so that the fire can take hold. Then, of course, it only takes a spark. Here, the ground was too sparsely grown.

But a bit of my bad conscience about my carelessness towards nature remained: fear, that she could avenge herself with fires, pyromanias — I was again afraid of the flying sparks, as it ought to be.

Suddenly we were standing in front of the dark trunk of a Saguaro which disappeared above us. Below us the headlights flew by and, for quick moments, glided over the mesh of shrubbery surrounding us. Very close by, against the background of the muffled highway noise, a soft sound could be heard — a high-pitched, steady hum, like a swarm of insects: but it was the thorns, set in vibration by the wind, as if they were strings. The whole cactus trunk sang — hypnotic, electric, alien.

We both listened in wonder — then we gave it up. It was getting darker and darker, we were both worried about rattlesnakes, and there was no point in driving on. The descent against the racing lights, back to Lukeville, was dangerous enough as it was. I drove very slowly in the farthest right-hand lane, ready to swerve off into the desert at any moment, as one RV right after another, with trailers even, upon which the broad outlines of ugly objects rocked, raced past us without lowering their high beams.

The insides of the RVs were brightly lit, full of people whose shadows danced in the windows.

Those are the inhabitants of Phoenix, you said, as if that would explain everything. The extended weekend, we hadn't thought of that, now they're on their way back from surfing, from the beaches on the Gulf, and are returning home to their heroic stone towers. Not glassy, light, and unreal, like downtown LA, but rather glowing red pillars of cement, forts or temples, cult statues with gleaming eyes, Egyptian or Indian, colored gold by the setting sun: A phoenix, you thought, in driving past on the high ramps of the freeway interchanges, just resurrected, almost terrifyingly indestructible, godforsaken, nothing human left: no inhabitants.

What may *they* look like?

There they stood — with their surfboards, motorcycles, go-carts, sailboats and deep-sea yachts on trailers — in the floodlights of the gas station, legs astride and husky, in front of the pumps, next to open car doors, in bright white swimsuits with bright blonde hair.

I was still half blind when we finally reached safety. We both stumbled towards the low bungalows, across the large lot that had suddenly come alive: curious dogs wandered about, goatsuckers swirled around in the rays of the streetlights.

Loud beatings of wings, bright chirping calls — I had never seen goatsuckers. What is that? Goatsuckers, we have them too, only one hardly sees them any more. But you could still clearly remember the image: Goatsuckers in the rays of the street lamps at the outskirts of town, nothing unusual, not too long ago.

The bar was gloomy and empty. The game machines blinked monotonously in the background, the jukebox was put away. We sat together at the counter, the only customers, Beba took us for father and son.

I corrected her.

I wouldn't have done that —

Did I do something wrong?

You didn't mean that too seriously either — just that it would have been easier to lie, you thought.

I didn't ask you what you suddenly were afraid of. My answer had been simple, a single word, harmless, neutral, without thinking about it, it just slipped out.

Friends.

In any case, she understood — you comforted me: it probably makes no difference to her; an impressive, old Mexican woman, with heavy make-up, in a long, loosely-fitting sky-blue dress, very low cut — an opera singer, we both thought almost simultaneously. On the tarnished mirror between the bottles stuck a photograph that showed what was probably her in younger years, all dressed up in black, next to a lighted Christmas tree.

An ancient woman, yes, but no accomplice. Proud and suspicious at first — condescendingly, almost reluctantly, she mixed us our first, and it seemed to me a weak, margarita, while carefully inspecting us, as if she knew that we were observing her as well. But it was she who asked the questions — I don't really know why she always directed them towards me, with occasional sideways glances, almost as if she still didn't trust you: too unapproachable on your too-small throne. I thought she said Finland, but she probably meant Phoenix, a hearing problem ....

Switzerland.

That, too, she took calmly.

You did not want to start, and I am not used to talking about ourselves in a foreign language, so she made us her audience.

Every time she wasn't able to negotiate the tower of Winstons on the high shelf next to the mirror, she would throw us a theatrical look of despair over her bare shoulder: we understood — before she took a deep breath and started to call her frail son out of the apparently extensive back rooms:

Semi...

She only had Winstons, and so you could only get Winstons.

They all yelled for cigarettes and beer, bursting in suddenly, impatient and greedy. They yelled at everything: at each other, to each other, for no reason, terse, high-pitched, with grating, raw voices. Restlessly, close to us, they hung at the counter for a while and grabbed hungrily, all over each other, right past our faces, into the big green glass in which hideous sausages swam in turbid vinegar.

A horde, close enough to smell, half-naked, still moist from the heat of the drive; quivering, wet flanks, gleaming torsos, their nipples fleshy and hard, their tight shorts bulging with half-erections.

You didn't know anymore where to look — silently, with a smile, up and down, left and right, in the mirror on the wall: surrounded — leaning your elbows on the counter, with your shoulders hunched, you finally decided to make yourself small, slouched, so that they wouldn't knock you off your stool.

The pinball machines blinked monotonously in the mirror, a gap yawned on the shelf where the tower of Winstons used to be; they had left, brown paper bags full of provisions in their arms.

For a little while longer I heard the commotion outside, the roaring of the engines.

We stayed seated, in the muggy humidity, in the haze of beer and sweat, suddenly alone again, next to each other, as so often in the end, having a Southern Comfort — a name you took literally.

Was it the little bit of tequila at the beginning or the Jack Daniels later on that had been too much?

You were already playing daisy wheel with your wedding ring on the wood of the small counter — not a good sign, this last thing that I saw, blurred in the murky mirror.

You didn't want to see anything anymore.

I didn't want to hear anything anymore.

It was easy, in looking back, to blame the alcohol.

(Translated by Tom Schnauber)

EUGEN GOMRINGER

Eugen Gomringer

Born January 20, 1925 in Cachuela Esperanza (Bolivia). Studied economics an
art history. 1967-1985 cultural manager of Rosenthal porcelain. 1976-1991 pr
fessor of aesthetics, Dusseldorf. 1987 Writer-in-Residence, Max Kade Institut
USC. Since 1991 guest professor in Germany and the US. Lives in Wurlit:
Founder of Concrete Poetry. Poems, essays: *konstellationen – constellations
constelaciones*, 1953; "Vom vers zur konstellation" (manifesto), 1954; *33 konste
lationen*, 1960; *das stundenbuch*, 1965; *manifeste und darstellungen der konkrete
poesie*, 1966; *Poesie als Mittel der Umgangsgestaltung*, 1969; *gewebte bilder*, 198
zur sache der konkreten, 1988.

At Home with the Missionaries —
Almost a Fairytale

Early on I was accorded the privilege of getting to know the Americans, that means, strictly speaking, the citizens of the United States of America, as missionaries — and as such, at least it seems to me, in their innermost nature. At first, however, just by hearsay: As a child in Bolivia I could occasionally hear more than understand from the conversations, that in addition to the Swiss missionaries there were also real Gringos, Americans from the North, who were also active in the same sacred task. As the Bolivian-Swiss childhood later changed into the fulfillment of compulsory military service, served mainly in southern Switzerland, I encountered the American missionaries in the form of traveling, relaxing GIs.

A single sense seemed to satisfy them all and made them appear, especially to young women, open and generous: They had fulfilled a difficult and necessary mission in Europe. The simple boy — he didn't even need to come from Utah — stands as a straw blond farmer's son from Oklahoma in my memory still, how he was superior to us Europeans — men of letters, art historians, wine and coffee connoisseurs, debaters — by means of his mission. Now, we did well, at first to listen to them. After all the missionaries came to us with all kinds of new gifts. Instead of with the holy scriptures and glass beads they marched up unbelievably relaxed with sousaphones and the new sound.

In the wake of their conquering — i.e. relief mission one of the most irresistible and effective gifts was bestowed upon us. The drink Coca Cola began its triumphal march at first in a bottle, which my generation, trained in warfare, was able to immediately recognize as an imitation of a handy projectile, for example, of a slightly elongated hand grenade. At the latest in the film "One, two, three" by Billy Wilder was the explosive force of this wonder weapon universally and humorously displayed in its amalgamation of economic and political potency. The joke circulating at the time could by the way be understood as an ethical counterpart, whereby the Holy Father in Rome should be convinced, by means of a lucrative counteroffer, in the future to end his prayers with "Coca Cola" instead of the usual "Amen."

In the last decades, I was able to repeatedly make myself familiar with the character traits of the missionaries directly on the spot in North America. In principal it must be kept in mind that not all Americans are willing to carry their missionary activities overseas, that quite a few even fight against it and still see, with not much less chance of success, their territory in their own country. This, however, to the disappointment of those overseas who gladly want to see a little missionary pressure employed as compensation for their own inabilities. Observations in the country of the missionaries always amaze Europeans anew. Because there the sense of mission comes to light so openly and friendly, that every European-cultural stubbornness melts away in a formerly non-recognizable readiness for joy and optimism. Being addressed by your first name, which is obligatory with every acquaintance, has a disarming effect — with which the missionaries who stayed home have an easy time, in any case with the European youth, who instead of allowing themselves to be lead like in the good old times to Hameln or into the Holy Land now follow in a never ending stream across the ocean.

Above all, persistence in sticking with the mission counts as one of the most important character traits of every missionary. And in a mission there is probably a duty, even a calling to be understood, whereby it must be distinguished between a higher calling, a being appointed by a higher authority, which the more unknown it is, the higher it is to be esteemed, and a self imposed calling. One speaks, therefore, about a sense of mission. No matter what happened back then — Columbus, conscious of his mission and unwavering, stuck to his course to the west. His persistence was rewarded. It lived on. It has been shown more than once in the history of America that even missionaries are not immune to being missionized. Thus, for example, the Latin American immigration — remembering the fantastic tourist attractions of the missions between Los Angeles and San Francisco — even the names of the two cities draw attention to this after all — can be seen as one of the many types of games in the give and take of missionizing.

It is also the case that the Americans are often willing to invite missionaries home, namely then, when they hope to garner from them spiritual and cultural gain for themselves. Take for example the mission of Concrete Poetry. An articulate and theoretically well versed missionary is given yearly the duty to propagate Concrete Poetry to the often still unconverted, anywhere in the vast country, which is equipped with little language material but a great sense of mission.

Whoever informs himself about our theme, encounters in every step a sense of mission, sees himself surrounded by missionaries. In this respect, not all of them treat their subjects so friendly and affable like it is done by the Americans.

So far I referred to the military, economic and political missionary activities of the Americans and mentioned some psychological characteristics. I saved for myself what is probably the most comprehensive mission which ever went out to conquer the world from American soil — most assuredly one can speak about a conquest, even if it proceeds quietly but openly. The following presentation and even the title of this Almost-like-a Fairytale pertain to this: At Home with the Missionaries.

One must imagine that in the first decade of this century a couple of Americans had lunch together in Chicago and that from this meeting, which most certainly could not have had anything conspicuous in the daily lives of the working people, a world wide organization developed. Out of this inconspicuous lunch meeting — the meeting remained inconspicuous — grew an international net of clubs, with far more efficiency than could merely be attributed to this weekly lunch meeting. Even the sarcastic word of Bernard Shaw, who answered the question "Where is Rotary going?" with "Rotary is going to lunch," could not harm this journey to lunch, today in 184 countries with 25,600 clubs with more than a million members, both men and women. It is more likely to find approval, considering that eating a communal meal after all possesses a large symbolic power from time immemorial.

The solidarity, indeed the optimistic, unending development of the world wide Rotary organization is actually founded on communal meals, is however only assured, when it — whether breakfast, lunch or dinner — can take place in the spirit of friendship and harmony.

The assembly of the participants is a written requirement. It is not restricted to any occupational group, nor is it a game or sport club, which get together separately, on the contrary, the participants belong to very different occupational groups.

However, membership is not open to everybody — he or she must be recognized in their own line of work, he or she should have also proven themselves steadfast in life. The "Spirit of friendship and harmony" is itself, however, only another requirement for the most noble goal of the world wide organization. This consists in its concise motto "Service above all": Service above all, wherever man and woman stand and in whatever they do.

"Service above all" is a plea which supposedly would not be trusted to another nation, to another country with some prospect of success like to the American nation, like America. Whoever investigates philosophical ponderings will come upon in this regard an American heritage and find for example, that the first and most effective American philosophy, the pragmatism of William James, 1842-1910 (1905 is considered as the founding year of the Rotary), has laid down of its most prosperous traces. William James' "The Will to Believe" gives the motto "Service above all" its persistence, which we have already mentioned as the core of their mission. The trace of simplicity of which the Americans are often accused finds itself as the foundation of a home-made philosophy, namely (in "The Sentiment of Rationality," 1879-1882): "The facts of the world in their sensible diversity are always before us, but our theoretic need is that they should be conceived in a way that reduces their manifoldness to simplicity. Our pleasure at finding that chaos of facts is the expression of a single underlying fact is like the relief of the musician at resolving a confused mass of sound into melodic or harmonic order. The simplified result is handled with far less mental effort than the original data; and a philosophic conception of nature is thus in no metaphorical sense a labor-saving contrivance."

Assuming that the world outside of America represents a "Confused mass of sound" — a mission, a calling formulates from it reducingly the will to harmonious order: Service above all! Ready to serve in daily life! The reputation of a leading power which consciously buys into a return from diversity and mental exertion for the will of international efficiency. Rotary, however, is their daily bread.

In 1992 I had the opportunity during a few weeks to more intensely experience this daily bread of a world wide mission than would have normally been the case with occasional visits. As a guest — let's say in Florida — with six families, who was moved on every three to four days or sometimes after a week, I not only learned about the spacious designs of the country houses, I not only learned to accustom myself again and again in new, however very similar guest rooms that had been vacated just in time by sons or daughters, I was from the kitchen, from breakfast to the television program and to the help you get-to-sleep drink included in the American way of life. I was driven in the country's roomiest limousines to the barber, to the photographer — also a Rotarian, naturally — to the shopping center, to the attractions of the city or the county. Above all, however, it was respected from both sides, from the sides of the guests and the host, that we appeared on time to the meeting of the host clubs, that means to the official ritual, ordered hierarchically and in the entire world where Rotary has become established, carried out in the same way. In spite of the simplification in a harmonious order, founded as we have seen from the philosophy of pragmatism, there are, however, through a world wide comparison, typical differences of interpretations to be ascertained from country to country, often from club to club.

In the land of origin of the Rotarian mission and thus also in the land of "The Will to Believe," the meeting is most emphatically embedded in devoutness. "We" begin mornings at 7 o'clock with a happy song, as a rule dedicated to Rotary and its mission and performed with robust singing, pray and ask for our own protection, and also for the protection of all the others in urgent need, and — only the Americans themselves — say the pledge of allegiance. Then comes breakfast and at the same time the daily agenda would be taken care of by the president, secretary, and other officers. In this point all the clubs in the world proceed relatively similarly. In greeting the guests they put forth substantially more effort in the home country of the Rotary than in the other places.

"We" can in America also celebrate the classic lunch-meeting, while the evening-meeting which is often practiced in Europe does not suit the Americans who prefer to go to bed early. Whereas the European in the club seeks a conversation, possibly within the circle of friends over drinks, the American is more likely to seek the spirit of friendship and harmony in mutual visits at their homes or during outings, often also across the street, where the missionaries are then so to speak among themselves. The engagement of the American Rotaries is often so significant that Rotarian service becomes a second, if not a main occupations. Among the members of the highest Rotary devoutness — please, one always keeps in mind the motto "Service above all" — the missionary or the missionary couple strive to set aside an entire room with writing desk and files as an action office in the service of this motto. One could classify that as the extension of a universal idea carried into the private sphere: It must begin at home ... (to quote a German-Swiss author).

Let us keep in mind at the close of this small study about the American as missionary, the missionary as American, that in his sense of mission, now aside from the mission of fast food, the category of necessity is inherent from case to case, that very often, when one must do "it," the American does it. He even sees, just this once, in the fulfillment of a mission something more, something other than a job. That surrounds his calling and himself with a nimbus of a world fairytale.

(Translated by John W. Arensmeyer Jr.)

EVELINE HASLER

Eveline Hasler

Born March 22, 1933 in Glarus. Studied psychology and history. Taught school for several years. 1990/91 visiting professor, City University of New York. Received several literary awards. Member of PEN. Lives in St. Gallen. Short stories, novels, children's books, film scripts: *Komm wieder, Pepino* (children's book), 1968; *Sonntagsvater* (children's book), 1973; *Die Hexe Lakritze,* (children's book), 1979; *Novemberinsel*, 1979; *Denk an den Trick, Nelly* (children's book), *1980; Anna Göldin: Letzte Hexe*, 1982; *Im Winterland*, 1984; *Ibicaba: Das Paradies in den Köpfen*, 1985; *Das Schweinchen Bobo* (children's book), 1986; *Der Riese im Baum*, 1988; *Die Wachsflügelfrau*, 1991.

The Wax Winged Woman

It'll all be over soon, Emily said, as she patted the cheeks of the youngest with the tip of her index finger, as is done to bring color to the cheeks of newborn babies, who struggle taking their first breaths.

Not again across the sea, not ever again .... The child's husky voice sounded heart-rending.

But I would, Gertrud protested. I want to go back to see Zurich, Grandmother, and the friends!

Then we will have to fly, like birds. Robert looked up to his father. Can't people fly? He looked expectantly at his father.

Two tried, Daedalus and Ikarus. Walter answered, but his heart was not in storytelling. Yet, the older children insisted on hearing the story, immediately, so Walter began reluctantly to tell the tale as he continued to survey the Hudson, over masts and sails, trying to make out Manhattan through the haze. Daedalus, a clever Greek architect or stonemason, decided one day that he wanted to fly in the sky like the birds. He gathered feathers, first small ones and then larger ones, and with threads and wax he made himself a pair of sturdy wings. Then, in the same way, he made a pair of smaller wings, shaped them carefully, and fitted them to Ikarus, his son. One morning on the beach, Daedalus told Ikarus: Follow me, don't fly higher than I fly; don't fly lower than I fly. No fooling around, no cutting capers ....

At this point, a yell for joy interrupted Walter. The ship weighed anchor and proceeded on course toward a berth which had become available at the pier.

Beyond the harbor with its tall masts and the gleam of white sails, the appearance of the New World was anything but romantic. Wooden shacks encrusted the dock. Wire fences held back the crowd that awaited the new arrivals. Uniformed porters began to work the crowd, one of them grabbing Emily's small suitcase. In the din, Agnes disappeared from sight and was lost for a few tense minutes until Emily finally found her standing in a line between the two-wheeled luggage carts at the immigration gate. The Kempin family took their turn in the slowly advancing line. The smell of the brackish harbor water was in the muggy air. The tall masts of the ships stood in bold contrast against the sky as sheet lightning illuminated dark clouds gathering at the horizon.

When the Kempin family reached the immigration desk, Walter could not understand the questions of the official and Emily had to push forward to speak for the family.

No, Walter did not presently have a job as a clergyman.

What would he do to earn a living?

Work as a journalist.

Where, for what newspaper?

As things work out.

The official, in shirtsleeves, no uniform, mumbled 'unemployed,' as he stamped their papers. He did not ask Emily for her occupation, but pointed to the abbreviation 'Dr. jur.' in front of her name and looked at her with furrowed brow.

What does that mean?

That is my professional title, Emily replied and added, almost apologetically, that she had graduated from the prescribed course of study in jurisprudence at the University of Zurich.

The official looked puzzled. He looked up at her as she stood before the desk, a small person, almost childlike. He seemed about to say something, but, conscious of the throng of those waiting in line, he simply continued:

Children?

Yes, three; Gertrud, Robert Walter, and Agnes.

Go ahead. The official smiled at her and waved to the children.

Next to the customs floor the possessions of the passengers were being unloaded and arranged alphabetically.

Walter and Emily had sent Elsbeth, the 16-year-old maid, to keep the children busy on the pier. However, three hours later, the Kempin moving goods, 22 boxes, were still not completely assembled for the customs inspection, and the children had come back, tired of looking and walking; Robert complained that he was thirsty, Gertrud that she was hungry, and Elsbeth's frustration manifested itself in tears.

Walter dispensed fatherly admonitions of patience. Emily, in her best school English, tried to get some information out of a passing customs official. For a while, the older children forgot hunger and thirst while watching their mother go through her efforts to get the right words out the right way. They even repeated some words they remembered from the English lessons Emily had given them on the ship: How long? Where? Oh, I see.

Finally, when it seemed to him that no progress was being made, Robert began to whine again. He wanted to take the ferry over to Manhattan. Why did they have to wait here so long?

As many times before, Walter urged patience. Then he took Elsbeth and the children to get some food.

Vending establishments dotted the pier. There were all sorts of drinks and huge sandwiches at twice the regular prices in New York, a Swiss compatriot warned him angrily.

A street vendor furtively offered Walter a switch blade knife for protection against the 'unlawful rabble roaming the streets of New York at night' but quickly dropped his display case into a sack and disappeared into the crowd when he caught sight of a police officer.

A man with a blond mustache introduced himself in resounding German as a representative of the 'New York Bible Society' and tried his missionary skills on Walter: With God into the New World, he urged. Walter tried to get away from him, finally telling him that he was a clergyman himself and believed in the teachings of the Bible.

Every word? the man replied from under the blond whiskers. When Walter nodded, the missionary laughed, and, with an all-encompassing sweep of his hand, he bowed down and presented a tiny thimble-sized Bible to Agnes.

By the time Walter returned with the children from the pier, Emily had found out why some of their boxes had been delayed. They had been misdirected to Castle Gardens. Because of 'your' mistake in labeling them only with numbers, not with letters, an official told them firmly. But the error had been discovered and the goods, on their way back, would arrive today. Emily's voice sounded thin and was almost drowned out by Agnes' piercing screams. The child had been stung by a wasp that had been attracted by the syrup in her cup.

Walter listened to the report quietly. His face was pale and he pressed his hands together. Emily could see his knuckles turn white. She knew his routine of shifting gears, when the going got rough. It was always the same scene. He seemed to lose his intellectual, positive register with reality, and shift into the accusatory mode, flailing with his arms: such junk, fuss, 'Spyri-stuff,' unnecessary fooling around.

Emily waited patiently until he suddenly fell silent, exhausted, looking about himself as if to make sure that he still existed.

He did not say a further word, but looked intently at the entirely uncharacteristic gleam on his shoes. It had been put on by a little black shoeshine boy, who had had his stand near the immigration gate. Beautiful into the New World, the boy had shouted; two pennies, Mister, beautiful into the New World for two pennies.

A new ship had arrived, with some 800 steerage passengers who had to be transshipped in boats to Castle Gardens; the crowd oozed from the hatches of the large ship like a mass of mud.

Towards evening, the missing Kempin boxes finally arrived, but could not be processed that day, because the customs office had closed. It would open early the next morning, before the first ship arrived. The children were tired. Walter had been given the address of a hotel operated by a Swiss couple. He read in the light of the lamps that frugally lit the pier: Hotel Naegli in Hoboken.

Take the children and get some rest, he said to Emily.

No, said Emily, you go. If necessary, I can get along in English. Walter yielded. He promised to come back in three hours to relieve Emily.

...ad not yet returned.

...customs building, Emily sat on one ...ht of a lantern. She still wore the ...band she had made from a remnant ...er plaid skirt. She drew the woolen ...hivering as she gathered the ends ...s passed back and forth, looking her ...ing questions and telling jokes. Emily ...he 22 boxes of 'Spyri-stuff,' as Walter ...cent pure bed linens, the silver tea-set ...piece table setting with the gold border.

She could still ...... mother remonstrate with her father, — she needs a hope chest befitting her station in life. You have refused her a proper dowry, but I insist that she get these things. She is a Spyri, Johann Ludwig, I just won't let you treat your own flesh and blood with such indignity — turning to Emily, she continued — take these things, Emily. Your husband and the children deserve to feel comfortable. Take good care of the heir-looms ....

Emily felt the burden of obligation imposed on her by these treasures from the Spyri halls in Zurich. And, worse, she felt the thinking expressed by these maternal admonitions as it obtruded on her consciousness; one does not just dispense with the maxims of generational wisdom, not by the facile, situational rationale 'forget that, leave all that old thinking behind you.'

Leave for the New World with the Old World on one's back, 22 boxes of Zurich, an unemployed husband, three small children, and a maid sniveling with homesickness. Without such encumbrance — how easily one would move, take the ferry to Manhattan. Alas, such was her life: existing in some traditional, restrictive setting, while ahead the apparent openness invitingly beckons.

The footfalls of a security officer approached, passed and merged in the noises of the harbor as he walked on.

Emily looked out into the darkness beyond the pier. She closed her eyes and called up, in her imagination, the mass of the ocean as it rose and fell. That ocean, it would cover her tracks.

That vast ocean between me and you, father.

I have physically removed myself from your life, from your plans, statistics, from your railroad tracks. I don't have to be afraid that you will appear to check up on me. I am safe from your interference, you, a man who needs to have firm ground under his feet, who goes to pieces, as it were, even on a voyage across Lake Zurich; I am safe from your interference.

Emily turned to look toward Manhattan, on the other side of the luminous green surface of the Hudson river. She envisioned the many thousands of immigrants that had arrived before her. Thousands, free of the bonds imposed by fathers, fatherlands, traditions. Like islands, cut off from the mainland. She thought of her future in New York: her better self waiting backstage, alone, relieved of the shadow of her father ... curtain, lights .... No stage directions ... and no sister, or mother, or anyone, who passed this way before. No wake in which to follow for easier passage. No father who, like Daedalus admonishing Ikarus, specifies the bounds, up and down, right and left, implicitly imposing a rule allowing only mediocrity.

Emily Kempin, the first European woman jurist in America. Other women will follow, sisters moved by the same spirit.

As time passes, the road will become wider, smoother. There will come the day when women will be able to move naturally in society. Like men? No, like women.

Twilight. The misty rain like dust in the light of the street lamps. Walter came running, open shirt collar, overcoat flying: he had overslept. His eyelids trembled as he told about Agnes' attack of sore throat and these aggressive spells, perhaps a form of homesickness. He had to sit for a long time by her bedside to calm her. Walter's eyes sought Emily's.

Agnes is so little; it will take time, Emily replied, shrugging her shoulders as if to underline her own uncertainty.

A uniformed official stepped into the light of the street lantern, bid them a good morning, and let them know that the customs office was about to open in anticipation of a ship that had already passed Sandy Hooks. The Kempin goods would be processed first, as the young lady certainly deserved to be relieved, after such a night ....

Don't you want to go to bed? Walter asked the question in rueful contrition putting his arm around her shoulders.

Emily shook her head, I am wide awake now.

Then we will wait together.

Walter was about to sit down on the next box, but Emily prevented him with a shriek. No, not that one! She pointed to the red label — 'Fragile.'

What is it? he asked.

Our wedding present from the congregation in Enge. He laughed, as he recalled how they had packed this treasure of white opal glass in layers of tissue paper and sawdust. This was the lamp under which Emily had studied Latin, Roman Law, and English. She would need the lamp. There was much to be learned in the New World.

They hired a horsedrawn carriage for the trip to the boarding house near Washington Square. It was ideally situated, near the University.

They saw their small, shabby rooms only late at night, because there was much to be accomplished. There were many visits to government offices, the search for permanent lodgings, registering the children for the school term, starting in mid-September. Emily had a conference with the secretary of the University at Washington Square which was, until 1894, known as the 'University of the City of New York.' Such activities filled the long summer days from dawn to dusk.

The family assembled for the evening and sat together as the cramped quarters allowed. The beds filled the small rooms like freight barges. Suit cases blocked the already narrow hallways. Despite the late hour, and the day's tedious errands, Emily was still wide awake and busy. She leafed through a dictionary, made notes for lectures she might give, some day, somewhere, in English. Gertrud and the maid shared a small storage room with a dormer window at the end of the hallway. Agnes and Robert were already asleep. Walter lay on his side, bracing his head on his left arm. He strained to keep his eyes focused on the dictionary in his left hand, but they continually wandered through the room, over the worn wallpaper, a floral motif on pink, which was wiped off at the head of the beds. On the ceiling, a kerosene lamp, converted to electricity, cast a weak yellowish light out over the room. The wedding present from the congregation in Enge, had, upon the advice of Fanny Weber, been sent away to be converted to electricity. Walter turned on his back and put the open dictionary face down on his chest. He was tired of looking at the words as they danced before his eyes.

Emily looked at him. Are you studying? He nodded weakly, suppressing a yawn.

Emily laughed, slid from her bed, stepped over a couple of still fully packed suitcases, and crawled into his bed. She slung her arms around his neck and looked into his eyes, drawing his face close to hers. Her eyes sparkled as in the days of their courtship and early marriage. He looked at her and asked, is it New York that keeps you awake? Yes?

Emily giggled and kissed Walter.

She was strengthened and overcome by a tenderness that made her yearn to make up for his way of opening up only reluctantly to the new customs and patterns of thinking in their new country. She was a model of patience and understanding also in handling the children. Somehow, she had the feeling as though she were responsible to all, husband and children, to make them happy in the New World.

Everything has begun so wonderfully, Walter, she said. Just think of the Webers, how they are looking after us.

After Walter had turned off the lights, Emily lay awake for hours, staring into the darkness. Ever since their arrival in New York, she had been unable to quiet down for a good night's sleep. She reviewed the events of the day.

The walk along Broadway with Agnes hanging on to her, and Fanny Weber leading the way and explaining. Every step produced new impressions, every street corner opened new vistas: commercial buildings rising to six or seven stories, with an occasional low, wooden structure, an incongruous remnant of a bygone age. Horsedrawn tramways. People of every shade of skin.

An ever changing scene that reminded her of the colored glass pieces of kaleidoscopes, producing new images at every turn.

Then, for a study in contrast, Fifth Avenue with its brown sandstone mansions overgrown with ivy. Stately carriages moving almost noiselessly on rubber covered wheels. The front yards resplendent with the fallen foliage of beech trees in the glory of fall colors. Glimpses of late Gothic spires, pointed windows. On to downtown, Broadstreet. Horsedrawn carriages before bank buildings with yellow-white awnings.

Men wearing black top-hats, their legs seem too short, jerky and tense gestures and movements.

Everyone rushing, pushing. The days pass more quickly in the New World. Every day with its assigned goal to be accomplished before nightfall. One has to swim with the stream of the moving humanity just to keep one's place.

Quick, Agnes, dear, move your little feet faster, we must hurry to get to that office before it closes for the day.

Eerie insomnia, night after night.

Emily lies awake in the stillness of the night, wide awake, as though a light were probing through her brain.

Like Dr. Wille, who, in the course of the monthly eye examination, comes closer and closer with his piercing little light, all too close come the age spots on his hands, his trembling yellowish goatee.

Have you passed on my letter, Dr. Wille?

What letter?

The letter to the pastor, my application for the advertised job as a domestic servant.

My dear, Mrs. Kempin — Dr. Kempin, many letters pass over my desk every day.

[. . .]

It is the end of January. The wind spirals dry leaves upward through the avenues. A cold wave drives many to seek free assistance at the local Arbitration Society Office. The office is open two days each week. Word is passed through the immigrant tenements and welfare shelters of Manhattan, to places like Pine Street, which are enlivened by hope as rarely as their meager dwellings are illuminated by the rays of the sun.

Fanny Weber and her assistants listen to the complaints. Legal problems are referred to Dr. Kempin in the back room. It is not yet certain whether she, a foreigner, will be admitted to practice law in New York courts. In the meantime, recently admitted attorneys represent the clients of the Office in court according to her instructions, for modest pay, but these ambitious men cannot be expected to stay on for long.

After a hard day, Fanny Weber and Emily Kempin take a walk in Central Park. The sky has cleared up and the snow covered park, its trees and bushes, gleams under the rays of the winter sun. In the distance, against the sun, the dark shapes of ice skaters move gracefully on one of the frozen ponds.

In the background, buildings rise into the blue of the sky.

It is about 5 o'clock in the afternoon and the park comes to life. As on the piazzas in Italian cities, the people appear, to see and be seen in what is seasonably in fashion. This year, the coats of the ladies are embellished with fur appliques, huge collar designs in blue fox, matched by bobbing hems and supplemented by muffs to protect the hands. The bridle paths and carriage ways bustle. It is well accepted that nowhere else in New York is it possible to see so many beautiful women. Emily observes the scene: These women are self-confident, more so than European women. They grow up under fewer restrictions. They take an interest in politics and business. Indeed, they even venture a little flirt here and there — it is said that they can confidently rely on the chivalry of American men. And yet, even these beautiful, sportive women, in spite of the appearance of freedom, are confined in an inexorable system of prejudices.

Only in the State of Wyoming are women allowed to vote. As a matter of principle, women in the upper classes do not work outside the home. Most universities still do not admit women. Emily Kempin, the first European woman to earn the degree of juris doctor, is the only woman allowed to attend lectures at the law faculty of the University of the City of New York.

As they reach a glade, a busy intersection of bridle paths and carriage roads, a young horsewoman turns out, dismounts and briskly approaches Fanny Weber. A lively discussion ensues. The woman is concerned with the solution of some urgent social problem involving a sewing class for poor women. As the conversation proceeds, Emily observes her: a young woman, who could be Fanny's daughter, elegantly dressed. She speaks with remarkable intensity; her face, with an almost childlike freshness, is dominated by eagerly attentive eyes.

Later, Emily learns that she is Helen Gould, the daughter of Jay Gould, the richest railroad baron, who is said to have absolutely no scruples in getting what he wants in business.

Helen Gould will participate in the next meeting of the *Arbitration Society*. The meeting is held in the salon of the Weber residence on 46th Street, a large room decorated with engravings of German landscapes in gilded frames. About 20 women are present. Fanny wears a bright yellow cashmere dress with pearls on the standup collar, that compliments her tall figure crowned by black hair. She is here and there, the all-gracious hostess. When guests arrive who have not yet met Emily, she takes pains to introduce her: Dr. Kempin, the first European woman jurist. She praises Emily's dedicated service in the Society. The latest developments are not good: Emily's application for admission to practice has been denied, because, as a foreigner, she does not qualify for admission to the bar in the State of New York.

Amelia Forman, the wife of Alexander Forman, a well known attorney, bluntly verbalizes what everyone feels: This decision threatens the existence of the *Arbitration Society*. It has become more and more difficult to recruit starting attorneys to handle cases in court.

An animated discussion ensues.

A lady who has listened attentively takes the floor. All fall silent. If there is what the feminists call the 'new woman,' she could be the prototype: Dr. Mary Putnam Jacobi, physician, writer, a lined face, authoritative manner, steely eyes behind rimless spectacles; she does not wear a hat, the characteristic feature of the societal uniform that is generally believed to mark ladies of quality.

Dr. Putnam does not mince words and her gestures and facial expressions cut right to the point: The law of 1886, that so piously specifies that women are entitled to be considered for admission to the practice of the law in the State of New York, is a pious sham. The lawmakers assumed that no woman can qualify for admission. As of now, the real problem is that the study of the law is reserved for men.

Not all states of the union are as backward as the State of New York. In 1869, Arabella A. Mansfield was admitted as the first woman to practice before the courts of the State of Iowa. Miss Lenna Barkaloo has been practicing law in the State of Missouri since the 1870s. Belva Lockwood fought for, and was granted, the right to practice before the Supreme Court.

It is time to remedy the situation in the State of New York. All present must unite to change the status quo.

Enthusiastic applause of the assembly.

Another speaker appears and calls for order. The new speaker is Mrs. Martha Buell Munn, wife of the well-known physician Dr. John P. Munn. Emily knows and respects her for her energetic participation in the work of the society's office. Mrs. Munn is one of the younger members of the Society.

The *Arbitration Society* is condemned to ineffectiveness, she says as an unruly lock of her red hair springs forth from under her hat. We need women who are trained in the law and can appear in court. Emily Kempin, who satisfies all requirements, has nevertheless been rejected by the establishment. Our offices are crowded with people who need help, yet we cannot render effective help. We must therefore organize a new society. We must organize a society to further legal education for women.

Another speaker struggles awkwardly to her feet, Mrs. Hewitt, a statuesque matron, the wife of the former mayor of New York. She adjusts her monstrous hat which does not want to keep its proper place on the wealth of her locks.

Dear friends, she says, as much as the concern for the welfare of the poor justifies the organization to promote the legal education of women, I can think of another reason, closer to our personal concerns. Don't we all have to concern ourselves with our property? Manage money? Sign contracts with employees? Make estate arrangements, in which knowledge of the law can be crucial?

I support Mrs. Munn in her proposal to organize the *Woman's Legal Education Society*; as you see we are making progress — we already have a name for our new project.

Dr. Kempin is requested to outline a plan for a law school for women. She makes one point clear: The ultimate aim is to provide solid, challenging courses, preferably under the aegis of the University. After the meeting, Emily has to answer many questions about her own career as a jurist. The ladies are utterly amazed to hear that she began to study at the age of 31, after marriage, and while raising three children and doing her part as a pastor's wife.

As a child, she was unable to assert her interests against the opposition of her parents, and against social convention.

I owe my liberation to my husband, she says. He was the first to recognize my abilities. In the evenings, after his work as a pastor, he taught me Latin and mathematics ....

Toward the end of the meeting, Walter Kempin appears at the residence.

He had picked up the two older Kempin children at their school, had taken them for a walk in Central Park, and had now come with them to pick up Emily for the cab ride to their new apartment at 14th Street, 207 East. Walter did not want to intrude and merely asked whether he and the children might wait in the hall until Emily was free, but the maid promptly announced his arrival to the hostess, who insists that he and the children join the assembled ladies in the salon for a cup of tea.

So he is seated in a place of honor at the head of the table, this modern man, the dream husband of the approaching Twentieth Century, who does not expect his wife to limit herself to the role of a low profile domestic servant, or an ornament, who willingly concedes that she is entitled to develop her own personality and talents, and even assists her in doing so.

The ladies strain to miss no detail of his person, as he sits at the head of the table next to his wife and the Committee members.

Is Walter also a lawyer?

No, he is a theologian, a clergyman.

The ladies study the peaked face of this man of 40. They observe the blond children who mannerly restrain their appetites as they nevertheless deftly put away the cake left over from the formal meeting.

The ladies want to know what he, a doctor of divinity, expects to do in the United States.

He wishes to work as a journalist.

A first opportunity had already offered itself — correspondent for the Philadelphia Democrat.

Walter's obvious bashfulness and his slow, hesitating way of expressing himself in English charm the ladies.

Fanny Weber and Emily help out when Walter's vocabulary fails him. He understands only bits and pieces of what they say about him, but he watches with wonderment, without even a trace of envy, as Emily holds her own in this circle of society ladies of New York. A few months only have passed since their arrival. She still wears her checkered Sunday dress, but a velvet cap has taken the place of the original straw hat. She is still the same person, the same oval face with the high cheek bones. Her dark eyes are as animated as they ever were when she found herself intellectually challenged.

He thinks of the first years of their relationship. She had been like a fragile little bird then, when he began providing her a few morsels of instruction in Latin and mathematics.

All that had changed. She flew far ahead of him now. Walter would never have believed that Emily would grow such mighty wings herself, mighty enough to cross an ocean.

He had been swept along, and was now sitting disoriented in a salon on the other side of the world, under the eyes of these beautiful, well-dressed ladies, who saw in him whoknowswhat. They leaned forward to miss not even one of his words, nor overlook even one of his gestures. He looked around. A sea of strange faces under hats; fancy designs in velvet and colored felt, riding the coiffured waves like ships, small ships, big ships; and bowls of artificial blossoms, fruit, feathers.

Mrs. Hewitt fumbled in the folds of her garment on her ample bosom for the chain of her lorgnette. She found it, and began carefully, systematically inspecting Walter.

Under these questioning, examining, penetrating eyes, he felt like the last specimen of an almost extinct species. A man: exhibited, admired, mourned.

As if to shake off this surrealistic dream, Walter turned to his children who were tending to the practical job of getting the last traces of the delicious cake off their forks in a mannerly way. His eye caught Emily, triggering another memory, running back 15 years in 'fast reverse,' as it were, when she first gleamed upon his sight in the Spyri garden in Zurich ....

[...]

Emily walked up and down the hall, memorizing the speech she had written first in German, and then translated, dictionary in hand, into English:

I think too highly of the office of law and justice in social life to recommend indulgence in any weak sentimentality. But I wish to point out in this connection, that the philosophers themselves are

still at variance as between Predestination and Free Will ...
The hall is narrow, without windows and receives its only light through the doors to the kitchen and living room. Why, in this already dark hallway, would one choose to paint the floor boards and the wooden wall finish dark brown?

Nowhere does the difference existing between these two schools come more conspicuously to light than in the administration of criminal law.

Doesn't that sound too complicated, Emily? Most of your audience will not be jurists ....

This lecture is intended as an introduction to a series. I merely touch the high points, in particular when I refer to Lombroso. These points clearly outline the conflicts.

Emily draws a deep breath as she looks into the living room at Walter who is outlined against the light of the converted lamp from Enge.

At the table, Gertrud and Robert Walter are doing their homework. As he writes, Robert's skinny legs are in constant motion. His teachers in Zurich complained about this nervous behavior and his new teachers in New York have already commented on it. Gertrud demurs: Quit your fidgeting, Robert, I can't concentrate.

The apartment on 14th Street simply did not provide enough room for a family of five. At best, it offered a temporary solution. The problem was money. They still lived from their savings. After a half year in America, neither Walter nor Emily had established a reliable income. As soon as they stood on firm ground, they would move on to a better place, in a quieter neighborhood. Emily needed a room to herself. With a sigh, she went through the living room to its street window and looked out.

At the Jefferson Theater, across the street, the colored lights had already come on. The elevated railroad on Third Street made the windows rattle.

Gertrud fussed with the ink on her writing finger and asked: Mama, what does it mean 'he is holding the newspaper upside down?' And Robert Walter, too, had a question: How do you say in English 'Erkundigungen einholen?' Emily answered absentmindedly.

Don't bother your mother, said Walter. You know she has to prepare herself for her lecture.

Emily returned to the hall and continued her memorization.

The other, the Positive School, plants itself upon the postulates of the alienist Lombroso. This clever investigator asserts that the difference between the insane and the sane can be stated by means and measurements ... the shape and structure of the skull, the length of the facial profile, the malformation of the ears and of the nose ...

Emily stopped suddenly, sniffed: The kitchen! Something was burning!

In three quick steps she reached the stove and jerked the frying pan from the fire. Elsbeth! You must not leave the stove. How many time have I told you that?

But Agnes asked me to repair her doll ... the arm has come off again ....

You must use your eyes and your nose when you cook and stay at the stove. Have you already warmed the vegetables left over from lunch? Agnes must eat what she left over at noon. Agnes stopped pushing her doll carriage along the hallway, and piped up in protest: But I do not like cauliflower, not for lunch, not for dinner, never! Her piercing whine carried through the entire apartment.

Quiet, hollered Robert from the living room table.

Emily picked up the sheet and read Lombroso's maxims: *There is no free will, hence no moral or liberty of choice, no moral responsibility ....*

As she walked up and down the hallway, Emily passed the wall mirror and stopped. Looking at herself, she continued: *The recent researches into criminal anthropology have demonstrated that the criminal is not a normal man, and that he belongs to a special class of individuals ....*

Emily stopped to examine her face more closely.

There was no concealing the obvious: Her eyes deep in their sockets, as if they were hiding. And these cheek bones — had they always stuck out so far?

And the hair, so thin, stingy, unruly. She would have to put it up to look presentable for the lecture tonight. Elsbeth would have to help her.

A scared mouse, that's what you are, she chided her image in the mirror.

Elsbeth appeared at the kitchen door: Madam?

What is it Elsbeth?

We are out of flour.

Go quickly to the baker on Third Street to buy a pound and at the same time pick up a loaf of dark bread.

After turning back to her paper, Emily became aware that Elsbeth was still standing in the door, her shoulders twitching as if she were about to break out in tears.

What is it, Elsbeth?

I am afraid to cross Third Street. There are always so many carriages; they come so quickly around the corner; and I do not know how to ask for flour in English.

Emily looked through the door to the living room: Robert, go with Elsbeth. Show her once more how to cross the street safely.

But Robert waived his hand as if to scare the assignment off, I can't go shopping! ... My school work will keep me busy until midnight!

Walter interceded. The stores would still be open later, on their way to the lecture.

Emily returned to the mirror and began to put up her hair. Her hands trembled. Her lips holding the hair pins were chapped, and they burned.

She glanced at her paper: *Statistics have shown that the increase of crime is uninfluenced by punishment.*

And then Agnes' plaintive voice by her side: My dress is torn and Elsbeth says she has no time to mend it ....

Just don't start crying, Emily thinks to herself.

I will mend it tonight, dear. When I come home from the lecture, I will do it. You will have it tomorrow, I promise, dear, I promise, tomorrow morning for sure.

Emily watches herself, as she utters these words, fogging up the mirror: for sure, for sure.

She looks closely at her image. It does show, the blue vein between her eyebrows; but not the incessant pounding, the crescendo in her head. One of these days, she thinks ... one of these days ... the whole thing will blow.

She imagines the thought particles, flying in all directions, a burst of mental energy rising like the fireworks image of a chrysanthemum.

Thereafter, a neat pile of ashes.

That was she, Emily, the erstwhile Emily Spyri.

What was she?

Everything to everyone.

It was just past six o'clock. Emily and Walter left the house. Emily looked up to the apartment on the third floor, to the corner window where, in the light of the kitchen lamp, the children and Elsbeth were now eating the evening meal.

I hope Agnes eats her cauliflower, she said to Walter, that child surely is stubborn.

Walter looked at her, managing a wistful smile: I wonder who she gets that from.

She scanned the front of the houses and the neighborhood up and down 14th Street. She carefully noted the red of the clean brick walls of the houses, like the color of flesh in a wound, she thought. She noted the adornments, cornices, stone masonry, the zig-zag of the fire escapes, black wrought iron winding up around the body of the building. The street level floor of their house, as of the other houses on the street, was occupied by stores offering various goods. Emily stopped at a window to look at various accessories: elegant handbags, leather belts, collars set with paillettes, gloves of various types displayed on mannequin arms, including the latest fad, gloves with long cuffs set with rows of buttons. Emily lost count at 20.

As they proceeded along the sidewalk, they had to step aside now and then to make room for ladies in puffed up gowns. They passed Tiffany & Company at Union Square with its display of precious jewelry and silverware. These stores served the employees of the many offices who shopped on their way home. Fourteenth Street was then crowded with women and men, eyeing the window displays. Emily noticed several displays with men's clothing, shoes and overcoats, all of better quality than on Broadway.

Soon after the stores closed, the crowd of shoppers would be replaced by the patrons of restaurants and theaters. This spring, the *Academy of Music* presented the 130th performance of *The Old Homestead.* From their living room window they could see a long line every evening at the ticket window of the Jefferson-Theater across the street. Its high white stone portal stood out as an attention getter among the other brick buildings, its bright lights like the maw of a legendary beast devouring the crowd of patrons.

Fourteenth Street was known throughout the city for its many good restaurants. There was the 'Lüchov,' almost directly across the street, in which men dressed in Lederhosen served dumpling dishes of various kinds, and every weekend a Bavarian band played its Umpapa-Umpapa late into the night to Walter's vociferously demonstrated dismay.

As they entered Third Street, a train of the *Elevated Railway* came up from the Battery toward them. Walter coughed as the mass of metal thundered overhead. Emily covered her ears. She could not shake her fear that the twenty mile-per-hour train might some day jump its tracks and come down on the heads of the people passing on the street below the elevated structure.

The bakery was still open. Having purchased the flour and bread, Emily and Walter continued and, at 20th Street, had escaped the noise of the commercial section. They entered Gramercy Park.

Emily drew a deep breath and stopped to watch a squirrel as it spiraled up the trunk of a tree, stopping to look at them at every turn. The Ginkgo trees were still devoid of leaves. She savored the quiet of this oasis in the hustle and bustle of Manhattan.

Walter, this is the place where I would like to have my home.

[...]

As on occasions in the past, Emily had the feeling of personal or spiritual enhancement, comparable to the acceleration she had felt as a passenger on her father's NorthEastExpress, approaching some as yet unknown destination, as the landscape, distorted by the speed, flew by.

In 1889, spring seemed reluctant to come to New York, and then it had come and gone overnight. Summer was in full bloom with a profusion of sunshine and stifling heat.

Emily struggled not to succumb to the mugginess of the weather that cast a sleepy spell on the city. Every day counted. The society ladies were already preparing for the move to summer residences. Lethargy began to set in. Any business not finished before the summer set in, remained for the fall season.

Walter noted Emily's stoic expressions.

Still no answer from the University?

No.

Let's go back, Emily. Our savings are used up. The experiment has failed ....

No, nothing has failed.

She looks through the window as if to force a favorable decision by sheer will power.

I will found a school, she says. I cannot wait for the University to follow through.

Walter clears his throat, a private school?

Emily nods. It will be *Emily Kempin's Law School for Women.* The Munns have found premises on 59th Street, where we can set up class rooms and also live.

Isn't that too ambitious, Emily?

She blows the hair off her forehead. Her cheeks turn rosy as the blood rushes to her head.

It is well planned.

And who pays for it?

I am assured of the support of the Munns, the Sutros, the Webers. The young Mrs. Gould, who lost her mother in February, and is her sole heir, will also contribute ....

The climate in New York is unendurable. Let's go back this summer, to Zurich. Her voice cracks: I can return to Zurich only after I have made my way here. Otherwise, my dear male colleagues would have me where they want me, on my knees — the cleaning woman who wanted to be an attorney ....

As she speaks, Emily stares out into the distance. Then she turns and looks at Walter. The man standing before her has lost weight. His breathing is labored. He cannot tolerate the heat.

A shadow of doubt flies over her face. She breathes deeply. Tears well up in her eyes: Walter, there is no other way. I must advance. Believe me: in this crazy place one must play with high stakes. In the fall, we will be over the hill.

In these muggy nights, many immigrants sleep on roofs and fire escapes, draped in mosquito netting. The simple task of breathing is work.

Add to this the emotional burden of being divided against oneself, with the desire to escape.

Emily cannot fall asleep. She listens to Walter's breathing.

She struggles with herself: It would be easy, too easy to go crawling back. Emily will not slink back like a dog, tail between the legs. Must she see everything through Walter's eyes? His hesitation, halfhearted existence, kowtow to convention.

Swiss popular wisdom: A head sticking out too far is likely to be chopped off.

This is a hard war on two fronts: against the inertia, even resistance, on the outside, despite the drag of inertia, lacking understanding, lacking perspective on the inside.

An insane struggle at cross purposes.

Florence Sutro plans a concert at her home, Riverdale Drive 102 West. It is to be presented before the summer recess as a goodwill action for Emily; pssst, no one must know about it, not yet.

Walter, hearing about it, confuses Sutro and Munn. Emily sets him right. The two are really quite different from one another: Munn has red hair, set in curls, a narrow face with light skin. She is the one who gestures when she speaks, usually with a lit cigarette between her fingers.

Quite eccentric, Mrs. Munn, given to theatrics, but really a wonderful person, alert and prepared for whatever comes her way.

Florence Sutro, née Clinton, is an altogether different type: Sporty, a handsome, friendly face with a perky nose. She is the darling of the social set, especially behind the piano. Yet, make no mistake about it, she can assert herself. You will see.

On this late afternoon, the trip from 14th Street to Riverdale Drive seems an endless journey. The horses pull the overcrowded omnibus with hanging tongues. With his cane, a pedestrian pokes at the flattened remains of a rat, which wagon wheels have, over time, ground into the asphalt like a seal.

Broadway is a sweltering canyon, on both its sides the tall buildings radiate the heat from the sun.

The end of the canyon seems to dissolve in the distance. Upon the closing of the stores, the omnibus fills with young sales ladies in rumpled blouses, wide sleeves, with worn makeup on their tired faces. The passengers move closer together to make room for the new arrivals.

The people sit quietly, stare into the void.

Riverdale Drive might as well be on a different planet.

Long concourses leading to portals designed for the ceremonious reception of guests in dignity. Windows fitted with striped awnings to keep the heat out.

Between park trees, a glimpse of water, the Hudson River, reflecting the sun light.

Emily and Walter arrive with the last guests. Double parked carriages line the concourse and the street. Even with the summer break only a few days off, no one would miss an invitation to the Sutros. A weekly society journal ran a feature on the young hosts, who had their entire house renovated according to the latest style, in exquisite elegance. The article included a picture of the couple:

He, Theodore Sutro, born 1845, in Aachen, Prussia, well-known as a brilliant attorney handling defense cases in the courts of New York ... for years one of the most eligible bachelors, almost 40 years old when he married Florence. She, the former Florence Edith Clinton, the exemplification of the New York ideal of 'beauty and brains.' Her musical accomplishments are noted.

At the piano, the light of the low sun plays upon her arched neck. The guests listen in rapt attention. The music salon is exquisitely decorated. On side tables of marble, longstemmed lamps, in shapes reminiscent of flowers, illuminate the upholstered seating arrangements in yellow brocade. Yellow roses in silver bowls, yellow azaleas in bamboo jardinieres, evoking oriental imagery.

There are no heavy damask drapes, no carved furnishings intended to impress by their bulk, as are all too common in posh brownstone houses, the Hewitts' for example, who are proud of the certificates affixed to their furnishings, attesting the fact that they were acquired in the liquidation of European castles.

After the concert, the guests do not separate, as usual, into a ladies caucus in the salon, and gentlemen in the smoking room. They remain seated, while the host serves refreshments in person, no costumed help hired for the occasion. No hired chefs.

Florence now among her guests, an indication of dampness on her nose as she circulates naturally through the room, fanning herself with her hand. Theodore Sutro, assisted by a young woman of the household staff, serves drinks.

Very well done, young lady. Precise performance, especially the modern, French 'Valses.' Judge George Thompson, the senior colleague of her husband, takes the lead in complimenting the hostess. An unusual event, because the man is known to be surly. The hushed silence following his comment serves to accentuate his praise.

Florence steps into the middle of the room, asking for attention to an important announcement:

Emily Kempin is preparing to set up her Law School for Women. The ultimate object of her effort is to make it possible for women to acquire the educational qualifications for admission to the practice of the law in the State of New York.

There is need for support. Moral support. There will be a news conference in October to announce the commencement of classes. All present are urged to attend.

You are bound to run afoul of the law, Judge Thompson interrupts, because the State of New York does not admit women to the practice of the law ....

Emily steps forward, faces the judge and begs to differ with him. She has conducted a careful study of the law. There is no doubt that women are entitled by the statute of May 19, 1886, to practice the law. Yet, no woman has been actually admitted because it is impossible for women to acquire the educational qualifications for admission. A law school for women would make this possible ....

I can see it, Thompson; it is the voice of Judge Kellogg, he continues, women jurists flooding the courts of the great State of New York three years from now. Our jobs will be next, Thompson.

The comment is intended to be jocular, but every joke has a serious root, this one is no exception.

Emily hastens to reply. It will certainly not be a flood, she says. Many women will study without professional ambitions, for use in their personal affairs or in business, she adds. She looks at Judge Thompson. He is uncomfortable, loosens his starched collar. A blush passes over his bloated face. His forehead, above the gold rimmed pincenez, glistens with perspiration.

He reminds Emily of her colleagues in Zurich, firmly entrenched in their chairs, listening to her argument why she should be admitted to the practice of the law.

I will be your first student! All eyes turn, in astonishment, to Florence.

My dear, are you not overtaxing yourself? A pianist *and* a lawyer? The wife of the railroad magnate Russel Sage, an imposing presence, all puffed up in a mourning dress of black satin, asks the question.

No, Florence turns to her with the graceful sweep of the neck that characterized her performance at the pianoforte, and holds her own under the older woman's steely gaze.

She pauses and continues. No affectation of a noble cause, just the natural desire for knowledge. The statement disarms even potential opponents like Judge Thompson. Of late, American society ladies are taking in increasing numbers to tennis and even to javelin throwing, and now, the law. Thompson affects a stance of calmness. With a bare indication of irony, he asks: What does your husband, my good colleague Sutro, have to say to this? He turns to the host who comes to the support of his wife. My wife likes to know what I am doing at the office. Should I consider that an undue interference in my life or spousal affection? Well, Thompson, what do you think?

The judge limits himself to an ambiguous nod of his tremendous head. Throughout the rest of the evening, he remains silent.

If you venture out into the open sea, you must be prepared to swim or drown.

Florence winks at Emily, as she works at her rosewood desk, making notes while typing the final copy of the press release. This will give the Dean of the Law Faculty plenty to think about when he gets up tomorrow morning and reads it in the New York Times. She looks out into the cloudless sky over New York. The city swelters under the heat of the summer.

Emily watches her, admiring her skill and the working of the machine. It is a novel thing, a black metal frame with a name in gold letters, levers marked with letters of the alphabet set in mother-of-pearl. Florence pushes the tops of the levers down with the tips of her fingers. Other levers come up and strike the paper, forming letters, numbers and symbols. Florence's hands dance on the keys, her staccato rhythms producing writing as expertly as she produced music the evening before.

Emily watches Florence and wonders when she will be able to afford a machine like that. With such a machine she would be able to produce her arguments efficiently, cleanly, as befits the dignity of the legal profession, and her writing would no longer reveal her personal history or emotional condition.

Florence guesses her thoughts. You would want a better model, she says. This is a cast off from Theodore's office. See, the 'M' is damaged and the low loops should not come out filled in.

On August 6, 1889, the following article appeared in the New York Times:

Dr. Emily Kempin's Plan to Found a Law School for Women

On October 1, this city will witness the opening of a law school exclusively for women. Its students will have the opportunity to qualify educationally for the admission to the practice of the law in the State of New York, pursuant to the amendment of the code adopted in 1886. The amendment of the law, together with the offering of the new school, will place women in a position of equality with men in the practice of the law. The founder of the school is Dr. Jur. Emily Kempin, a graduate of the University of Zurich, Switzerland, author of several treatises on the law. Dr. Kempin, a resident of this city for one or two years, has become prominent as a champion of suffrage for women. She claims to have the support of several prominent jurists in this city.

The 'Dr. Emily Kempin's Law School' will be organized under the laws of the State of New York. Its curriculum will be equivalent to the curriculum of any law school in the state and will therefore satisfy the educational requirement for admission to the practice of the law. Dr. Kempin does not expect that her school will flood the city with women jurists, at least not in the near future as has been suggested; because the number of women desiring to enter into the profession is relatively small. In any event, the full curriculum will be comparable to the training of European lawyers.

Although Dr. Kempin's effort is clearly designed to make it possible for women to enter the legal profession, it is expected that many women will enroll in order to train for positions in business, either because they must support themselves and want to be prepared for positions of higher responsibility, or because they want to be better prepared to manage their own businesses. The faculty of the School will be selected from specialists in the various fields of law. Dr. Kempin has tentatively scheduled an orientation meeting for September 1, in order to work out the details with those interested.

On the day on which this article appeared, the Kempin family moved to their new quarters on 59th Street.

The children were happy to have Central Park nearby, and Walter had hoped to overcome the feeling of being boxed in.

Instead, as he walked through the apartment, he felt lost. He would never come to terms with the enormity of it. The rooms intended for the use of the family were huge. He finally sat in the far corner of one room, on one of the high window sills, made a few notes in the fading daylight, and awaited dusk.

One thought possessed him: Emily, what are you doing to us? You are dragging us into a lifestyle that is too expansive for us.

Emily entered briskly, turned on the desk lamp, then walked over to the window wall and drew the drapes, shutting out the twilight. She sat down at the table and began to arrange her papers. The curriculum had to be described in detail, but first the personal notes to the many donors and patrons. Looking up from her vantage point in the lamplight, she could barely see Walter in the darkened far corner of the room.

Our article came out very nicely, didn't it? she asked.

The light of the lamp blinded her, but she guessed that Walter was nodding. She continued: Judge Noah David and Pastor Crosby have assured me of their support. Isn't that a promising start?

She laughed like a little girl.

The impish exuberance of the early years of their marriage had returned to her eyes.

Despite this happy turn of events, Walter could not escape the ironic implication of another article that had appeared in the *New York Times,* that same morning on the same page as the article announcing Emily's new law school. It had appeared under the heading *Miscellaneous.* Walter should have pointed it out to Emily when he first read it, perhaps with a pointed comment. He had not, and in the meantime, the story had come to dominate his thoughts:

A countess in her mind: As the 'Servia' discharged her passengers yesterday, a woman with sad eyes appeared before the immigra-

tion officials. She claimed to be a princess, the curator of the Unified Kingdom. Upon detailed interrogation, she further stated that she had already purchased parts of Italy and planned to buy New York, if she found the inhabitants to her liking .... She was denied an entry visa, and was greatly surprised and outraged when the officials laughed at her, stating that her designs on New York would offend the local capitalists ....

Just think, Walter, even Judge Thompson will come to the press conference in October, Emily said, raising her voice. Even Thompson? I wouldn't have expected that.

Walter looked at her as she sat by the table, shuffling her papers, sitting as if on an island of light in an ocean of darkness. Her left cheek glowed from the heat of the lamp, as though it were being warmed by a faithful lover.

[...]

Emily experienced a renewal in early 1890.

Snow fell heavily, covering all of Manhattan, creating the illusion of picture book serenity inside her new home on Nassau Street.

Her existence was still dominated by an ebbing melancholy. Closing her eyes and setting the focus of her mind's eye to transcend the physical separation of thousands of miles: She saw her two older children walking, across the Stadelhoferplatz in Zurich, on their way to visit their grandmother Kempin.

It shocked her somewhat that she hardly missed her husband.

She realized now to what extent his ever present, sneaking uneasiness about everything had arrested her attention, stifled her initiative, distorted her being. His hesitations, his ifs and buts — his very outlook on life had held her back, dragged her down. She became inclined to the notion that she had merely granted Walter refuge in her life, and had finally been forced to concede that she was not strong enough to carry both of them.

Her vitality returned gradually.

She awoke earlier in the morning than before, with a clear concept of the work to be accomplished during the day. She enjoyed preparing each day's lectures, and was settling into a routine.

The classrooms were still located on the premises on 59th Street. Four new students had been recently enrolled upon scholarships provided by Helen Gould's committee, bringing the total to seven. These were all strong willed women who made teaching a joyful challenge.

Stanleyetta Titus, intelligent, full of provocative questions. She studied in order to be able to help her family out of some financial bind.

Cornelia Hood, a tall, energetic woman with a double chin that was quite remarkable for her age. She had originally intended to become a midwife. The practical bent of her questions and, especially, of her challenges to all too glibly taken positions kept the whole class on the ground of hard reality. Especially Florence Sutro, whose artistic nature all too often collided with hard reality, benefitted from Cornelia's pragmatism.

Isabella Pettus, a chubby girl. What the others readily grasped, Isabella labored to comprehend. Yet, once she had understood, her memory kept her on the true path, and she served as the resident reference for the other students.

Twice each week, Emily conducted evening courses; one of the many good ideas hatched by the Committee. Anyone who paid the membership fee of one dollar was entitled to attend free of charge.

The entertainment season was at its height. Word had passed among her friends: Emily likes the theater, she sits enthralled in the darkness like a child, eager for the plot evolving on the stage, happy to be a spectator for two hours without any obligation to produce effects herself, to keep others engaged.

The Webers and Sutros invited her regularly.

Yet, her preferred entertainment was spending a quiet evening in her apartment on Nassau Street.

She had left the large living room practically unfurnished in order to avoid that the light entering through the large corner windows be swallowed up by upholstery and dark wood.

Here she liked to sit after dark on the old carpet, the one with the woven design of blue triangles and green moons, that had adorned her room in the old Spyri house in Zurich. Sometimes she read professional materials; but, of late also, increasingly, stories by Walter Scott.

On many evenings, Emily and Agnes sat together to talk about the events of the day. The child's health had improved. She was much quieter, as if, upon the departure of Walter and the two older siblings, she, too, had been relieved of a source of tension.

Yet, at times, entirely without an apparent occasion, Agnes asked, what are Gertrud and Robert doing now?

They are fast asleep, because, in Zurich, it is now past midnight tomorrow.

That's strange, so far away, like day and night!

That's right, Agnes.

While Agnes sleeps, and while the other part of the family is ready to get up for the new day, Emily is still wide awake, planning, organizing. She needs little sleep; yet, in the morning, when she sees herself in the mirror over the wash basin, she looks at the other Emily, the one for which she has long searched.

In February, Dr. Munn asks her to give yet another lecture on hypnosis, this time before the young physicians at the Woman's Hospital. The interest in this topic is fueled in America by continued and growing interest in Europe. Emily, who knows Dr. Forel personally and is thoroughly familiar with his experiments at the Burghölzli Hospital and his publications, is recognized as an expert in the field.

After the lecture, a lively discussion ensues. Dr. Munn is pleased. He considers the presentation a success, in significant part, because Emily speaks clearly, with conviction. Her enthusiasm infects the audience and carries it along.

Would she care to join him in the theater tonight? He has two tickets ... his wife ... she could not join him tonight ... his wife ... sometimes she has her own plans ....

He seems to be somewhat uncomfortable under Emily's probing eye: This renowned society physician turns into a supplicant, with such soulful hound dog eyes, protruding ears, a bundle of romantic incongruities enough to melt the heart.

She would have to decide quickly, the performance starts in half an hour.

But that would not leave her any time to change.

Not necessary, Dr. Munn reassures her, indeed, this velvet dress with its lace collar, it makes her look delicate, feminine, and the emerald hues complement the dark tone of her blond hair ....

You should be a fashion writer, she replies with a smile.

The box is in the most expensive section of the theater. The piece is too complicated for Emily to follow. Champagne is served between the acts. At intermission, all society opera glasses are trained on the box: Dr. John P. Munn, the wellknown physician of the Goulds, is also renowned for his liberality in sharing his box with various ladies. Who is it today?

Emily sips her champagne and imagines how she must appear to the many eyes straining to catch a glimpse of her from afar: a small head, barely clearing the plush balustrade, pinhead sized eyes; and Munn's head beside hers: standup collar, silk scarf, protruding ears, monocle, hair slicked back, the carefully trained and blackened mustache. The scene is unreal, Emily feels easy, light, as if she were about to be carried off.

After the performance, in the cool air of the night, she regains her sense of reality.

Munn insists on taking her home. Just over on 59th Street, isn't it?

No, she still has her school there, but her apartment is downtown. A taxi will safely take her there, no need for him to be concerned.

A lady alone in a taxi? So late at night? No, he insists.

It is a long drive along Broadway, over many frozen mounds of snow. The blanket of lambs' skin and the presence of the other's warm body make the trip quite comfortable. He reaches for her hand and she tolerates the gesture, her small hand finds a berth in his.

Are you comfortable, Emily? he asks.

She nods.

A snowflake caught in his mustache melts into a drop of water. His signet ring digs into her hand, she moves it to relieve the pressure. More demonstrations of tenderness? Hardly, the air is too cold for more. Besides, the journey is about to end. The landmarks fly by: Maiden Lane is coming up where they should turn left, but the driver overshoots it and continues to pass Trinity Church, where the lamps barely illuminate the scene. Left into Wall Street. The columns of the Sub Treasury Building stand out in the snowy landscape. Washington's frozen statue at the top of the steps. They turn into Nassau Street. A few minutes later, the taxi stops in front of the house.

Munn looks up to view the front of the building, mumbles something, presumably a favorable comment about the new architectural style. His breath makes a cloud before his mouth. A cup of warm coffee, perhaps, asks Emily, to fortify you for the long trip home? She looks at him while she wipes the snowflakes from her eyebrows.

Do you want me to wait, the taxi driver asks.

No, Munn replies and pays the fare.

The taxi turns and is nearly instantly swallowed up by the driving snow.

Emily lights the lamp in the living room. She quickly looks in on Agnes. The child seems to be having a bad dream, as happens frequently. She asks Munn to look after the fire. As she carries the coffee into the living room, he has succeeded in getting a lively fire going. They sip the coffee, savoring its warmth as it drives out the cold of the trip. Munn has draped his arm around her shoulders, drawing her closer. She willingly complies with the tender pressure of his hand in turning her head toward him. His thick, sensuous lips move closer to hers, twitching under the mustache, in anticipation. He must wear a mustache trainer at night, she thinks and shudders. Still, she allows him to kiss her. A love story, with a predictable conclusion: They will make love. And he will come back day after tomorrow, and next week, the beginning of a round of secret encounters, and all the while she will become more and more dependent.

Does she want that?

Does she want that now, having just emerged from the bonds of one confining relationship?

She hears Agnes's breathing and moaning from the next room. She gently withdraws from his embrace and gets up, in control once again.

It is late, she says in a firm tone. You have a long trip home.

The taxi is gone, he pleads, leaning back in a defiant gesture and producing his best hound dog pout.

There is a taxi stand around the corner, on Fulton Street, she replies.

She stands in the window, watching him as he passes through the light of the street lantern: an awkward bundle of humanity, done up, top-hat, pittypatting legs dressed in gaiters, patent-leather boots, disappearing from sight through the snow, withdrawing in silence, as if from her dream.

Emily undresses and then slips under the covers next to Agnes. Agnes awakens and, recognizing her mother, turns and snuggles up to her.

A vague feeling of loss comes over Emily as she falls asleep with the child's cheek pressing against her throat, her breath warming Emily's chin.

The next day, there was much paperwork to be done. Toward evening, when her eyes begin to tire and play tricks on her, she stops to watch a snow storm outside; the falling snowflakes are mirrored in the pupils of her eyes. Then sitting down on her shepherd rug, she strokes the blue and green design.

This room would make a cozy love nest, she thinks.

Munn? No, she does not regret having sent him home.

She begins to conjure up her ideal love story.

Since the days of her childhood, she has read Walter Scott, has lived in his stories. If he were still alive, Walter Scott, a fellow jurist, could be her ideal lover, telling stories, more stories. Like Scheherazade in that old tale — why couldn't Scheherazade be a man? On her rug they would love, their bodies entwined in the natural state, naked, in the light of the moon as it stood over Manhattan, protected from the other people in the city by the walls through which the noises of the world are barely audible. She had read in the *New York Times* that Walter Scott kept adding rooms to his house, rooms decorated and furnished to resemble the rooms in his stories. He had been forced to keep writing to finance the overambitious project.

So they would lie on this rug and love and he would add to their love — covering their love as if with a magic carpet of stories; it would be a story ever changing, ever new. She stretches out in all directions over the navy blue pattern on the carpet. Her hands stroke her breasts: come, Water Scott, fellow jurist, entangled in the struggle to sustain dreams come true, I am waiting, come, let me caress you, so that I can feel myself — come, my male complement, come to make us whole.

The weather was stormy in April.

Between two downpours, Emily took Agnes to the harbor and, without knowing it, stopped at the same place on the dock where Walter had stood with Agnes on the day he left.

Beyond this ocean are Robert and Gertrud and Daddy, said Agnes. When will we be together again, mommy?

In the summer, dear, when the water is calm. We will go on the ship and you will not even get sick then.

Emily looked out over the ocean. It seemed to breathe, as though it were alive.

She thought of Walter who, seeking to escape from her by returning to the Old World, was now following in her footsteps ... having enrolled last semester at the University of Zurich to study jurisprudence.

Agnes tugged at her sleeve and looked up at her, wide-eyed: Daddy told me about Daedalus and Ikarus .... What happened after Ikarus learned how to fly?

Daedalus told Ikarus ... to follow close behind ....

And then, Mommy?

After some time, Daedalus looked back and could not see Ikarus.

Emily fell quiet again, because her thoughts were still with Walter. She imagined him in the lectures of Schneider, Meili, or Liliental. He was trying to catch up with her, to meet her halfway.

And then, Mommy?

She continued: Finally he saw him high above, flying toward the sun. He called out to warn him, but Ikarus was too far away to hear his father's voice.

Up above, a seagull, silhouetted against the sun, glides upon its freedom.

Cumulus clouds made patterns in the blue spring sky as they approached the University.

The carriage passed through Washington Square Park, approaching the main building. It stood out like a relic from the Middle Ages. There were the high, Gothic windows, spires, architectural features intended to be imposing, authoritative and, like a medieval fortress, menacingly defensive. Every revolution of the carriage wheels seemed to enhance the ominous menace. Emily felt vulnerable and checked her appearance in a pocket mirror to make sure her hair was properly disciplined for this encounter, for which she had longed for months.

You are going to make it, said Fanny Weber, who sat in the carriage next to Helen Gould. Helen, a small spot of sunlight dancing on her check, smiled.

Still Emily worried: Would they find real, live people in this bulwark of science? Does this university have something like a face or a soul?

The closest approach to the 'face' of the University was looking through a window on the third floor of the East Wing. It belonged to Vice Chancellor Mac Cracken. He watched the carriage drive up to the portal, wondering what these three amazonians would look like.

He knew only one of them, Helen Gould, whom he had met quite casually a few years before.

She had sat next to her father Jay Gould, an alumnus of the University, in front, at the speaker's lectern, among the very important persons. There was good reason for this honor, Jay Gould ranked among the most generous contributors. The young girl next to him, in her white muslin dress, looked like a butterfly, refreshingly young. Now she was a young lady who had become widely known for her zestful promotion of social causes. Vice Chancellor Mac Cracken felt that it was high time for the University to confront women's issues.

The conventional approach was to simply exclude women. That had kept them out, but produced a ubiquitous, amorphous threat to the status quo. Not only the tabloids and the boulevard press, but of late also serious gazettes, carried articles dealing with women's rights or particularly glaring instances of their denial: transcripts of Salem witch trials discovered, women in men's clothing marching in support of the right to free love, fur seamstresses on the Lower East Side striking ....

One might easily dismiss such cases with a laugh as sensationalism without popular support. But these reports about a newly established law school for women needed to be taken as tocsins of serious social development.

Reports, as they appeared shortly before Christmas in the *Mail and Express* were taken seriously by the established professors:

> *Dr. Emily Kempin, herself rejected at Columbia University and the University of New York, will make it possible for women to acquire the educational qualifications for admission to the practice of the law before all courts in the State of New York. The intent is to achieve for the women of New York full equality with men in the pursuit of the legal professions. Similar movements are known from other states. Thus, four women attorneys are practicing in Boston. At least a dozen are believed to be established in the profession in the states west of Missouri and Mississippi ....*

Dr. Kempin had petitioned to be allowed to establish her school under the aegis of the University. The University ignored her. That was barely a year ago. She turned around and established her school in competition with the University. Certainly in the long run, the existence of the entire establishment is threatened ....

The only way of effectively dealing with this rash of distaff revolts would be to incorporate them into the conventional system where they can be disciplined and directed. The essential proviso being, of course, that the essential objective of the University, the training of the young men of the state, not be impaired by the reception of these rebellious women into the system.

The present effort began in March with a second petition by Dr. Kempin, essentially a repeat of the earlier attempt — with one significant difference: The name of Helen Gould, in its almost childlike simplicity, appeared among the signatures of the sponsors. Without any of the usual ado, the petition was immediately referred to the Committee of the Law Faculty for its consideration. The committee promptly requested the Chancellor to invite the ladies to this interview in order to explore the issues and possible approaches to their resolution.

Emily was happily surprised about the 'face' of the University. Fifteen minutes later, the ladies had been ushered into the office of the Vice Chancellor. The surprise was that this gentleman, sporting one of those beards that had long gone out of style, had an open, kind face, attentive eyes, and a sense of humor.

Fanny Weber gave a summary report about the work of the *Arbitration Society* founded by her, about the needs served by it and the functional restriction imposed upon its work by the lack of staff sufficiently trained in legal matters. The sponsoring ladies had helped Dr. Kempin to establish her law school. It would be desirable to operate within the University system in order to avoid the administrative burden and concentrate on the substance of educating women in the law. It should be understood, however, that Dr. Kempin would be in charge of the new school and be allowed to pursue her objectives.

Mac Cracken then asked for a presentation of the concept of the school.

As usual, when she talked about her school, Emily's enthusiasm carried the audience along.

Mac Cracken found Emily's presentation remarkably concise. He did not see any difficulty with the idea that the proposed *Law Class* remain academically autonomous, within the framework of the University, even though it would be attached for administrative purposes to the Law Faculty, preferably under the patronage of the *Woman's Legal Education Society*, as soon as it came into existence as a legal entity. When would that be?

Fanny Weber stated that the work of incorporation proceeded apace and should result in official registration within a few weeks. The principal reason for the delay was the desire to lay a sound, enduring foundation, since the effort was certainly not a passing whim but intended to create a permanent institution. In the meantime, the Vice Chancellor was invited to inspect the list of persons who had so far declared themselves future members.

The Vice Chancellor scanned the list, noticing with great satisfaction the names of promintent and wealthy citizens.

He then approached the most difficult aspect of the reception of the new school into the University system: It would be necessary that the class be financed for the first few years by the Society ... the University would not be in a position to assume any part of the costs for several years.

Fanny Weber stated in her simple, dignified way that the Society would provide the salary of Dr. Kempin for the first four years and also make contributions for scholarships.

This will amount to a considerable sum, Mac Cracken said. Have any funds been secured?

We are about to establish a foundation to collect and administer the trust fund, Helen Gould said, intervening as if her part had come. May I have a sheet of paper, Reverend Mac Cracken?

Mac Cracken handed her a blank sheet of paper across the desk. Helen Gould wrote, starting at the upper margin: Helen Gould pledges for the *Woman's Law Class* $16,000.

Then Fanny Weber reached for the paper and wrote: Fanny Weber pledges for the *Woman's Law Class* $1,000.

The Vice Chancellor watched with bulging eyes.

He rose and bowed formally: I am looking forward to your class, Dr. Kempin. If everything goes as planned, I will be elevated to Chancellor next year. Please be assured that your class will enjoy my personal attention. It will be one of my great satisfactions in office to advance the cause of women.

Emily looked at him; overcome by joy, she could not say a word in reply.

On May 5, Emily received a letter from the University Regents:

The University of the City of New York authorizes the Vice Chancellor to allow Mrs. Emily Kempin, Doctor of Jurisprudence of the University of Zurich, to conduct lectures for auditors who are not immatriculated, in particular for women in business.

The honorarium due Dr. Kempin is set at not less than $1,000 per year, for a total of four years, and will be paid, upon their promise, by the friends of Dr. Kempin. A certain percentage of the student's fees will be paid to the University to cover administrative expenses.

The *Woman's Legal Education Society* was formally founded on June 14, 1890. Fanny Weber was its first president, Mrs. Field vice- president. The wife of the attorney Alexander Forman assumed the function of secretary; Dr. Mary Putnam, physician and well known for her promotion of women's rights, became the treasurer.

Among the members was also Mrs. Abraham S. Hewitt, the wife of the former mayor of New York.

Emily Kempin's lectures were scheduled to begin in October of 1890.

(Translated by Sandra and Ewald Schlachter)

HANNO HELBLING

Hanno Helbling

Born August 18, 1930 in Zuoz. Studied history, German and comparative literature. Since 1948 editor, from 1973 to 1992 chief editor of feuilleton for *Neue Zürcher Zeitung*. Guest professor in Switzerland, Germany and the US. Translator. Received several literary awards. Lives in Zurich. Short stories, novels, essays, historical books: *Goten und Wandalen*, 1954; *Saeculum Humanum*, 1957; *Schweizer Geschichte*, 1962; *Das Zweite Vatikanischen Konzil*, 1965; *Umgang mit Italien*, 1966; *Kirchenkrise*, 1969; *Der Mensch im Bild der Geschichte*, 1969; *Das große Provisorium*, 1976; *Kaiser Friedrich II*, 1977; *Politk der Päpste*, 1981; *Die Zeit bestehen*, 1983; *Eine Bürgerfamilie im 19. Jahrhundert*, 1985; *Tristans Liebe*, 1991.

Discovering America

Columbus was not the first one. We know that and like to repeat it. But that does not change anything. The America to which European emigrants came and which emerged as a result of their colonizing work was the country it was and the country it became, regardless of who was the first to lay eyes upon its shores and to set foot on its soil.

What does matter is that Columbus was not the last one. What would have become of America if he and no one after him had discovered it? Try to imagine that, considering the choice offered our historically oriented approach by the colonialism. (For history shows, even where it does not "teach.")

To encounter inhabitants, later to be dubbed native Americans, and to chose to treat them in ways, such as segregating, integrating or corrupting, dislodging or exterminating — one discovery suffices and for either of the other two, this was already one too many.

Now such a first and simple type of discovery was in time overlaid but not annulled by other kinds of discoveries; yet it did not undergo a revision until much later. Museums for a destroyed culture and reservations for a ruined people are "better than nothing," but they really signified nothing, when measured against the wanton acts committed by earlier generations, acts that cannot be undone by anyone.

*

Who was the last person to discover America? The respective self that one day landed, presumably after a flight, in New York in the afternoon or in Los Angeles in the evening. Or in Chicago? That one really should know, for America can be discovered here as well as there. It is always the same, yet not alike everywhere.

It was a long trip. What a huge country! We had imagined it to be big, but not that big! We found the continent between the Atlantic and the Pacific Ocean to be vast and empty beyond all our expectations. Would there ever be an end to these plains and these wheat fields? We already had four days and four nights of travel behind us and it got hot in our Pullman car. Outside there was nothing but sandy wasteland. It was the desert we were crossing. Would this journey ever end?

Here we have Klaus Mann's "discovery of America" in 1927. Not a word here that others before and after him have not written or could have written. And now his comments on his earlier encounter with New York.

... a fata morgana of floating delicateness and titanic dimensions; the silhouette of the skyscrapers; the much lauded and yet forever astonishing, incredible, overpowering 'Skyline' of New York ... It was a new kind of beauty, almost Gothic in its sharply upward-reaching construction and its slender perspectives, which I found striking here; a boldly experimental, soberly grandiose style that took my breath away and made my heart beat faster. 'Now that is colossal,' I stammered with some effort. We were now on 42nd Street between 8th Avenue and Broadway with a view of the mightily towering New York Times building. 'Hard to believe,' I whispered, 'that anything like that exists ...!'

Not a word here that not anybody else could have written, perhaps even better, as could Klaus Mann, when his feelings were not running away with him. Finally, to top it all, here is what he had to say at the end of his trip to the West coast.

But on the morning after the fourth night, the scenery outside seemed magically changed. A mass of luscious gardens in place of the barren flatlands! The Promised Land, bathed in sunlight, with a rich measure of color and fertility, with its orange groves, cypresses and fig-trees, its proud palm-lined avenues and blossom-surrounded mansions. This was worth spending those four long days and nights, to be sure. It was a paradise that greeted us at the end of our trip. Our disappointment started in Los Angeles. How amorphous and barren it seemed after the hard and dynamic beauty of New York! Los Angeles is not a city but an enormous conglomerate of streets, buildings, vehicles and teeming human masses.

Here the author unabashedly resorts to a description that is put together with clichés. Did one have to travel to America to compose sentences like these? But then, Klaus Mann did not undertake that journey for our sake — or for those readers' sake, for whom his experience is just the usual, but for his own sake: in order to have seen for himself — to have discovered what others might know. However, of what use was that to him? And when he then uttered the usual, it was not the final version of what he had encountered. His last word about Los Angeles was not yet spoken in his *Wendepunkt (The Turning Point)*.

*

At this point I feel obliged to mention the strange creature that I personally saw in 1610. Once, when I stood on the shore near the seaport Saint John very early in the morning, a wondrous creature of the sea came swimming toward land with great speed. It was quite beautiful though, its face, eyes, nose, ears, mouth, neck and forehead resembling that of a maiden. It also had hair that was bluish in color and hung over its shoulders. The hair seemed real to me, for I had a long and good look at the creature together with my servant who is still alive. But when it was no further than a long spear's distance away, I was so startled that I began to retreat. Seeing that, the creature submerged quickly in the water, but it soon emerged again and made for the spot on land, where I had stood. From a distance I watched it a bit longer and it seemed to me that from the top of its head to its navel it looked like a human being and from the navel down like a fish.

That is what Sir Richard Whitbourne reported in 1620, and this passage was included in Bry's travel accounts in 1627. For an experience of this sort, one surely need not have traveled to the "Newly Discovered or New England" at some risk to one's life and facing many deprivations, lest one aspired to being recorded in literature as the archetypal European, which was hardly Sir Richard's ambition. "Well, here I am," Melusine could have called out to the startled onlooker, whose imagination was so lively or so limited that after crossing an ocean it had to avail itself of the repertoire of myths and legends.

When at his first sight of California Klaus Mann speaks of the "Promised Land," alluding more or less consciously to (Goethe's)

"Do you know the land," then he acts in a manner similar to that of Whitbourne, that is, he relates what he sees to what he already knows in order to establish a relation between himself and the unknown. One cannot help asking whether thereby the known is not placed slightly in front of what is seen. And the more or less intentionally banal answer must then be that no great harm is done, the shift being only a slight one. Only when someone puts whatever he "knows" in the place of what there is to be seen, will doubts arise regarding his discovery. But what discovery is free of such substitutions? In order to discover a country *ab ovo*, one had best arrange to be born there, but of course, even that is no protection against disappointments.

*

Columbus was not the first, but he had the right to feel he was the first; and he did not necessarily have to be the last to have this right. After all, this right does not cease to exist until the advent of dialectics. Only he who declares that he had imagined the country to be "not *that* big," gives away his being a latecomer; he compares. Only he who can maintain that Los Angeles is no city is a belated discoverer; for he has found a correspondence between New York and his *idea* of a city, and in Los Angeles he does not find New York again, let alone his *idea*. The example is doubly instructive. You could visit Los Angeles at the end of 1984, when it was as much or as little of a "city" as 57 years before. And you could return in 1991, at which time it displayed its towering downtown, its "Sky-line" and said: See, I can do that, too. *And* even in 1984 you could stay a while and find that you were very much in a city — at the expense perhaps of your idea of a city that you had brought along and which indeed well befitted San Francisco or, while we are at it, Naples.

The dialectics of the America-"experience" (as it is now called in preference to "discovery") has, however, gotten an additional twist after World War II. Visitors now arrived from an "Americanized" Europe — or so they thought — and thus as initiated travelers, so to speak. "This music sounds familiar to me," they would recite, and they were prepared for encountering all kinds of life-style characteristics. But when at breakfast in the hotel the gentleman at the next table asked, "How are you this morning?" they had to cope with the just barely suppressed counter-question of precisely where *we* had kept company the evening before. The fact that language at times serves not so much to transmit the factual states of affairs as it does to create moods, you could learn back home from notorious smarts, but could not recognize it as the germ-free drop of oil in the machinery of daily living.

In other words, even a short stay in the United States more than suffices to make one comprehend that Europe is no more Americanized than America (apart from New York) is Europeanized — and that the continent beyond the big pond is strange enough for Europeans to still merit being discovered 500 years after Columbus. Not only the "vast and empty" land, but also the small towns with the varied versions of their social structure (varied in degrees that do not necessarily impede the new inhabitants' orientation); also the ghettos of the millionaires, of the Mexicans, of the middle-class in the big cities. It is a different kind of life, and it can easily happen that someone yearns to break loose from it and later on wishes to return to it. It is not the purpose of discoveries to simplify existence.

*

What is it that is being discovered? Land and people. Often that satisfies us — often it satisfies even persons who would do well to pay attention to governmental establishments and social mechanisms. We need not believe that it is dangerous to "stroll under palm trees," as Goethe (who hardly was thinking of California) figured, but that it can be dangerous to simply stroll under palms and not be informed about the land in which they grow, as many an emigrant's life has demonstrated. Discovering has over a long period of time come to signify a great deal of adaptation. Five hundred and also four hundred years ago life was still easier. Sir Richard Whitbourne could equip, with impunity, the lady who swam toward him on the coast of New England with the tail of a fish. Today he could not rely on the contexts brought along from home. He would have to inquire into the given nature of things there.

Yet, in the meantime it has in fact become possible to tie the contexts together as well.

> Am I to assume that the Creator created man to wander forever aimlessly around within the spiritual misery that surrounds us? I cannot believe that. God offers the European people a more constant and calmer future. I do not know His intentions, but though I cannot see through them, I do not cease to believe in them, and I would rather doubt my insight than His justice.

> In this world there is a land where the great revolution of society appears to have more or less reached its natural limits. It took place in a simple and easy manner, or more to the point, this land enjoys the fruits of our democratic revolution without having had to suffer through this revolution.

> The emigrants who settled in America at the beginning of the 17th century liberated, so to speak, the basic maxim of democracy from all doctrines, against which it had fought in the old society, and transplanted it in purified form to the shores of the New World. There it could now flourish in freedom and grow peacefully within a life-style guided by law.

Thus wrote Alexis de Toqueville in 1833 after his return from the United States, where on behalf of the French government he had studied the practice of executing penal sentences. The three short passages contain a lot that is characteristic of Europe's perception of America. Clearly there is an echo here of Goethe's "(America) you are better off," an utterance he put before the world without having to worry how it would be interpreted. Also there is the motif of freedom, along with the concept of a "pure" pragmatism — which could not prevent linguistic usage's clinging to the well-known "pure theory," that in itself remained theory-suspect.

Above all, one discovered the new continent's "lack of history"; not only at the expense of the country's pre-Columbian history – the discovery of which took an extraordinarily long time – but also at the expense of the historical assimilation of those emigrants whom de Toqueville looked upon as harbingers of an undogmatic democracy. He did not let himself be distracted by the fact that the passengers of the Mayflower had turned their backs on their homeland for more or less "purely" dogmatic reasons and that they had committed themselves not merely to finding freedom from the old clerical oppression, but at the same time to practicing their own rigorous discipline, religiously, morally, and socially.

He envisions a "more constant and calmer future" for the European people, not a statement one tends to quote with regards to de Toqueville's prophetic vein. Such calm and constancy he sees exemplified in the United States. What he finds exemplary is undoubtedly the evolution of the law, which he knows to be a historical but not a "historically burdened" process — a view that is not entirely free of idealization. The conceptual basis revealed here was intended by de Toqueville to be elaborated on in a description of America's middle-class society, its habits, thinking, and customs, "but," he says, "my eagerness to carry out this plan has subsided." "Someone else" will "depict the main features of the American character and, softening the seriousness of the images with a light veil, endow the truth with a charm with which I could not have graced it." He had in mind his friend and travel companion Gustave de Beaumont and his novel, "Marie ou l'esclavage aux Etats-Unis."

*

Beaumont had only been four days in New York, when he supplied his father (on May 16, 1831) with a detailed account of life in America. "Les mœurs y sont extrêmement pures," he reports. To be sure, he would never marry a woman in a strange land — "parce qu' une telle union entraîne une foule de circonstances fâcheuses" — but de Toqueville and he meant, nevertheless, to settle down in America if in France they should become victims of an "événement politique." What causes the two friends' enthusiasm is the private happiness which they see realized — in no way at odds with a business spirit that inspires greed, fraud and "mauvaise foi" — in society and especially in marriages. The high morality that underpins this great happiness is rooted, on the one hand, in the "esprit religieux" that prevails in everything: "nulle part les idées religieux ne sont plus en honneur." All credos are respected here; only to have *none* is a disgrace.

On the other hand, it is precisely that excessive business spirit that contributes to the fact that men are always busy, and that there is not — as in France — a larger number of individuals "qui, s'ils ne s'occupaient à séduire les femmes, n'auraient rien à faire." Beaumont does not anticipate Max Weber's thesis. He sees no inner connection between religiosity and striving for success. He merely notes that their coming together has a salutary effect, since the chase after riches protects men against the vices of idleness. — "On n'a pas le temps d'être mauvais sujet," and in addition there is, incidentally, a "tempérament plus froid," which he detects in the Americans (which he will come to have doubts about again after a closer look at the southern states). — Our brief sketch of this no longer early but not yet late discoverer pertains to a period when the concept of the simple, the unspoiled, the nature-like (as opposed to the refined and corrupt Europe) is still adhered to, but when at the same time one is also aware of what one is dealing with, as regards the New World: a civilization of its own.

(Translated by John Frey)

URS JAEGGI

Urs Jaeggi

Born June 23, 1931 in Solothurn. Studied economics and sociology. 1964/65
professor of sociology in Bern and Bochum. 1970/71 professor at the New School
for Social Research in New York. Since 1972 professor of sociology in Berlin.
Painter. Lives in Berlin. Short stories, novels, poems, essays, scholarly books: *Die
gesellschaftliche Elite*, 1960; *Die Wohltaten des Mondes*, 1964; *Die Komplicen*,
1964; *Für und wider die revolutionäre Geduld*, 1966; *Ein Mann geht vorbei*, 1968;
Macht und Herrschaft in der BRD, 1968; *Ordnung und Chaos*, 1968; *Literatur
und Politik*, 1972; *Brandeis*, 1978; *Grundrisse*, 1982; *Kopf und Hand*, 1982; *Fazit
und Johanna*, 1985; *Heicho*, 1986; *Rimpler*, 1987; *Soulthorn*, 1990.

Brandeis

It is early spring weather. Brandeis steps into the still bright evening light. I shall not tell any more stories; there will not be another story, not by him. He will call it life, as far as is feasible. Move. Hang in there, hold on tight. The main thing is, Gleen had said, that it is about to start. Any time now. Somewhere. It's going to start, everything is prepared. If we were just there, where we could be; if just we were there, even if it cost us dearly. Life. Perhaps. Sometime or other our ships will sail, sometime.

Nothing is moving anymore. He lies on the couch, many things are possible, everything is possible. He takes an opened wine bottle out of the refrigerator. Days pass by, weeks. The bottles are piling up. There is old, stale bread. He has draped his windows with cloths, lies in the dark, in the dirt. The ticking of the clock as precious seconds. He hears voices, noises. "Take up arms, citizens!" he hears people shout. He can no longer tell from where the yelling comes. It comes from everywhere, from left to right, from above and below.

Fever.

It is here, burns and spreads, garish colors like those at a fair, sweeping over everything, strangling, crushing. He hollers, paddles with his arms, yells himself unconscious, comes to again. The windows rattle, the light-bulbs flicker. He feels the urge to go outside. First he walks slowly up Fourteenth Street to the corner of Fifth Avenue; he crosses it at the intersection, descends into the subway shaft, climbs up again on the same side of the street. Suddenly the lights go out. He seems struck with blindness. "No, those aren't cops, they are soldiers," someone says, and somebody sings *Blue Moon* in a very loud and high-pitched voice. Another one recites a poem, screaming piercingly. One hears someone crying. Brandeis runs in the direction of Washington Square;

loudspeakers blare out the message: CITIZENS! THIS IS THE GOV-
ERNMENT SPEAKING! WE ARE FIRMLY IN CONTROL OF THE SITU-
ATION! DO NOT PANIC! EVERYBODY GO BACK INTO THE HOUSES!
CLEAR THE STREETS ....

THOSE OBEYING THESE ORDERS HAVE NOTHING TO FEAR ... WE
LIVE NORMAL LIVES, ALMOST NORMAL LIVES! WE LIVE QUIET
LIVES, MANY OF US HAPPILY! MANY OF US ARE LUCKY ... DO NOT
LET YOURSELVES BE INTIMIDATED! SO FAR, THERE HAVE HARDLY
BEEN ANY DEATHS! FEWER HAVE LOST THEIR LIVES THAN THE
REBELS WOULD HAVE YOU BELIEVE. GO HOME! WE NEED OUR
UNIMPAIRED COURAGE AND STRENGTH! STAY AT HOME ... !

CITIZENS, THIS IS THE GOVERNMENT SPEAKING!

Colorful rockets explode over Washington Square. On a platform, surrounded by military personnel, stands the President of
the United States, wrapped in the American flag. He looks seriously and solemnly at the square full of military personnel. Jet
fighters dive from the sky in close, immaculate formation; the
military observers from friendly countries hardly have time to lift
their heads when the planes streak past with a loud roar. Tanks
surround the square.

In Bleeker Street Brandeis runs into his mother, who is sitting
on the sidewalk, next to a dead child with a bashed-in skull. "Come
along," he says, "come on. You can't be of any help around here
anymore, we have to get away from here." Then he shouts, "Come,
let's go to the museum ... *There* it is quiet."

Resignedly, she lets herself be led away. At the museum, a few
adults and children stand around, all of an indefinite age, silent
and almost motionless. The pale hue of the emergency lighting
makes all the faces here look alike, man and woman, Blacks and
Whites, children and grown-ups. Large mirrors multiply the people standing around, cut them up. Bloated corpses pulled out of
the water lie around, bullet-riddled soldiers, heroin and brain
cancer victims. Jackals run around among the people, light-footed
and avaricious. "Come mother, come," says Brandeis and drags
her, panting and gasping for air as she is, through a long, white-
tiled corridor where slot-machines are placed. They are equipped
with silvery claws that play against each other. Little lamps light

up, numbers: silver, gold, red, a lot of red, and yellow. The machines are talking to each other, says the mother and he says: Of course, and it isn't witchcraft. It's tape recordings, those are not *real* voices.

Brandeis I: What is to become of us?

Brandeis II: Children cannot stay with their parents forever.

Brandeis I: Just the same. Where does all that brutality come from?

Brandeis II: It is now quiet in the street *(he looks out)*: There is even a store open at the corner. Calm down!

Brandeis I: We have missed too much, left too much behind.

Brandeis II: I still have to do some work today, mother, my seminar ...

Brandeis I: I can't see anything anymore ... It's all in a dark fog now. I don't feel you, have no sense of your presence, and I have yearned for you so much.

Brandeis II: Let's go on! Come on, mother!

Brandeis I: The quiet this evening is unusual, isn't it?

Brandeis II: Come off it. Don't be fooled. It's nothing unusual, nothing at all. Just be yourself again. *(long pause)*

Brandeis I: Help me ... I am suffocating here. It's freezing.

Brandeis II: That! That's too bad ... Really, that's inept, too bad. But don't get all excited. It'll pass. It'll pass.

Brandeis I: Stop!

Brandeis II: *(vigorously)* Oh, you know, I was beginning to like you, there were such times ...

Brandeis I: *(pleadingly)* Kurt!

Brandeis II: There, my dear, it's alright already ... I have settled down. *(pause)* Can't you be quiet at long last. *(annoyed)* When I am cold, you pull the blanket over my feet ...

Brandeis I: For hours I stood next to you, patiently. I wanted to talk ...

Brandeis II: Naturally. *(rudely)* Patiently. Sacrificingly. Blackmailingly. I can't think of any word but deadly.

Brandeis I: *(vehemently)* Yes, I have tried, again and again. *(pause)* Forgive me!

Brandeis II: *(apingly, wickedly)* Forgive me, forgive me! *(pause)* Couldn't you be quiet ... Disappear. *(rudely)* Beat it!

Brandeis I: *(serious)* I thought of it, honestly, I'd do it for you ... Honest. *(pause)* Believe me, please.

Brandeis II: Who do you take me for, who do you think you are?

Brandeis I: Oh yes, I know.

The next hall is empty, no furniture, only red, patternless silk wall paper. A handful of people sits around, loosely grouped, everyone in physical contact with his neighbor. The people form clusters, cram close to each other. They talk about what they are feeling when they touch. "I feel it, yes. It is soft and gentle like the coat of my dog — It almost hurts, it hurts as if you were in the grip of a vise, but not unpleasant, not at all ... A pleasant pain. It is cold, I am freezing, although my hands are sweating. You feel like a, like a, how should I say it ... your skin is chapped ... I don't want this, I find it repulsive. It is as if I touched a stone." — "You are awake," a voice rises that Brandeis cannot identify, "you are being truly reborn, painfully but also joyfully ... We are lying here, immobile, but everything is moving gently, very gently. You do not have to talk, not now. The least movement suffices. Let yourself fall, it works ..." In the next room two men confront mother and son, and with a quick grasp twist their hands to their backs.

"Good," says one of them, "yes, very good. Turn on the searchlights ... The peacock fan, we'll try the peacock fan ...."

They laugh. The solid grip with which the men hold them as if in vises has something calming about it in spite of the pain. Then all of a sudden a salvo of commands. "Climb up this ladder, go to the crossbar ... knees over the bar, now put your hands on your lower thighs, press everything nicely together, nothing will happen ... now *let go and drop!* The younger man gives mother a shove, starts the swing going, her body is swinging. "With a bit of practice you'll be able to swing in circles like a wheel," says the older one, "like a wheel! Just remain nice and loose, do not tense up. That will do it. Swing loosely and keep on swinging."

Mother gyrates, her skirt puffs up; her thick thighs, heavy with age, are covered with varicose veins that swell up like blue worms. "Throw up, get it out, for Pete's sake," the younger one jeers. "At your age it no longer pays to keep stubbornly silent ... Go ahead, holler, try a few more octaves! Don't be shy ...."

Mother —

"I can't help you," Brandeis roars, "our science is powerless. People die without recognizable causes, are shot dead. People die hanged or squashed by tanks. People die as gasoline torches, are reduced to ashes. Without warning. Just like that."

"Look," he says, "the museum is burning, it's in full blaze, the city is burning, the trees. Listen to me," he yells over to his mother, "we have to become virginal. Close your eyes, close your ears ...."

"I always wanted the best for you," gasps his mother, "I have tried hard. There was no sacrifice that I minded, none was too big. You should be proud, ah well. Perhaps it was in vain, I know it now ...."

A patient, Minkowski, says: "I didn't know that death looked like that. The soul is no longer being taken back. I want to seek the world. It's been an eternity since I left, there is no hour, no noon, no night. Life on the outside goes on. The leaves on the trees move back and forth. The others walk through the hall, to and fro, in all directions, but for me time doesn't pass. The clock runs as it always has. Sometimes, when the people outside in the garden walk briskly back and forth, and the leaves fly vigorously in the wind, I would like to live again as I did before. In spirit, I would like to be able to run along so that the time passes again, but then I get stuck, and I don't care. How does all that's going on outside concern me? To me it's all the same, trees, clouds, people ...."

Blinded. The trees in Washington Park split apart; the fountain in the middle of the park explodes. Brandeis hears how people around him collapse. There is shoving, stepping on toes; there are sweaty faces. "Fellow citizens," the loudspeaker bellows, "do not listen to the government. We are not making a revolution. We do not want a blood bath. They lied to you; they hoodwinked you with the slogan: No state without parliament, no state without force! But where is parliament now, *where* is your government? ... Swept out, everything swept out ...."

Trucks carrying soldiers drive by slowly, without a sound. The loudspeaker squeaks and gurgles: *Te arrancaré los ojos y me los pondrés me arrancaré los ojos.*

Brandeis again hears the rhythmic sound of boots. On Fifth Avenue, soldiers in khaki uniforms gather, gas masks on their faces, truncheons and automatic weapons in their hands, while on the other side of the street, rebels stand, gigantic, bigger than life figures. They are wearing multicolored bird masks, yellow, white, black gigantic beaks that open and snap shut noiselessly. The rebels advance slowly, machine-gun salvos perforate the masks. A few figures stagger, but the advancing wall cannot be stopped. Cars are tipped over. Billboards, hot dog stands, pretzel stalls, trees. The rebels keep advancing. Their immense bodies squash everything. The fog rises. A steel-blue sky appears. The wind whips up ashes. Now the day is over, Brandeis hears a black man say.

Somewhere a clarinet plays in F sharp.

He hears the clarinet endlessly holding the same note. You wouldn't mind, would you? We let the Venetian blinds down, let go of each other.

On the radio, a monotonous voice chats away. "I saw a young captured Vietnamese woman. Rumor had it that she sympathized with the Viet Cong. She refused to talk during the interrogation. They stripped her of all her clothes and tied her down. Then she was raped by each one of the soldiers in the unit. They sewed her vagina shut with ordinary wire, rammed a brass rod through her head and hanged her. I also saw the daughter of a Vietnamese village elder being tied down. We heated a bayonet over a fire. We drew it across her breasts and thrust it into her vagina. She was still alive. We had a sergeant with us, who pulled a leather shoelace out from his boot, wetted it, tied it around her neck and let her hang in the sun. Leather shrinks when it dries. The sergeant refused to let any of us end her suffering. He sat next to her, heard her screams and later the fading rattle in her throat." That's how it was. Brandeis feels the fever rising. Big, heavy trees crash down around him. He gets covered, entombed by immense granite blocks. He works his way out from under and writes the message he received on the nearest wall of a house: UNDER THE PAVING STONES THE BEACH!

Violence, as we know it, is dead, sterile and monotonous, says Brandeis, standing at a lectern. Non-violence is colorful and cheer-ful, he says. We know that, but this is not enough. Our power must prove itself, must be equal to that of the enemy, must be better, inventive, agile, productive; must be condensed, solidified, organ-ized. We must destroy the regime of untruth. Quickly, before it is too late.

The faces that are looking at him, that are trying to speak with him, start to blur. He holds on to the lectern, leafs forlornly through his manuscript. That's odd, he says. Slowly his legs are giving way under him, he feels himself sinking, uttering some words. EVERYTHING WILL BE ALL RIGHT, matter is ever present. The faces continue to blur, they slowly dissolve. Now all is silent. The earth might be uninhabited, he says. It depends on us. We must find a precise strategy, clear, careful thinking. While talking on in a whispering voice, he flaps his arms up and down like a confused bird.

Delirium.

"The view over the great landscape" was the message he had been writing in vain on all walls over the last few days. THE VIEW OVER THE GREAT LANDSCAPE.

Tumbling. Falling forward. Joe's bar is engulfed in gray fog.

It is cold. Brandeis sits under the bright light of the search-lights, chained to a chair. Once and for all, shouts the one across from him, the revolution is not coming. It is hopeless, give up!

Brandeis downs whisky, glass after glass, hour after hour. Don't worry, you are finished, says the one opposite him in an aloof, gentle voice. Step by step, there is no escape. Keep going, go on.

He saw it coming, it was only the specific time that could not be foreseen. He saw it coming, and now he also seems to know the exact time, no, not know, but it seems that way, it creates that impression. Millimeter by millimeter something advances which he is unable to recognize clearly.

Waiting, forgetting. A last effort. You have arrived. Have no more fear. All roads now lead away from you. Let yourself fall. Fall at long last. Fall down, and keep on falling.

Have no fear now.

It's all right, this kind of light. A part of night, a part of day. Outside the birds are flying by, back and forth. Their movements grow calm. Let yourself fall. It's snowing. He is sitting there with his teeth clenched, his carotid artery beating rather feebly. Dense blackish white snow, which slowly fills Joe's bar. Slowly falling. "Help!" "Help!"

All voices speak simultaneously, without him being able to understand what they are saying. The sun outside glows fiercely — he is falling. There are no screams, no names.

[. . .]

Let's go, Anne said, now nothing can happen to us anymore.

Anne and Brandeis are traveling. A long tale is coming to an end. Suddenly they see no more connection between their experiences and the now.

UNDER THE ROCKS OF OROVILLE, UNDER FORMATIONS OF CLOUDS IN THE BLUE SEPTEMBER SKY, ACROSS THE BORDER INTO THE USA, TREE BRANCHES HELD UP BY POLES BEND UNDER THE GLOWING RED APPLES —

IN OMAK, A HEAVY-SET GIRL IN WORKING PANTS, LEADING HER LARGE BROWN HORSE ALONG THE ASPHALT HIGHWAY ...

NEAR NESPELEM IN YELLOW SUNLIGHT, A SIGN POINTING TO CHIEF JOSEPH'S GRAVE ...

AND GRAY WATER SPLASHING AGAINST THE GRAY SLOPES OF STEAMBOAT MESA ...

IN MESA, PAST A NEW GRAIN ELEVATOR, ON THE CAR RADIO WALKING BOOGIE, SWEET TEENAGE VOICES ...

ON THE PLATEAU TOWARD PASCO, OREGON'S MOUNTAINS ON THE HORIZON, BOB DYLAN'S VOICE ON THE AIR, MECHANICALLY MASS-PRODUCED FOLKSONG OF A LONE SOUL "PLEASE CRAWL OUT YOUR WINDOW ..."

LAKE WALLULA IN THE CANYON BETWEEN THE BROWN FLATTOP MOUNTAINS, IT SMELLS OF RAIN AND SAGE, GREYHOUND BUSES WHIZ BY ...

SIGN UNDER PONDEROSA PINE: ACREAGE FOR SALE — 45 DE-GREES LATITUDE, MIDWAY BETWEEN THE EQUATOR AND THE NORTH POLE — WEATHER FORECAST ON THE CITY RADIO: CLEAR NIGHT WITH TEMPERATURES BELOW FREEZING; LARGE YELLOW DAISIES, BALES OF HAY STACKED UP IN RECTANGULAR PILES SEV-ERAL STORIES HIGH, NEVADA ...

COYOTE JUMPED IN FRONT OF OUR CAR, DOWN THE BANK, CROSSED THE RIVER, RACED THROUGH A FIELD AND UP TOWARD THE EDGE OF A FOREST ON THE MOUNTAIN SLOPE, STOPPED SUD-DENLY, TURNED AROUND AND STARED ACROSS THE FIELD AT US ...

MOUNTAINS LIKE THOSE ON PICTURE POSTCARDS. FOSSIL RIVER BEDS NEAR DAYVILLE ...

Anne and Brandeis drive through the Appalachians, through Harlan County; they pass through and cross many little neighboring valleys and rock-covered hills. They pass the same signs over and over again: KENTUCKY BLUE-GRASS, BAKED CHICKEN A LA KENTUCKY, HOLIDAY INN. The air is steamy; they are traveling on bad roads and across bridges in ill repair. It is coal that makes Kentucky something special, someone says on TV. The man they talk to, the drugstore owner of the place, says, while the two are having a cold beer in the *Blue Moon*: the bosses control everything around here; it's a company town, the homes, the hospitals, the schools, the jails, and the bars. The miners shop at the company store, they send their children to the company school, and in the end they die in the company hospital.

Down in the center, the lights go on. Someone near to Brandeis says: "We have been on strike for eight months now; we are demanding an all-inclusive contract, a pension fund and health insurance. The company's response has been hired security guards ... ever since then we have been in a state of war; every night there is shooting ...."

"Since the beginning of the sixties, monster bulldozers with a scooping capacity of more than 200 tons have been tearing up the earth to lay bare the coal," says the drugstore owner. "The ridges of the whole hill range get ripped off and moved away. The resulting avalanches of rubble keep on moving, uproot trees, block the brooks, and squash houses ...."

When Anne later wants to take a shower in the hotel room, nothing but air comes out at first, but then enough boiling water gushes out to flood the room; they drink a beer and study the map.

While driving along, Anne sits deeply sunk into the seat of the old, blue Chevy. She is wearing a long skirt and a T-shirt. They do a lot of talking. There is nothing forced in their conversations any longer. They talk quietly, without unreasonable expectations; they talk because it's fun and because they are getting reacquainted. They eat fruit and sandwiches; now and then Anne hands him the Coke can, and every three hours they drink a cup of hot coffee in one of the ice-cold bars. Some anonymous voice on the radio gives a report on the war, which has now entered its main phase. During our training at the Marine base at Beaufort, South Carolina, says the anonymous voice, we received instructions in how to survive in the jungle. We also were taught how to tie the electrodes of the communications equipment to the genitals of prisoners. There were drawings on the blackboard that showed how to attach electrodes to the scrotum of a male and to the body of a woman. We were shown what one can do with little bamboo rods, how to stick them under finger nails or into ears. We were told to take off the girls' clothes, spread their legs and ram pointed sticks or bayonets into their vaginas; furthermore, how to open incendiary bombs without detonating them and then rub the phosphor on parts of the body. Our instructors had fun telling us how they tied the arms and legs of a prisoner to two helicopters and then took off. When we went to the mess hall, we had to yell three times kill, Viet Cong, Viet Cong, kill, kill, kill. Gotta kill, gotta kill, 'cause it's fun.

They got higher and higher into the mountains.

They stood in front of fossilized trees which, being as high as 100 meters, draw all the light toward them. Anne placed herself with her back against one of these Miocene-giants, posed as one once did for an old fashioned photo album ("Lady standing in front of a tree with turned-up collar.") It was really a sight: a petite, happy-go-lucky creature in front of a species dating back to the Miocene epoch. The trees exuded a refreshing fragrance.

They drove through hundreds of variations of red, blue, silvery gray, and white. The landscape presented a riot of colors. For days they drove in sunshine, through rain. They ate "home-made pancakes," trout, peanut butter sandwiches. Their blue Chevy dragged a glowing white cloud of dust behind. They pitched their tent among other camping nuts, hauled bags of cans, bottles, apples, potatoes, tomatoes. In the evening, they watched the Ed Sullivan Show. The Mets decided the game against the Giants in the 15th inning and became the champions with a score of 12 to 10. Indians assemble in front of cameras. They had driven through Elvis Presley's birthplace; the stone pine-covered hills of Berkeley. SAN FRANCISCO.

The journey is over. In thirty-six hours they'll fly to Frankfurt. Brandeis spent decades in this country, it seems to him. He doesn't remember exactly whether Kurt and Gleen are one and the same person (and he doesn't know whether Anne and Suzanne really behaved as he describes it; but that isn't important. He knows people who do act that way, and it really doesn't matter in the least whether Kurt, Gleen and Brandeis are one and the same person). He can project himself into all three of them, and he in fact has played all the roles he describes. (He could have played all of them.)

Gleen was real. Gleen who, when he visited him after midnight once, went to a bar with him, took the saxophone away from the sax player and improvised for two full hours: IT COULD HAPPEN TO YOU. His laughter in his dark face. During his improvising there was something religious and grand in his eyes, something desperate, and an unbridled desire to shake off the despair. Gleen, the giant — in this situation.

Later, Gleen sat in front of his beer again (he called it *Humpen* using the German he had learned as a GI in Heidelberg). "You are a funny people, without strength. Without self-confidence. You let yourself get paralyzed by your own history! Why don't you start all over again, but in a really new way?" (Although he knows that Brandeis is not German, at least not a native German; he says: "You ...")

Brandeis hears Kurt talk. In one of our last conversations, Kurt expressed the opinion that people nowadays no longer dared to have wishes. We hide our wishes. To talk today about wishes is to talk about something unknown, taboo, he said, and I answered: No, you can't look at it that way. Dreams, fairy-tales, myths, these things are still around, likewise psychoses, all kinds, as a symbolical wish-fulfillment.

Kurt standing by the open window drinks wine out of a cup. Naturally, he says, but everything you say points backward, into the past. No one will deny that the civil ideals of liberty, equality, and brotherhood have turned into their opposites and that the consequences of this reversal can be felt in every fiber of every person, he said. But the emotional catastrophe was that we were no longer able to cope with the external constraints, were locked up in our private lives as in a prison, and that it was our duty to blow up this prison.

Kurt and Brandeis drink Beaujolais, eat the ghastly-tasting German bread and Appenzeller cheese. Kurt says something unintelligible between two bites. In the sciences that concern themselves with the well-secreted boundaries a fear-ridden strategy was raging: the conceptual lexicography of theology, psychology, philosophical anthropology, and medicine, for instance, — their intent was to conceal those problems that focus on death and sexuality. But that gave rise to the question: what remained in this world, in which everything turned into dust, in which everything one hoped for was *not yet* realizable. When Brandeis asks Kurt to elaborate, Kurt says that he doesn't have any precise notion either, and he added in his rather off-hand manner that that was just the way it was, because wishing was now banned. Our deafness for everything that could undermine this was growing. All kinds of all too hasty and ill-considered substitute solutions were being offered: slogans like repression and oppression — and with that being so, it inevitably had to culminate in explosions. One also could not prevent our lives from turning into an arena of destruction, a place of mass annihilation, of tortures, and terror.

It is New Year's Eve. Outside the first rockets are launched and explode. We are sitting across from each other, arguing amiably. Even if we were allies of death and thus irrevocably united with it, it does not necessarily mean destruction only, I say (or he says), and Kurt indulges in his tremendous laugh which clearly contains a trace of contempt toward my objections. You misunderstand me, he says. Law and infringement are interconnected, are chained to each other exactly as is the reduction to zero, to the sterile, the dead on the one hand. Just as with self-capitulation it is, on the other hand, in the case of ecstasy, of orgy: it's the same, as is six of one and half a dozen of the other. We had not differentiated carefully enough: speaking does not mean dancing, writing not laughing, yelling not touching. We were blinded and we persisted in our blindness. You are full of pathos, much too full of pathos to be really fit to act, says Brandeis.

Kurt's face now looks inquiring and friendly. The rebellion of the oncoming generation would, allegedly scientifically proven and uncontested, be presented as neurotic conflicts, as a danger to the system, as destruction (all of which was true enough), but what was forgotten was this: the erupting revolts set into motion the age-old mechanism of psychotisizing and criminalizing, a mechanism which turns the aggressors, the subjects, into victims, into objects — erroneously and fatally. Our problems, all of modern thinking, had in reality the imprint of the question of revolution on it, the question: what is going on here, how can and must we change things? And what can and must we do, so that we intellectuals, this necessary and superfluous group, can become even more superfluous in this era of transition ....

Kurt abruptly ends the conversation and practices a handstand at the book case. Of course you are right in your objection, he says with a very red face and breathing hard; of course, there are criminal acts that are disguised as political ones, bank robberies with a deadly outcome, for instance. But don't make it too easy for yourself. The lawlessness has deep roots, the delinquency is criminalized in accordance with our yardsticks. But don't forget: among all too many it all begins with the experienced loss of oneness with their "mother," which urges to restoration by all available means, even the abandonment of reality. The aim of this childlike wish is the return to the womb, the search for immediate gratification. It's not by accident but in the normal order of things that incest with the mother is being interpreted as a death-wish and a yearning for rebirth. There you have it. And that isn't all; it's merely *one* interpretation. The bold flame of rebellion was understandable, explainable, was comprehensible, to start with, as a reaction against the existing order of things.

Kurt now argues ever more excitedly, and Brandeis says: alright, let's make a fist, even load a rifle, but start a fight, *actually* pull the trigger? Was that what he meant, did he think that was the right thing to do?

Let the father, the law, step in as a border, a barrier, says Kurt and he once again gets aggressive in his reply when Brandeis does not answer. The simplest dreams of a child show wondrous or forbidden objects, things dreamed of, things envisioned and things realized. Therefore for us, children would always be figments of the imagination, an idea, wish-children, wish-mirror, and we would do anything to kill off these ideas. Strangle them. Anything complex, inexplicable, anything new, all that was being covered up with patterns of the factual, the law, jurisdiction, and sanctions: erroneously. The law, the penalty, the punishing, says Kurt, was only the one form, the answer of the ruling class, the answer of the powerful, to dam up, to kill off everything that runs counter, everything innovative.

Kurt, sullen and unfriendly, enjoys eating what is left of the cheese, and he empties the opened bottle of wine. It had been rightly said that an infringement was a gesture that had to do with limitation, that at this thin line the lightning of transgression flashes up, the unexpected, but also perhaps its whole flight path and its origin. Perhaps the point of this transgression was just that, a point and no more. The game rules of the limitations and infringements were of a simple tenacity: infringement meant repeated cutting across a line in order to retreat anew to the horizon of the impassable ....

I repeat: with your pathos, your waiting for miracles, for the whole, the absolute, you'll get nowhere at all.

Kurt's combative, excited voice now turns thin and hoarse: you still have to hear the end of these thoughts, he says. This game surrounds its elements in an uncertainty — certainties namely, which can be reversed at any time and which our normal thinking ability cannot comprehend. *That far* you have to go.

Picking up the plates, cups, and bottles and carrying them into the kitchen with quiet and pleasant movements, Kurt says: for me politics is no substitute for what we just talked about, and he says before parting: politics and wishes are the same thing.

SAN FRANCISCO

I walk along the bay, my hands in my pants pockets. Fisherman's Wharf, Alcatraz on the horizon. Alcatraz as a factory of power, as a prison for lifers, terribly magnified by a telescope put up for tourists, forsaken today, empty, as a tourist guide says. It is a crystal-blue morning in May, a morning of peaceful, fragile charm. The sea around Alcatraz; to the left and to the right of the island there is light and water. A white bird soars motionlessly above it, hundreds of seagulls, perhaps thousands. Along the bay, collected in crates and glass containers: lobster, shrimp, starfish. All the smells here are strange. I sit in a café under a big ventilator. Looking back over the past years, I could talk of mourning; of grief. I understand the Japanese for whom white is the color of grieving. Bleaching: Faded by sun and history, Snow. Snow-white.

At any rate, things happened in a way that warrants reporting them. One was a professor, another one a bank employee. One was committed to a psychiatric clinic, not in Konstanz to be sure, but in New York, because he had set fire to his bed several times and succeeded twice. One does time in a Bochum jail for attempted murder of a policeman. Suzanne is assistant professor of sociolinguistics in Paderborn. Gleen was accidentally shot and killed as an innocent bystander at a gang war in Harlem — in 1976. Friends wrote me about it.

Facts render my imagination helpless; my imagination renders the facts helpless; something is changing, however, something has changed. We begin.

A wind comes up, it gets darker. I go into one of the restaurants to eat a cheeseburger. We stay in an old hotel that is run by an old Chinaman. The building is dilapidated, deteriorated, but the staircase and the terraces are monumental. I sit down on the terrace. The rain now whips through the city, drives trash, newspapers, household articles, and dead animals through the streets. The sea: black and beautiful. I wait under a sky that is now a venomous yellow.

As night falls, the letters spelling out LINCOLN shoot up into the sky from the building across the street. A gigantic papier mâché cow in rose-colored illumination advertises MILK, the healthiest food there is. Anne wears a silver chain around her neck, her hair is spread out on the pillow, blond and then dark. Gleen has sent a telegram. Just picture New York as an all Black city, he writes. All inhabitants make their own decisions about everything. The schools are places of joy, the pupils learn without any coercion. The workers in the factories do their jobs in accordance with their own ideas. And so forth. Imagine the US being all Black. We produce with our labors whatever we need, whatever gives us pleasure. And now imagine the whole world being all Black. We are alive.

Expressions like mourning are sheer impudence. When the real angst hits you, there is no room for pain, you are numb; there no longer is talk of fear and grief. If we, beyond this fear, make use of the openings, the gaps, the caesuras, if we do that, then there is a chance for us. When we learn to make wishes again, writing becomes dispensable.

I wait, wait at the airport beside Anne who is reading; I sit there with a half-emptied, dripping Coca Cola glass before me, put my notebook aside; tear it up. An imagined figure is not a real person. I smoke a cigarette, a Pall Mall. Several policemen on patrol, automatic weapons at the ready.

Your attention, please, your attention, please — Flight PA 1341.

Is there such a thing as a right side, I hear myself ask, a perfect society, a country we can live in; is there such a thing, and I hear Gleen answer: wherever there is power, there is also resistance. Your attention please —

(Translated by John Frey)

HANNA JOHANSEN

Hanna Johansen

Born June 17, 1939 in Bremen. Lived for two years in the US. 1985 Writer-in-Residence, Max Kade Institute, USC. Translator. Received several literary awards. Lives in Kilchberg. Short stories, novels, radio plays, children's books: *Die stehende Uhr*, 1978; *Trocadero*, 1980; *Die Analphabetin*, 1982; *Über den Wunsch, sich wohlzufühlen*, 1985; *Zurück nach Oraibi*, 1986; *Ein Mann vor der Tür*, 1988; *Die Schöne am unteren Bildrand*, 1990; *Über den Himmel*, 1993; and the children's books *Felis, Felis*, 1987; *Die Ente und die Eule*, 1988; *Die Geschichte von der kleinen Gans, die nicht schnell genug war*, 1989.

Ideas

I am Hungarian, said the driver. So I speak German.

I did not want to speak German. He did. I could not understand his German.

Is this Armenian? I said.

No, he said. Not Armenian. He did speak Armenian though. He spoke Rumanian, Bulgarian, Czech, Russian and a few more languages I could not keep in mind.

No, I finally said. I don't need a drink. I never do. I just need a taxi.

This is a taxi, he said.

What a town. This was the day of my arrival.

As soon as it starts raining in New York City, the corners are crowded with busy males, each of them at an age where you would still like to start a business of sorts. They are selling umbrellas, mostly the kind of automatic American umbrella I had brought along from Switzerland. They are all manufactured in Japan. These umbrellas being an obvious example of vendibility on a rainy spring day made me think of the times ahead. I used to imagine how the males would sell harpoons and fins in New York summers.

Philadelphia is different, I've been told. As soon as it stops raining there, the flower vendors move on to the smelly islands in the highways. Philadelphia drivers suddenly stop in the left lanes to buy pretzels and roses. They seem to need more flowers than anybody could offer. I never got to Philadelphia. It was close. But why should I go there?

Once I was looking for an apple. All I found was tiny shoes in expensive colors. When I was looking for a record, I found homosexual bathing suits. I liked them. I might have gotten a hot dog and a variety of sweets. No postcards. I felt new. Nevertheless I aged in hours by disappointment.

My lover gave me a lecture about ideas. I had never asked him to, but all of a sudden I seemed to like the idea of ideas. And besides, he was not my lover then.

I told him about Swiss cows, Swiss sumo and Swiss wedding candies. Everything seemed to surprise him then.

Is this true? he said.

Yes, I keep telling my countrymen. They do have butterflies in New York.

He lacked quite a few things men usually have. In the first place, he did not have a wife. Which was a good thing if you were looking for love. Next, he did not have an ironed suit, which I really appreciated for reasons I don't want to reveal now. He did not have a beard. That made him look rather naked. But he seemed to think that his face was worth looking at and I agreed. Then he did not have an apartment. What I thought was that this must be a very uncomfortable life. He shrugged and smiled when I asked him. But as I did not have an apartment either, I could at least be sure he did not want me because of a cozy home of anykind that he might be offered.

There are more things he lacked. He never let me find out whether he loved me or not. But that is nothing to complain about.

He did have a bank account. He showed me the card. He avoided mentioning the code number. He went to work all day. So he did have a job, I thought. One night he grabbed my hand and took me to his bank account. The bank account talked Mexican, Puerto Rican and Latin. It did talk English if that was what you wanted. We were asked to announce our wishes. We took the Latin way. Then the computer decided to give us the exact amount of money it had been asked for.

There is always an opportunity to talk about ideas. That's the way life is. Didn't you know that? I didn't.

To be serious, I never saw a single butterfly in New York City. I hate to admit it because it was my fault. It was not exactly winter. But I mostly went to places where they could not possibly survive.

Places like subterranean subway stations, planetariums, inexpensive hotels, expensive hallways and bank accounts. I would not call these sterile environments, but they certainly don't provide what animals like butterflies or even cows might need. I did see a bird. That was on a rainy Sunday in the park when I tried to keep up my usual pace among an innumerable crowd of scattered individuals moving around at incredible speeds. None of them stumbled or dropped dead as I had been told they would. I felt ashamed because I was so slow and tried not to look at them. It was not easy.

I try to remember everything I avoided. I avoided three youths in a well-lit subway station. They seemed to be waiting for someone like me. They had suddenly stopped their conversation. I did not like the idea. I never know what people are talking about, I thought. It makes me feel foolish. I left the station in a hurry. When I returned the next day, they were still waiting.

I tried to avoid men leaning against sunny fountain rims. You could meet them close to cozy walls, too, faded men putting vague questions to themselves when somebody happened to come along. They looked starved but did not talk about it, which was quite unlike older men waiting for the travelers who came riding down the stairs of the bus terminal. Dutifully I read the cardboard signs about them being hungry. The fountain man had a sloping voice. He did not mind his yellow hair hanging down his face while he asked himself whether I or anybody else might want his services.

I had been told never to say thank you in a case like this. Not in New York City. He moved his head and did not expect any answer. In fact, he did all he could in order to avoid being confronted with the wrong kind of answers. The only one he could accept was: Yes, I'd love to.

I avoided older women with plastic bags.

They reminded me of quite a lot of things that had lead to anxieties in my interior soul a long time ago. Their faces used to show the very features of childhood if you were prepared for the encounter. The way they moved reminded me of the future.

The smaller streets around the corner were crowded with garbage bags. They seemed to have been waiting there for some time. They had holes in their sides as if they hadn't been looked after well enough. Some of the garbage bags looked alive. They were sitting on one another. Every once in a while one of them was sloping. They never go to the Frick collection.

I did. There they don't have men leaning against their fountain rims. They want you to come in. Heartily they welcome everybody who is not a garbage bag.

I was told about Mr. Frick. But now I have to admit that I forgot what it was he sold. It is such a long time ago. He must have sold something in order to buy all these heartbreaking examples of art history. He probably sold goods of the kind that a large percentage of the population seems to need. Or if it was not goods, it may have been his services. Men with unusual abilities usually make it in our societies.

I was supposed to meet my sister in San Diego. After two weeks I called her.

What happened to you, she said.

I was so surprised I could not answer the question. It was such a simple-looking question. Then I discovered it was not only because of the surprise but I really did not know what had happened to me. I am still in New York, you know, I said. But how would she know.

Do you need money, she said.

Oh no, I said.

Call me collect, she said.

I never did.

She was supposed to have her baby soon.

How is your baby, I said.

Fine, she said. He is just fine. He started to smile at his daddy.

I hate rainy airports, I said.

You might like ours, she said. They seem to have the most beautiful airport in San Diego.

Spread your wings and fly when it seems to be the worst moment or the last.

Why do you say so, I asked him.

Because it is difficult to get rid of ancient ideas, he said. Sometimes you don't even realize you are wrong.

That's right. I used to think of true love as of something that happened only once. Everybody seemed to. So why shouldn't I?

Do you know what he did? He let me sit on his lap until the night was half over. I was delighted. But he had forgotten to tell me that in the second half of the night he had to leave for work.

The day I found out that he only worked daytime hours I started to weep. But I never told him.

You look funny, he said.

Do I, I said.

I guess I was too young for him. He liked women with experienced faces. He once said so. On the other hand, sometimes I can look rather old. It's easy.

As a baby I used to talk Swiss. Now I forgot. He told me how he had kept his Swiss watch for decades. It needs repair though, he added.

How I would like to sit in his skin for just one day. And then maybe one night. What good are wishes if they are not fulfilled? In the leaden morning wind I would slip back into my own wrinkled dress.

The coins in his back pockets accompanied his lovely slow steps with the constant whisper of a cosmopolitan life. His coins were all colors and sizes and came from far away countries. He showed them in an open hand.

This is democracy, he said. They all live together peacefully. And in fact, that was what they did. Some of them were created with a hole in the middle.

These are my favorites, he said. You can wear them as an earring.

He had participated in one of the undeclared wars. No fighting, he said. We just moved around.

Right in the middle of his belligerent heart he kept those few words I always wanted to hear. He had in fact promised to give them to me some day. So instead I kept this hope because I seem to need something that can be kept.

I looked for some place to buy used records. The number was 607. They didn't have a single garbage bag waiting outside. I walked right in through a shiny crystal door, embarrassed because I had expected a rundown environment. My shoes felt wet inside. The beautiful doorman took my umbrella and placed it in a special corner of the container where he promised not to mix it up with the others. They all seemed to be twins of mine. It was not sunlight that poured down on us from the ceiling five floors above.

I asked for Alice, which to me sounded like a more appropriate request than used records.

Mr. Frick, shouted the lady with her good, soft voice. Do we have an Alice? No, there is no Alice here, she whispered. Lots of ladies. They were reflected by the black mirrors that surrounded us. They all whispered.

But this is 607, isn't it?

It was. They had a jewelry exhibition. I had managed to drop in on the opening. So I left. The doorman picked my umbrella.

You are welcome, he pronounced with a beautiful smile. Ma'm.

Outside I took a good long look at the construction work which was still going on in the higher floors of 607.

I said good-bye to my love.

Do you know how it feels, I said.

Yes, I know, he said.

I called San Diego. It was a strange connection. The cackle of the runways could not stop to sneak into our communication.

Where are you, said my sister.

Who is crying?

It was Jeremy. He wanted to talk to me.

Why is he crying?

He never wants me to answer the phone, she said.

Still raining in San Diego? I said.

Oh no. That's a funny idea you've got.

I am still in the East, I said.

I'll send you a ticket.

Please don't. This is my last day.

The New York sun has a beautiful way of coming around in the morning. It starts lighting up the east sides of the tallest buildings. Millions of people open their eyes. Sixteen hundred pages of phone numbers are waiting to get busy.

At this time, I stopped being concerned about how much of my money I was allowed to carry around. I was ready to hand my cash over to anybody who would force me to give it to him. There seemed to be enough people who needed it.

One of them had one day started to love gypsies. He had from this time on been searching for gypsy women in the city. Although he never succeeded, he had detested all the other kinds. He had stolen a gypsy guitar that looked abandoned in the park. Then for years, he had tried to learn the music. That turned out to be difficult because he never had played the guitar before. He did not want the dream of his life to be drowned in his incapacities. That's the reason why he did not give up. He had even thought of cutting off one or two of his fingers in order to have a better chance at getting the sound that was waiting in his head to be taken out into reality. He had spent a night in a burning house. He had gone to the country but immediately returned because he could not stand the smell.

I met him when he was sitting in the lead and oxygen mixture of a downtown parking entrance surrounded by soda cans, leftover doughnuts and the usual oily stains on the pavement. He refused to give his guitar back to a tall figure that approached him from behind, recognized his former possession and finally hit him on the head with a bottle. The bottle was filled with something that looked like orange juice. The man fell to his side without a sigh. The bigger man took the guitar and pressed it against his naked chest. Then he left.

We had a beautiful morning. No rain at all. The driver told me how his wife had left him. He was still sad.

I know how you feel, I admitted.

My name is Steven, he said.

He wanted me to call him on weekends.

I gave him my umbrella. It was still in good shape. It actually looked new.

You may need it, I added.

He gave me his card. It said LOVE TAXI. Day and night services.

I am only one in a crowd, he murmured while he was writing down his home number on the back of the card.

Thank you, I said.

A woman never gets a man back if she wants him. Didn't you know that? I took his watch along. It slept in the depths of my bag. It needed a real Swiss repair, not an ordinary one. But he had never asked me when I was going to give it back to him.

Again I tried to buy a postcard. This time I found one. It was a duty-free photograph of our spinning universe with an arrow that said: Here am I. The postcard arrived at its destination a few weeks after I had gotten there. I read it aloud with my new voice which was stuffed with memories. It read: Please don't take the garbage out of my room. I will need it soon.

Daddy said: Sorry, we could not possibly keep it. He was wearing an extremely new summer suit.

Oh Dad, I said.

They kept asking me all sorts of questions about the United States. I had no idea what they were talking about.

I once met a man in Manhattan. I told them because they were all dying to be told at least some of my experiences. He wanted to show me something. No, I said. Come on, he said. He did not move out of my way. Come here, he said. What he meant was a basement entrance around the corner. He kept a briefcase pressed against his lower front. He looked disgustingly unhappy. I don't want to see it, I said. But I could not help taking a look at what he took out of his briefcase. It was a fine female hand, covered with black skin and a yellow paper cuff.

They all stared at me in dismay. What did you do, they said.

I ran away, I said. Don't run away, I heard the man cry. But I did not want to hear it.

The dong-dong sound of the cowbells had seemed rather slow and sleepy for a few days, or for a similar period of time, but now it suffered some sort of revitalization going hop hop with every imaginable sign of a growing spirit of hurry. This might indicate some hope in their minds, I guessed, if it wasn't anxiety. Despair would not sound like that.

The cows now watch me leaning against our natural apple tree while I watch them chewing a couple of meals they have had before. Three more weeks, and somebody will take the fences down. The cows that don't know about beef will go to the slaughterhouse. In the meadow I will be able to watch the annual festival of Swiss sumo and after that the growing of five medium-sized apartment houses. And in between I will be surprised by the sight of a little Swiss wedding with all the children from the neighborhood gathering to collect as many of the colorful Swiss wedding candies as they can. And I will go to New York City, where, if you are old or insane, life is said to be hell. It's going to be a lot worse if you are a woman. The reason is money. That's what they told me.

JÜRG LAEDERACH

Jürg Laederach

Born December 20, 1945 in Basle. Studied mathematics, physics, French and English literature, music history. Lived in New York, Graz, Paris, Vienna, Berlin. Jazz player. Translator. Received several literary awards. Lives in Basel. Short stories, novels, plays: *Einfall der Dämmerung*, 1974; *Im Verlauf einer langen Erinnerung*, 1977; *Das ganze Leben*, 1978; *Die Lehrerin verspricht der Negerin wärmere Tränen*, 1978; *Ein milder Winter*, 1978; *Dummweg, das Hermelin*, 1979; *Wittgenstein in Graz*, 1979; *Das Buch der Klagen*, 1980; *Fahles Ende kleiner Begierden*, 1981; *69 Arten den Blues zu spielen*, 1984; *Flugelmeyers Wahn*, 1986; *Der zweite Sinn*, 1987; *Passion*, 1993.

Emanuel — Dictionary of the Enchanted Loafer

In Guinea-Bissau, the doctor told the tardy Emanuel, there is a fellow who is a night watchman. His job is to guard a hospital. In the evenings, he arrives at the long drawn-out building and, to start with, lays down his club, a cane that has a nail driven into it. He lies down on the ground next to his club, pulls a rag over his face and goes to sleep. The doctors leaving the hospital climb over the sleeping watchman. One evening, when the night watchman cannot fall asleep, he goes into the hospital hall — a prototype of all halls in this world — stands around for a while, disappears in one of the corridors and ends up with the doctor on call, whom he asks for a sleeping pill. The doctor on call has AIDS. His handing over the pill leads to a brief altercation, in the course of which enough viruses jump over to make the night watchman tired after a while, so that he goes to sleep on his own, as the stars come out. We want to get married, but never have anything to do with each other. We have children, naturally, but we never see these children. They live in their house, we in ours. We don't live in our house either. You live in yours, I in mine. We only get together to eat some rice, drink a glass and make a baby. No good would come from anything else. Oh yes, we do take a walk at Easter every year; it takes us to the hill outside of town. There we stand still and think about everything; we shall have done the right thing. Let's take out letters from the bag to begin our scrabble game. Draw without looking. Emanuel draws an *M*, Perkins an *E*, and Pannonica, the Austrian baroness, a *G*. Quick as lightning Perkins opens with the word *Gnus*, 5 points. The Austrian baroness follows with *Teils*, 14 points. Emanuel gets 4 points for the word *Ger*. Second round. Perkins offers *Finte*, 8 points. The Austrian baroness comes up with *Lid*, 6 points. Emanuel has a big one, *Teilstreik*,

26 points. Nip on the glass. Third round. Perkins puts down *Erde* and collects 6 points: the Austrian baroness throws in *Feige*, takes back an *E*, leaving her 14 points. Emanuel casually lays down *Teilstreiks*, giving him an additional 14 points from the same turf. The fourth round nets Perkins 20 points for *Eber*, 12 for Pannonica, the Austrian baroness, who offers *Quer*, and 18 points for Emanuel, giving the genitive of *Fenchel*. The foundations are laid. The fifth round goes faster. Perkins gets 27 points for *Ähr*; the Austrian baroness squeezes out 16 with *Top*; Emanuel matches the balance of the two with 43 for *Maya/Fa* (that could be two names for soaps). Perkins exceeds his last score by one, making it 28 with *Quelle*; the Austrian baroness, adding 2, gets 28 with *Jede*; Emanuel falters and loses 23 with *Nischen*, down to 20. The seventh round tightens the net. Confusion, because only 11 for Perkins with *Lüge*, only 13 for the Austrian baroness with *Ion*, 11 also for Emanuel again with *Bö*. Eighth round, a bonus. Perkins 43 with *Hosanna*; 18 for the Austrian baroness with the impossible word *Dussel*; 10 for the embarrassed Emanuel with *Wird*. The ninth round nets Perkins 27 for *Chic*, the Austrian baroness 9 for *Wob*, and Emanuel, parasitically cashing in on the contribution of Pannonica, the Austrian baroness, 33 for *Umwob*. Round 10. The end is near. The bag, emptied with eyes averted, is nearly empty. It's pretty certain what the final scores will be. Perkins gets 5 with *Uran*; the Austrian baroness racks up 67 with *Exile/Böe*. *Böe* is contested, but then is accepted. Emanuel cheats a little with *Huts*, but gets 8. Eleventh round. Two inhalations, the table top sweats wax, the edges of the scrabble board grow frayed. Perkins takes advantage of what scares Emanuel: 16 with *Kitz/Zion*; *Zion* is questioned, but then is accepted. The Austrian baroness asks about *Tao*; *Tao* is accepted, 20 points. Emanuel tries slyly to get away with *Erden/Nö* for 16 points; *Nö* is written down and found unacceptable, but he successfully sulks his way through. Twelfth round. Actually it is all over, as the board is full, the bag empty, and the letters having been placed. Perkins gets 4 for *Im*, the Austrian baroness 16 for *Kitzel*, Emanuel 8 for *Chics*. Since *Wumm* is met with silence, Perkins can finish with another 25 for *Jedem* and block any further moves on the part of the other two. The line-up of the players at the end is the same as at the beginning:

Perkins in first place with 225 points, Pannonica, the Austrian baroness, in the middle with 213, Emanuel last with 211. It is also the winner, Perkins, who adds up the scores; the others are no longer interested in the outcome. Now it is time to fold up the buckling, sweating scrabble board, stuff the tiles into the blue, opaque bag, stash away the tile holders in the pasteboard box, put an elastic band around it, and then tell for three hours how one drew letters to end the game as quickly as possible. Next time we'll allow more words, says the Austrian baroness, and we'll have a lot more fun. She, this Pannonica, is one of those people who start telling an anecdote and invariably forget the details. At the beginning she still saw a man with a dog, then she forgets the dog, then doesn't remember whether it was a man, then doesn't know whether she saw anything, and she asks herself whether she is crazy in even telling an anecdote. Then she wonders whether someone who has trouble with such a simple anecdote must be crazy. Finally she reactivates her own power of observation, brightly puts back the gentleman and the dog, and with renewed vigor starts again: I saw a gentleman with a dog, and it is all the same to me whether they walked or floated. They probably soared to extreme heights, the border of the human sphere, where the possibilities of survival can be evaluated only by some trick. The topmost floor of high-rise building X: sensation of flying, of being able to lift off. If one stood a few yards from the building out in space, at the level of the gable rim, gravity would never pull one downward. Around the high-rises, specifically in their air-space, nothing has any weight. Understandably, the world is being ruled from the two highest ones, the World Trade Center towers, each 400 meters high and housing 50,000 employees. New York is narrow, but it is built on granite. The world is broad, but it is a swamp. There is no question as to who in the end dictates whom. The red-light district at one time earned its name. With the appearance of the AIDS virus, it shrank quickly as the clients suddenly took an interest in other things. They stayed home and did it themselves. For a while the photography business flourished, when they took the ladies home as photographs and did it with them and afterwards used them to wipe things up. But the photographs tended to tear, causing that branch of endeavor to come to a quick end. All its employees rushed into the selling business and began to hawk picture postcards, key pendants, radios and cameras. The virus stuck to the articles for sale, too, but it died after forty-five seconds, and all was clean again. When I won against one of the hagglers in a camera and radio store, he spoke to me in a tone of voice as if he wanted to ram a knife into my body. I left the store in high spirits, although he had refused to sell me the article, after I had won the haggling. Without any purchase but happy, I stepped out into 42nd Street. Later it occurred to me that the man might belong to the Mafia and actually did mean to ram a knife into my body. I shall later come back to the techniques of haggling. Intermission. Now it's already later. A certain amount of time has passed, which I spent doing lowly things, those of everyday living, purely psycho-pathological. The problem in question was a door that slammed shut at the wrong moment; the other one was my reading a newspaper article that dealt, as it were, with an author, who had written a book. Its outside appearance seemed so good to me that I wanted at all costs to prevent my book looking anything like it. He had chosen the Bronx for himself, I intended to focus on the Bronx only fleetingly. So far, all was fine. He had chosen the crime of the Bronx, and that was, of course, my topic, too. The coincidence excited me enormously; perhaps unexpected coincidences are the only things left that still can really excite us. Fate decrees the worst vexations and leaves the lowly mortal alone with his lot. In the eyes of fate, I was dirt, that much was clear, but fate was naturally also rather dirty. When it comes right down to it, it solely inflicted on the worms what it itself had been for a long time, a fact that the worms in turn did not dare know, for then they would have done away with fate. But in doing that, they would have gotten into definition difficulties and gotten deprived of the resigned expression "that's fate, you know," and would have had to take things concerning their lives into their own hands, something one could not expect of them. A contest between the aforementioned author and myself developed — who stole from whom? — which I promptly lost, however, since his book apparently was finished already, while mine was yet to be written, that is to say, was lying in front of me and inviting me to finish it. My relation to my own books was one of danger. If I did not write them, they wrote me. I may say that in my short life I have written only perfect books; but whether the texts I did not write and that therefore wrote me were good authors, I would doubt. Although I am, as the author of texts, quite sure of myself, I am less sure about authorial qualities of texts. They commit a great many grammatical errors. I am not overstepping the bounds of propriety in saying that the texts suppressed and not written by me have, in that they wrote me, made a mess out of me, ruined me, distorted me. They have robbed me of my original gestalt. They have sneaked into my character as viruses; they have made an evil monstrance of one who peacefully, like a shepherd from Devonshire, began to write and then, when there were enough there, started to suppress them. It came to severe, unresolvable controversies regarding our position in point of time between that author and myself. Since his book was already finished, he obviously was, in point of time, ahead of me, who was struggling with it and possibly, in the search for motives, had to come across the article dealing with him. I was already deeply into comparing exactly what he had written and whatI was about to write, and how the similarities and the avoidance points of parallelism were constituted. He had located his crime of the Bronx, which clearly fascinated him, in the police headquarters, where the crime now squatted like a criminal, but with the difference that it was not handcuffed and could move about freely. Thus, his crime plagued also the criminals, whom it soon forsook, however, in order to penetrate the minds of the policemen, the lawyers, and the police chief. It did not choose to go via the anus, that is to say, via a seat, from where it entered the body, but it forced its way into the brain directly by the route of morality which, at least in the case of the police chief, was lodged in the brain. As for myself, I had constructed a similar plan. However, I was not concerned specifically with the crime of the Bronx, but with crime in general; and that, from the author's point of view, complicated matters, because mine was now crime in the abstract and thus just barely manageable, but also universal. Mine was EACH AND EVERY crime, each single, committed crime, to be sure. In this sense I could well claim that I was working on a super-novel about crime, in which the already finished novel of my predecessor-author would, at best, be an episode, perhaps only a footnote.Clearly, it was a clever idea to choose the Bronx as a metaphor for "the whole world," since its condition, laid bare and spread over the whole world's surface with the planetary butter knife, corresponded better than any other to the condition of the whole world. So I had probably better avail myself of the Bronx, too. His thinking had something compelling about it. "Der Scutt" is the name of an architect. The "Der" is a given name or a nobility prefix like "von," "de," "van," "of"; in every respect a more dignified name than the one of that Otto, who wanted to lift the lake up onto piles, so that one could walk through underneath, and who conducted with me in the manner in which Klemperer wielded the baton. Klemperer came first; he had made the recording. Then, thirty years later, we came and imagined Klemperer, how he conducted Bruckner's Fourth and unleashed the London Philharmonic. "Do you know Der Scutt?" I asked Otto right after the trombones had come in. "He built the Gengalowe-Building, not much glass." I am recalling that as I ride down in the elevator from my room. The hall below has already changed. I climb into a taxi in the hotel. It comes into the entrance hall. After it has driven out, the entrance door is lifted back into its hinges. The taxi bumps along. I hang on to the handles above the door. It is a long ride. I see endless straight rows of traffic lights, which from in front toward the back turn green. During the trip I think of something entirely different. Suddenly I stop in front of a skyscraper. The doorman looks at me suspiciously. But he doesn't see me. The rays that make me invisible work. I enter the elevator and ride up to the thirteenth floor. There all doors have the number thirteen, and to each one is a different letter attached. I ring the bell at 13 D. A young pianist opens the door. He gives me a lot of tonic water to drink. He sees me; I have turned off my magic rays. His mother emerges from the kitchen. She is Viennese. Many New York mothers are old Viennese ladies. *Ach Gott*, you are really here, she cries with a sigh of relief. Viennese ladies tend to express their relief with a reference to God. It is the Jewish God, and the lady's name is Kahn. The pianist pours me a new glass of tonic water. The quinine cools me. When he sees that I am conscious, he begins to talk about Waldheim. That I didn't anticipate, when I entered the taxi in the hotel. Ah yes, Waldheim, he will stay. In contrast to Finkel, who lives further south in town and finds the Austrians to be filthy swine, young Kahn is more understanding. He gives Waldheim three months. I ask him whether he means that as a time-limit he grants him, a deadline, so to speak, or that he can objectively last only that long, don't fool yourself. We get around to the matter of the Austrians being Nazis, but agree that the Nazi generation is slowly dying out. I chatter about all the Viennese pianists I know. He say that they play Haydn badly, play Mozart badly and collect immense sums of shillings. I forbid him to utter such blasphemy. He has fetched the last bottle of tonic water from the refrigerator. I empty it while I fiddle with the switch that turns on the rays. *Jo mei Gott*, there stands Mrs. Kahn in the door frame, the lady from next door beside her. Both are wearing high, heavy boots, hiking boots. We are going to a so-called reception, says the elder Kahn to her son. Take good care of him. Are you still thirsty, young man? She remembers that she forgot to put on her glasses. She doesn't see me clearly. When the lady from next door also rubs her eyes, confusion reigns. My invisibility rays begin to work. The young pianist no longer sees me. Nobody in the family sees me any longer. And all of them forget me instantly. That's a nice bonus of the rays. I go to the kitchen and take a swig of mineral water from the refrigerator. Provision for the ride down. Below, the doorman punctures the empty space with a mean, forewarned look. In the street stands a taxi. The driver is a Chicano who curses like all of them. A species doomed to die out. The people in the hotel are tightening the last screw of the entrance door as my vehicle pushes the two wings open and comes to a stop at the reception desk. My key, please, and is there any mail for me? Trembling, the cautious Japanese hands me a crumbled piece of paper which has a number on it. Please call at seven. I hand the piece of paper back. Upstairs, on my bed, I sleep for an hour and a quarter. Then I dial a number at random. That's easy to do in the US. Everybody you call is talkative and a bit lonely. I am polite and ask about the children. That's always a good opener. A woman. We get into a fairly long conversation. After she warms up, she asks me why I am calling. I tell her that I was to call someone at 7 o'clock, and I called someone. I don't know you at all, she giggles. May I introduce myself, I say in my deepest telephone bass voice, I am the Ray Man from over there who would like to come over here. My children are coming home from their evening class. How many, I ask. Two, one is older than the other. Leave them at their evening class, I say in a tone that is now more intimate. Evenings all children like to be in evening class. And what is it we are studying there? Piano, she says. Ah, now she must notice that I am astonished. And what does the lady teacher say? Their teacher, he is very pleased with their progress. Hm, I pause pondering. Schönberg, I then ask. Haydn, Mozart, he brought their atmosphere along from Vienna. Let's meet tomorrow, nice you called, she says. Leave your children with the pianist and let us tune our own piano. Vienna is not everything, and so the conversation seems to come to an end. In the beginning I admired him, because he talked about Vienna; but then I noticed that his was the Vienna of old, and I didn't like the way he played K 488. I let that have its effect on me, stretch out on the bed and hold the receiver a few feet away from me for a minute with a stiff arm, as if I could get rid of her that way. Then I bring it back to my ear and become stern. No idea whether that will help. Well, are they going to come home now, or do you leave them with Haydn, I ask impatiently. I'll take a taxi, she says, where do you live? They are repairing the entrance door just now and, tell me, do you have the AIDS virus? What, she asks. I don't insist; instead: it would be better if the children didn't stay up there too long, it is late. I'll call Kahn, she says. Don't, I say; then: I have an important date. She is blond and tall and has a big heart. Want to come along? Gladly, she says. She has an art critic with her, thus my rejoinder, that makes four of us. At 4 o'clock I sat in my gabardine-covered chair, never dreaming that a few hours later I'd sit around as part of a foursome, she said enthusiastically. Oh, we are not sitting around. Abruptly I put down the receiver and roll sideways across my double-bed, over the edge, until I crash down on the floor. An arm comes to lie under me, now it hurts a lot. With the other one I pull myself up on the chest of drawers and go slowly past the TV to the bathroom. There I stand before the mirror and think to myself of something. I think of something for myself. I arrive at conclusions, the same ones as yesterday. We are more or less the same every day. I am barely finished with my deep thoughts, when the telephone rings. I am at Elaine's, are you coming up? Are you picking me up, I ask. I don't absolutely need you, she says. Then leave me alone. Scooping up a little caviar at the Petrossian on 6th Avenue, but dropping the spoon contemptuously, getting up, taking three steps from the table, throwing down the money, pulling the fur hat over my forehead, heading on to the Irish Mulligan's, where you get served hot beans and dark beer in a two-liter pitcher with a few cans of Budweiser to boot. On the giga TV screen, they show the Olympic games in Calgary, and a friendly lady, whose true identity is not ascertainable, whispers into your fur-covered ear: wherever Katharina Witt walks, stands, or lies, Alberto Tomba is not far. When even the modest Mulligan wants to get paid for the drinks, you jump up, gather up the tails of your sable coat and race back to the Petrossian, where the waiter in Tartar costume is just now clearing the table. "Do you have a Chekov," you ask, "volume 4 of the complete edition in English." "Which?" he asks, while he wipes the Ndoja-silk table-cloth clean with the sleeve of his Tartaric blouse, unabashedly vulgar, as it seems. "Volume 4," you say, hold up your fingers and make a gesture of leafing through with your thumb. What you want but do not dare communicate is this: in volume 4, Chekov suddenly runs out of money in Paris, and he reveals a trick of how to get a new supply. That passage is gone from your brain, the brain of a simple Komsomolskite; looking it up would enable you to take care of your bill at modest Mulligan's establishment. As long as you do not pay there, you only get beer, not hot beans. The founding of the Reality Club in the middle of New York takes place in a run-down house that can look forward to being renovated instead of being torn down.The Reality Club is an organization without a fixed number of members and is waiting for lectures. The members should really do their part, but they do nothing, chatter away behind their cocktail glasses and get fearfully embarrassed when a thin, high-pitched voice asks them to give a public lecture. That is so even when the public consists only of the club, whose male and female members know its make-up by heart without exception. Thus the club finds itself living in a great lecture-drought and combs the city feverishly for possible speaker candidates. The topic is immaterial; the length

176 / *Jürg Laederach*

of the speech should not exceed thirty-five minutes and should not
be much over ten pages. In the attic of the ramshackle house lives
an old painter, a drug-addict, who never pays his rent and has,
therefore, been sentenced by the landlady to rent-free living. From
that moment on, he produced no more paintings that formerly had
comprised a sort of blackish-brownish linear pattern which
stretched across the canvas horizontally or vertically or, in recent
years, diagonally. With the diagonal arrangement, he explained,
he was giving consideration to the optical appearance of the harbor
cranes; one of his painter-excursions during the past few years was
devoted to search out such a crane and to standing reflectingly
under its arm for quite a while. Contrary to his expectation, the
hook did not come down, the crane did not hoist him up.   "Had
they laded me, I would not have objected, they didn't, and so I lade
myself." Like the members of the Reality Club, he is overcome by
abject shyness, when he is asked to say something about his
lading. The "in the neighborhood of ten pages" was suppressed,
since it is secretly assumed that he would read his talk from one
of his blackish sheets and ad-lib something in addition, as the
whims of the moment dictated. "When will you renovate my
abode?" he asks the owner of the house, who just now succeeded
once again in not becoming president in the Reality Club's latest
election. "Why should I renovate?" she asks in turn. — "I am cold.
I am freezing," he says. — "In which of your conditions?" she asks.
The give and take ends in a tie, since he does not dare remind her
that renovations cost money. What she had succeeded in was to
make money a taboo topic, since he paid no rent and did not want
to hear that either. As silence sets in between the two, another
member, male, full-bearded, is reminded of the awkwardness of
the silence that would again and again plague the Reality Club at
its meetings. "May I take the plane real quick?" Fullbeard asks
the never-yet lady president. "Take the smaller one." He accepts
and in no time lands in the Balkan near Fertörákos, not quite the
Balkan yet, although he already thinks Balkan. It's the Hungarian
border, but close to the Balkan. The Balkan, Fullbeard says to
himself, now becomes a possibility to be reckoned with; I must not
lose sight of my goal: to find a speaker for the New York Reality
Club. No one knows whether this is his consciousness that says

exactly that, or whether the search for a speaker is an electric impulse in his head. All signs at his landing indicate that Full-beard seeks a speaker, whom he will tell only after he accepts in principle, *where* he is to speak. The little plane of the never-yet lady president is pushed into a sinking hangar at the edge of Lake Neusiedler, the waves of which lap at the hangar's foundation. Seaweed is clinging to the padlock. From the cabin Fullbeard heard the croaking of the frogs, Hungarian frogs, of course; between each croak a little plum brandy. What is about to happen in Fertörákos becomes a race between the locating of an Hungarian willing to lecture as well as having at hand approximately ten pages of his thoughts and the hangar's and with it the plane's sinking into the lake. That would mean that Fullbeard, who a minute ago was still swirling his cocktail glass in embarrassed silence and secretly seconded the painter with "Well said, I am freezing my ass off in this place," would be stranded in Western Hungary and could be rescued only by helicopter. Who is that sitting next to me anyway? At first only a stray person, who comes and goes and comes again, as it suits him at the moment, says Botho Strauss through his female travel guide.

Once nature gets involved in the destruction process, it produces an amazingly rich variety of results. After exposure to nuclear radiation, nature is the most luxuriant thing in existence. There is a contamination of forests that stimulates growth. In the case of total pollution we should not expect the result to be prairies but jungles. To look at jungles excites us; wild animals have always fascinated us; pollution upsets us greatly, but growth inspires us no end. We can't get our feet down on the ground anymore. Thanks to the enthusiasm over this growth all rooms grow into light-filled, lofty halls for us. No sooner is there growth in nature, and our enthusiasm soars. It is a genuine enthusiasm, an unbridled rapture over the fact that something is growing bigger. True, we could drape ourselves in black, give up all hope, pitch tents in a tunnel because the contamination is spreading, but it is nature, after all, which responds to extreme pollution with extreme growth. And have you noticed that growth conquers pollution, because it is a matter of unconditional growth. This growth of this nature offers no mercy, although filth begs growth for mercy, because it wants to expand. It asks nature to be so kind as to permit being destroyed by it. But nature throws out its chest, enlarges, swells to overflowing, draws a deep breath and fills its muscular thorax. No way, filth, you will be conquered and knocked to the ground. I roll you flat, just so you know you make me great. It is because of you that I, nature, am coming back into my own again. Already jungle strips are crossing the freeway; proliferating palm trees are competing with high voltage masts; the dirt-coated lion roars evenings beside the garden hose in the back of the house. Nature and its Blitzkrieg. Filth experiences its Stalingrad. Emanuel hears the roar. The contamination sends Hess to nature in a plane. He is to conclude a peace in good time; yet the tank columns incessantly form a pillaging phalanx and burn, cauterize, squeeze out dirt. End of the pollution, it steps onto the podium: nature, place number one; we lift its right arm, in order to give us a victory-wave. Grown big, thanks to its deadly opponent. Yesterday still moribund, today bursting with strength. Nature needs a burst-protecting attachment round her belt. *Sieg, Heil, Sieg*. At nine a jungle picnic, please bring empty preserving cans, we want to do some scattering. Berlin is a city that is well aware of its deficits. First there is its space deficit, and this shortage of space is all that is to be reported about Berlin for now. It is a simple report initially, until Emanuel recognizes the almost incomprehensible ramifications in which this shortage keeps affecting the people and their private as well as public systems. This process is made all the easier the more decisively the forgetting, displacing, or the Berlin variety thereof, the ironizing, is practiced. Whether land deficit or freedom of movement deficit, the city has developed forms of compensation. Nowhere in the world is literature put to work on behalf of the survival-oriented collective, the survival-oriented state, as it is in Berlin. From a given subsidies level on, Emanuel can, as a literary man, not shake off the impression that in return something definite is expected from him. These expectations are never put into words; everything points to the conclusion that they do not exist. And yet, Emanuel senses them, but cannot respond to them, since they refuse to become explicit. This view produces a chilling as well as a positive effect. One morning, the Americans had once again hurled a No into the Russians' faces, I said to myself, better inform yourself about China, seek refuge in China; only the Middle Kingdom can still be of help.The TV was on, it showed the final minutes of the human rights conference. The Americans demanded that Jews be permitted to leave the Soviet Union; the Russians demanded that a black Jew become President of the United States. To anyone watching it was clear right away which was the free country and which imprisoned all its citizens for life. Compared to both systems, the Chinese had an advantage: they were far away. Emanuel talked less about them, they had an evident sense of humor, and Emanuel did not understand them too well. Hence the only logical thing to do was to study Chinese history. "Jews don't have a chance in your country; in ours they can become lawyers, doctors," the American negotiator shouted at the Russian. Both wore rimless glasses, the colors of each one's tie were those of their national flags. "The soup you serve the Blacks in your soup kitchens for the poor doesn't contain enough proteins; they are condemned to die a creeping death," shouted the Russian negotiator back. A Swiss headwaiter stepped between the two super powers to whisper: "Should the gentlemen want to become neutral, it would pay off, would bring in dividends; whoever is a super power, will be even stronger, if he becomes neutral." — "And what would Switzerland do, if the USSR became neutral?" asked Wroslow Maleschinski, the second embassy attaché. Switzerland, asserted the headwaiter, would then play the part of both super powers who had drifted off into the neutral zone "and play it better than they." It is only the speed of light's insurmountable wall that denies man a cosmically viable existence, Hans Blumenberg annotates the Copernican optics. The one who has forgotten his self is not the one who has turned inward by a long shot. Getting rid of one's self is not enough to find oneself. The one who has turned inward has taken the first step toward finding himself, he has something resembling a chance, but of course only a modest one. The self-forgetter, however, heads straight for his own worst detriments, since he has now simply forsaken his interest in everything and therefore cannot come into possession of anything again. Common to both is the motivation to want to get ahead, in that they choose a way to which nothing is attached that smacks of transportation. But the one submerges into himself and loses everything and perishes, and the other has made a first weak important-unimportant choice, that opens a tiny view to the outside. As a rule, he also perishes, but he then looks different from the other one who can indeed smugly call himself the self-forgetter but fails.

(Translated by John Frey)

HUGO LOETSCHER

Hugo Loetscher

Born December 22, 1929 in Zürich. Studied political science, economics, sociology and literature. Journalist and editor of newspapers and magazines. Lived in South America and the US. 1981 Writer-in-Residence, Max Kade Institute, USC. 1981/82 guest professor, University of Fribourg and City University of New York, 1988 University of Munich. Received several literary awards. Lives in Zurich. Short stories, novels, essays, plays: *Abwässer*, 1963; *Die Kranzflechterin*, 1964; *Noah*, 1967; *Der Immune*, 1975; *Wunderwelt: Eine brasilianische Begegnung*, 1979; *Herbst in der Großen Orange*, 1982; *Der Waschküchenschlüssel*, 1983; *Die Papiere des Immunen*, 1986; *Vom Erzählen erzählen*, 1988; *Die Fliege und die Suppe*, 1989; *Der predigende Hahn*, 1992.

From Coast to Coast

*A merica, the USA reflected in the work of a contemporary Swiss
writer, this collage could be called as well "from Coast to
Coast." I would like to present you texts about New York and Los
Angeles, about the "Big Apple" and the "Big Orange." Let's start
with New York: The visit with Liberty.*

I was on her island, too. You pay only one way. Everyone comes
back. There's no place to stay on Liberty Island. Except for the
guards. But their jobs attach them to Liberty.

Entire school classes are slouching around and shouting on the
gangway. This morning they are not having geography or math, or
biology or dictation. Like me, they're visiting Liberty. Only, the
teachers already told them the story of Liberty before the trip. And
the pupils are equipping themselves with french fries and chewing
gum.

The statue of Liberty acts as if none of this affects her at all.
Nobody would suppose that she was once reddish-brown in color,
the way copper normally is. She rises greenish-gray against the
backdrop of the blue sky. In the course of the years she's turned
this vert-de-gris color. The patina, which is itself the result of
decay, protects from further erosion.

She stands there ramrod straight. Nobody has ever caught her
squatting down. Maybe they left no leeway with the pedestal so
that the only thing you can do on it is stand. A figure whose feet
do not give away whether she's walking or remaining stationary.

At any rate, she's holding the torch high. You can't make out
whether she's showing others the way or is looking for it herself
and is standing there only because she hasn't found it yet.

You land at her back. You've hardly left the ferry when you hear, not only in English, but in French, Spanish and German, when the next boat will be going back. Not only school classes or individuals like me visit Liberty. Families and travel groups are always underway to see her. Very many Blacks and, of the Orientals, one or two Japanese who are changing film for the second time.

Liberty is hollow. Once you're inside, you see how thin the dress is. Maybe it would be better to say "robe" because of the many folds. They are held together with clips, so the wind cannot blow them away.

But even though Liberty is hollow, she's not empty. She may not have any intestines or other organs that you might expect in the body cavity. There is a tall structure including braces to ensure safety. But bars and screws can rust. That's why Liberty once almost lost the prongs from her crown.

Her backbone stands in the middle, and circular staircases wind their way around the pillars. Before you ascend, you read that the temperature in Liberty varies. It is colder down below than it is in the middle, the temperature is at its warmest in the head and crown.

You are also warned that you are ascending at your own risk. There are one hundred sixty-eight steps to climb. So climbing in Liberty is not for those with heart problems or whose nerves or legs give them trouble.

But there are small landings at regularly spaced intervals, just large enough for one person to step aside and catch his breath. But who wants to step to the side and watch someone who got a later start pass and reach Freedom first?

The distance between steps is unusually high, so you concentrate on your own steps, one hand on the inside pillar, the other on the handrail. You have to be careful not to come too close to the person in front of you, otherwise his or her heel will be in your face. You yourself are careful not to swing your feet out too far so as not to kick the person behind you in the face as he or she is climbing, a few steps below, into Liberty.

Once you're on top, the circular stairs widen to become a viewing platform. You are now in the crown of Liberty. From here you can look out through the windows. Toward Manhattan, Long Island,

Brooklyn and toward the harbors. The panes are murky and dirty, but even though they do not afford a clear view, even skyscrapers and steamers look small from up here. The view from Liberty shows the world behind a veil.

The glass in the windows is shatterproof. Otherwise someone could break one of the panes and crawl out. There are also bars in front of the windows so someone arriving at the top of Liberty doesn't take the liberty of leaping into the depths.

But you can't enjoy the view into the distance for too long, because others are pushing forward from behind. You can hear their impatient voices coming from below, asking what there is to see up there in Liberty. So you leave the barricaded view and make room, descending, one after the other, urging the person ahead of you and being pushed by the person behind you. You are careful not to put your foot in the neck of the person climbing down before you and yield to the one in your back so he doesn't kick you.

To start with New York is not an unusual beginning for a Swiss coming from Europe and crossing the Atlantic. New York determines — for most of us — the first ideas, the right and the wrong ones. To such a degree that we are inclined to take The City for the rest of the country, for the rest of two hundred million.

I'm not the only one who had to learn that Manhattan lies on the Hudson and not on the Mississippi, that the hills at 130th Street are different from the Rocky Mountains, that besides the Atlantic coast there is a Midwest, besides The New York Review of Books *a Bible belt.*

Crossing the American continent I ought to make a stop in Chicago if my collage were not only to regard my purely literary work but my job as a journalist, too. In 1972, I wrote a text for a special edition of du, *a cultural monthly, where I used to be junior editor — a special issue on Chicago with photos taken by Magnum photograper Rene Burri.*

In the introduction of that issue you'll read sentences like the following:

Chicago is an American city.

Have you ever been to New York? Then you have not been to America. Go to Chicago, then you'll be in the center of things.

The fact that Chicago considers itself so American is the reason for its pride and its credo, its arrogance and embarrassment.

Chicago was propagandized as an American city: happiness can be created, and now those who came here, even the Blacks, believe that.

Ghettos and slums and modern architecture were invented - a range to take your breath away.

But, as an American city, Chicago is breathing despite and because of all resistance and when it has to breathe against itself, it does not want to suffocate, not even on itself. And it breathes with everything it has at its disposal:

With smoke-stacks and skyscrapers, with its railways and expressways, its parks and dumps, on a lake and in entire city blocks being wrecked, in its stadiums and in its museums, with advertising and balance-sheets, with its crime rate and its projects.

Despite the various breath fresheners, you can still sense the wild onions that flourished here on the muddy ground and, known as Cheacagou, helped give the city its name.

Nowadays, without disputing the status of Chicago as an American city, I would feel obliged to make amendments to my former judgement. But these amendments would not change the fact that Chicago became important for me to correct my first impression; later on I had to correct my second impressions.

But what does "the first impression" mean? In my personal map of America the first name I had to notice was Cincinnati. My mother was German, and in the German branch of our family, I was told, that an uncle had done something wrong, that's why he had no other choice than to go to America, to Cincinnati, where a large German community was. As a child, when I did something wrong like breaking a glass or lying, I asked myself whether this would be the very moment to run away and go to Cincinnati. I did not go to Cincinnati, I went to Los Angeles.

I came to Los Angeles thanks to an invitation by the University of Southern California (USC), where I was a writer-in-residence — an opportunity I did not want to miss. After the lectures at the University of Chicago in 1972, it was my first contact with an American university again. To what degree I was a freshman you will realize when I confess that on my tour across the campus I stood in front of the Hall of Fame with devotion, convinced that this is the monument dedicated to all big and small Einsteins. This was not the case. Later on I realized that my academic stay was not complete unless I went to the football game between USC and UCLA. Not knowing the rules, it was hard for me to behave correctly, in solidarity. Sitting among nothing but UCLA fans, my enemies, I shouted when the people around me were silent and I didn't move when the UCLA fans stirred up their team.

A year later I had the honour to become the first holder of the Swiss Chair at CUNY (City University of New York). This time I wanted to prove to myself that I was an academic teacher fully aware of his duties. I asked for the football team, they looked at me with astonishment. Indeed, my appearance was not athletically convincing.

Let's go back to L.A.

As a writer-in-residence I was not obliged to write. I had to reside and talk about writing, about my own writing and about the writing of others because there are always others who write, too.

But I am a word addict — an expression you can translate from the Latin "nulla dies sine linea" — not a day without line. I could not part with it.

First the journalist was activated — I wrote articles about the Spanish-Mexican heritage in California and about the Chicanos, articles that continued and followed up stories written earlier on Puerto Rico and the Puertoricans in New York — hispanic matters that could not leave anyone indifferent who had been interested in Latin-American issues since the mid-sixties and who — in the Spanish manner — likes to put America into the plural "las Americas."

But then I happened to make a discovery — not a sensational one. I only discovered the two lawns around the house where I lived

— a natural and an artificial one. A banal discovery, but a moment of inspiration. I felt the Muses. I had been kissed by grass.

That explains the opening of my book about Los Angeles that reads as follows:

Los Angeles, the "Big Orange" — a lot of slices around nothing. He had spent his fall in slices like those. How green this fall had been.

He had two greens. One that you sowed, and one that you bought by the yard from a roll. A lawn that grew by itself with so much chlorophyll, as if it had been produced in a laboratory. And a second lawn that you attached, so irregularly structured, as if the arbitrariness of nature had been at work instead of a machine. If both were lying next to one another outside, it was not clear for which he would need the mower and for which the stain remover.

It was an autumn among newcomers.

None of these trees that had put down roots was embarrassed to have left continents and countries behind. They did not put on an act about eternal nature as if they had always had their roots here.

Some of the trees were proud to have been through nurseries and that they weren't illiterate weeds, even though the dwarf cypresses behaved like poodles, trimmed as if the gardener had used a scurler.

Not only the wind had sown the seeds throughout the Big Orange, the postal system had also done so. The trees, bushes and flowers had not multiplied because of an arbitrary bee or because of some intermediary carrier. Seeds had come first by covered wagon and others came later by airplane. Most of them had been rushed through the immigration bureau, even though innumerable illegal seedlings flourished. So the plants had not only a Latin name but also a work permit. Not even the weeds are indigenous here.

Trees that had been imported and bushes that had been replanted, ones that had put down roots, emigrants and immigrants: they made it possible for this fall to be greener than any before. But this green fall was not fall only because of season.

This fall H. also had more than one sky. First the one in California and then the one from Paramount.

One hung over the Big Orange and its slices, it spread out over the deserts and the ocean. It preferred to be found in the swimming pools painted blue, it sparkled in the chrome of cars and was reflected in the glass walls of the skyscrapers.

The other one leaned on a facade, behind that a strip of the entire length of the recording studio, a chain of hills set back and above that, the first sky.

This upper sky could darken and turn overcast. The clouds remained white throughout the giant screen and did not have bad breath. If the material was slack, they stretched it out again.

H. had two sorts of blue, one changeable and one repairable.

But H. was nowhere nearer the two skies of the Big Orange than in the thirty-fifth floor of the Bonaventure Hotel in the Top Five Bar that rotated once every hour. The two heavens merged on the horizon and yet remained separate. When Lyra hung above, other constellations of musical instruments could be made out, below a guitar with amplifier or a synthesizer. And not only the upper sky told the story of Perseus and Andromeda.

When you have so many skies, and skies with such tales, H. wondered if you shouldn't be with someone to show the sky with all its tales to.

Look, the signs above are stationary. The flashing lights that are making their way through belong to an airplane on a night flight. The stars glow with the same white, however varying their colors of origin might be.

And below them, look, another sky. The red taillights massage each other, up to four and five lanes, one next to the other and in dense convoys. In the opposite direction the white headlights, also crowded, one behind the other. And the yellow turn signals. The blue lights of a police car in between the lights. And there, orange letters and the green company logo. Neon colors that turn on and fade away. Even the facades of the neighboring skyscrapers change continuously from floor to floor, and from moment to moment depending on the cleaning crew, overtime and security checks. The streets and freeways with their lighting draw definite lines and curves across the horizon; even the flat light of residential areas seems to be laid down once and for all. But between all the fixed points are mobile lights, innumerable cars making everything flow and keeping everything in motion.

H. had wondered what sort of horoscope could be read from this lower sky; after all his Sagittarius and Capricorn rose across the autumn sky above. But before he could begin to ask what this fall might bring and whether something might follow it, the constellation had already shifted.

I was fascinated by a world where nature and artificiality could hardly be separated. Daily life looked like a stage set, and the stage set behaved like daily life. The decision was made: This world should become a subject of mine. But a decision is not yet a book.

During my stay as a writer-in-residence, I started with outlining and sketching, back in Switzerland I had finally gotten my general idea, but I had to come back — "coming back home," as my landlady said, that I took for a good omen. I finished my book not only by writing it, but also by looking for specific places and by visiting places at random. A direct result of this literary mobility is reflected in one chapter of my book called "Between Sand and Sand," between the sand of the desert and the sand of the ocean — passages from this chapter follow:

This green fall lay between ocean and desert, between aquariums and ghost towns, between cacti and that seaweed that was collected for its algae, used in ice cream and cosmetics.

This was not the first time H. felt the desire to advance so far into the desert that the parked car was no longer visible and no street could be sighted, that only sand dunes presented themselves to the eye, massifs and ranges of hills, endless valleys and an invisible horizon so that each direction was one possibility among many and all were equal in importance and indifference.

And then to say "yesterday" and mean "four or five hundred years ago." Long ago when there were still fresh water lakes here and the inhabitants carved out depressions in the stones in which they crushed the beans of Mesquita trees to mash; when women used the thorn of the agave as an awl and the hunters carved into the cliffs the outlines of animals they tracked down and killed.

To think of a time twenty or thirty years ago and not mean the time when you were young yourself, but something that went back much further to a fall that lasted five hundred million years, from the Cambrian to the Tertiary, time enough for the invertebrates and the first fish to develop, amphibians and reptiles, mammals and birds. To count on the drop by drop patience of water and include in the counting the forbearance of the wind, to calculate such that a thousand years plus or minus made no difference, a margin of error in which your own life and your own era could fit many times over.

For this desert, which appeared to lie before the beginning of everything, was itself an end result with its sunken valleys and grooves, the extinguished volcanoes and the mountains of ash turned cold; even this desert knew its "once upon a time" and this was full of erosions and faults.

The intention of telling a situation created problems because I didn't want to write a historical or sociological work — the goal was fiction — even I would have been embarrassed if I had to define clearly what literary genre I kept in mind. It was neither a novel nor a short story. But anyway these worries concern the academic reader more than the author — at least it was a press text.

My personal concerns were different. Nevertheless, a situation is limited, as a world it stands for itself, a world that seems to become endless and boundless when you start to deal with it. How to get a good grip on it? True, reality fixed in words is always a reduction compared to the reality we aim at. But how to reduce it without giving up the essential parts? A possibility was to choose a hero. In my case a protagonist called H. — H period. Don't remind me what Tom Wolfe said recently about heroes who have only a letter as ID and not a full name.

This protagonist is a visitor coming to LA for a conference and staying here longer than planned — thus the discovery of the scene or the situation was a logical and self-evident topic, because the stage set was not a frame but the subject itself. It is due to this protagonist that the subject gained a personal face.

When H. arrived in the Big Orange, he was still a walker. And so he had struck up a friendship with the other pedestrian.

At first he had assumed he was a dinosaur. But he was younger by one stratum. On the calling card that the museum had handed him there was no telephone number listed but rather the era.

H. had already noticed the black pool the first time he'd ridden past it. As the bus drove back, H. saw behind the trees and bushes that the elephants were still stuck in the same spot in that sticky goo.

H. got off the bus, walked back and climbed up the lookout. From there he watched the demise: the tarry ooze reached almost to the stomachs of the female and the baby, and even the larger elephant in the back was struggling to free itself from the mire. The animals reached with their trunks for some sort of hold in the air; but the air smelled of the asphalt against which they were struggling with their feet.

On a boulevard between skyscrapers, billboards and picnic tables, elephants were drowning forever, frozen in the moment before their final ruin.

The glossothenium's place was in the museum not far from the cashier's desk. Whereas the other mammoth animals supported themselves on all fours and the birds spread their wings with the help of wires, the glossothenium had stood up on its hind legs.

H., the last pedestrian of the Big Orange, said hello to the first. They introduced themselves. H. was from Switzerland and Glossothenium Harlani from the Mesozoic; it suggested: "You don't need to call me Giant Sloth, just call me Sloth."

His friend the sloth explained that he had walked on the edges of his back feet and on the ankles of his front feet, he let himself roll along rather than actually take steps. Those were the days, when walking upright had meant courage and avantgarde. His species had not been content with what was to be found on the ground; they had gotten up on their hindlegs in order to reach the youngest branches of the trees. That had not been easy considering

their sickle-shaped claws. They had also had to support themselves with their tails. Understandable at one thousand five hundred pounds' weight. But he had never been overweight.

His skeleton was bronze in color, like those of the other animals
standing on pedestals or in exhibit cases. The bones were not the
sickly yellow you see elsewhere but had a tan color as if even the
skeletons lay out on the beach every day in the Big Orange.

When H. congratulated his friend the sloth on his good looks,
the sloth remarked that lying in tar made you tanner than any
cosmetic tanning lotion. Then he hesitated briefly: you shouldn't
tell a story in America without having taken out a patent on it.
But, he continued, the thing with the tar pits had actually been
quite different from the way it was presented in the film in the
exhibit hall next door. Oh well, but the museum was designed for
family outings, the ruin had to be suitable for youngsters.

Of course he had died in the tar, otherwise he wouldn't be
standing there. Slowly he'd sunk, each attempt to free himself had
brought him that much farther down. The ooze had clung to his
legs. Of course, the vultures had argued on the edge of the pool as
he'd tried to save his head by stretching his neck. Before he had
perished, one of the birds had stabbed him in the eye with its beak.
The bird that had torn out his flesh piece by piece had flapped its
wings around him, which in turn came in contact with the tar that
then covered the feathers. As the animal had clambered around
on him, it had slipped off into the tar. As the vulture tried to take
off, it hadn't been able to get up into the air. The tar had attached
them to one another. For several thousand years he had lain bone
to bone with the one who had gorged himself on his death.

All of that was correct. It was also true that many animals had
simply wandered into the tar pits. Especially the gazelles, who
were so playful in their surroundings. Not all the tar pools had
shown themselves out in the open. Sometimes there had been a
layer of humus on top of the oily swamp, a green trap, a ground
that collapsed under the slightest weight; then the black liquid
that relinquished no one had gushed forth. Bucks and prehistoric
horses had been caught in the midst of their trotting and racing;
they had kept running — no longer forward but downward.

That's how everything had been according to the bone analysts. But he, on the other hand, he had been one of those who had known about the danger of these pools; but they had gone there nevertheless. Sure, they had hesitated on the bank and checked to see whether the ground was soft or not. But then he had dared to take a first step and a second, until only the last one remained. There had been an odor there, an odor of asphalt and tar, he hadn't been able to resist it, it had drawn him from the edge into the center, you just had to breathe it in, it had filled his lungs and given pleasure to his head, it had become easy, this odor had made the act of dying attractive, even though it was a slow death.

The day that H. decided to rent a room by the month, he flipped through the yellow pages. He called a driving school. The next morning the driving instructor rang the bell; he was from Lebanon. He gave H. four forms to study on the way. They were driving to take the written test. There were five forms all together, but the questions were the same or similar. For the multiple choice questions he should mark the ones that contained the word "legal." He probably had some background information as a pedestrian; he would have to memorize the speed at which one was permitted to drive past hospitals and schools, and of course it made sense that having an open bottle of alcohol in the car was not allowed.

With his Levantine driving instructor, H. got to know residential areas of the Big Orange which he would otherwise never have discovered. There was room to maneuver in the villa neighborhoods. H. parked in front of Greek pillars ("Lean back, judge the distance from the curb more accurately"); he drove up to a Norman castle ("What do you think the rear view mirror is for?"). He stopped at a Moorish tower ("Easy does it, you don't want your wife to go flying through the windshield"). He turned right toward a log house ("Not so sharp, not so sharp"), he turned left toward a Japanese garden ("If someone had been coming just now"). H. yielded at the entrance to an Indian adobe garage ("The trash collection is more powerful, but you have the right of way"). As H. made a turn in a cul-de-sac, someone watched him from a veranda. H. parked once more ("And the parking brake?"). He backed up

("Pick something to focus on — like the ceramic dog"). But as he started to put it in reverse again, he suddenly felt his abdomen cramping; his foot slipped from the gas pedal to the brake ("You'll brake yourself to death one of these days").

The man who administered the exam was black with short hair. Upon greeting H., he told him that he would be singing in the Church of the Seven Truths that Saturday. As H. took the first curve, the expert said "Thank you" and as H. later changed lanes when asked to do so, he said "Thank God." The more H. shifted and signaled, the louder the praise of the man on his right, and the more he looked in the rear view mirror, the greater the jubilation: a pedestrian's soul found its way home. They did not return to the Department of Motor Vehicles, but to a piece of heaven. When H. removed the key from the ignition, the black cherub next to him proclaimed: "Welcome, welcome to the Big Orange."

Since H. was planning on an extended stay, he had some money from his savings wired to him. The woman in the bank leafed through his passport and hesitated at the stamps and visa. She returned the passport and looked behind her; the man at the main desk was on the telephone and the teller next to him was entering data into the computer. The teller asked him what sort of document it was. H. took the passport out of its case and pointed to the white cross: "A Swiss passport." Didn't he carry an I.D.? Then she discovered his driver's license in the passport case. She took it out, scrutinized the photograph and checked H.'s face; then she took down the number. Because it was a large sum of money, she would need a second I.D. H. presented his passport once more, this time open. The woman removed his credit card from the case and wrote down the number and expiration date on the receipt.

H. gained a new identity by means of a driver's license and a credit card, and he got a message from his friend in the museum.

"The streets," said the sloth, "they're all paved. What if the animals and plants that the tar is made of were to move again? If the streets themselves were set in motion, what would be their destination? Tell me, aren't the explosions in the motor really the cries of the tar animals?"

"How's that small tar pit in your chest doing?" asked the sloth without waiting for an answer: "It wasn't much different then from what it is now. Only that we searched for months for our pools of tar. And now I'm standing in a museum where smoking is forbidden. Sometimes, when the entrance door is open, the odor comes in from outside, then it's like it used to be. You with your exhaust pipes and smoke-stacks, you have it easier. You have matches and lighters in your pockets. Everywhere and at anytime you can produce your own tar. Even in bed. And when you are buried, you'll bring your own tar with you. Will they use your tarred-up lung someday to pave one of those streets that you so loved to travel?"

The protagonist brought a plot with him: A man coming to LA, staying longer than planned, discovering a city and learning that he was ill, maybe even fatally ill.

As helpful as this plot always was — it offered a story or a skeleton of a story —, it could never make up the sense of the book. The protagonist served as a guide to talk about the real subject: The Big Orange.

With the assistance of our hero, even a chronology was gained: The book begins with his arrival and ends with his leaving. Yet looking at the titles of the chapters, we clearly see that another order of events is intended: "The Green of the Newcomers" and "The Mobile Skies" are followed by the chapters "Between Sand and Sand" and "The Message from the Tar Pit," "The Staged Nights" precedes the last one "On the Edge and at The End."

In this case composition is more inspired by music. I dare say that we read a prose sonate: Each chapter takes up the general theme, changing and developing the subject. Each chapter can be read for itself, like a movement can be played for itself. It's evident that a movement is never the whole.

The decision to choose a hero as guide was just one way to limit the situation. The other possibility of reduction or concentration is illustrated by the title "Herbst in der Großen Orange" (Fall in the

Big Orange). For the English version I preferred the word "fall" to "autumn" because of the ambiguity of the word "fall" — meaning a season and a downfall.

Although the fall was drawing to a close, H. felt as though he hadn't even arrived in the Big Orange. Like the Big Orange, his fall began nowhere and everywhere, ended nowhere and was still unmistakeably over.

On his trip he might come across a city limit sign. But the same street with the same houses kept going beyond the sign. H. returned to the city not by turning around, but by driving straight ahead.

Whenever the last skyscrapers disappeared from view into the hills and no more houses were visible on poles or supporting walls, he could have supposed each time that he had left the city behind him. But on the other side of the pass it was there again, it stretched itself out and divided itself behind other hills.

Downtown, the administrative and court buildings formed a center of their own. But this one had nothing to do with that of the banks, insurance companies and other firms located a few streets to the west, and this one in turn had nothing to do with Broadway a few blocks to the south, were the Mexicans shopped.

Behind each center of town there lay another, and near each noman's land lay an everyman's land. The agglomeration was overgrown and lost, on another spot it shot out of the ground and grew into the horizon with satellites and enclaves and into the valleys and canyons. Every suburb was the suburb of another suburb.

H. had approached the Big Orange from all sides. Not only from the east, when he had landed in the jet. Also from the mountains and hills, from the desert and from the ocean, from the southwest and the south, and as he came from the north, it had almost been like coming home.

But no matter from which direction he approached the Big Orange, he could never say with complete certainty whether he had already arrived or was driving through the city. He was always halfway to the place to which he'd started out and never actually at his destination, never in the middle, but also never on the outskirts.

To resume: We have a situation guided by a protagonist and marked by the keyword "fall." But it is not a fall in the usual sense of the word, it is a threefold fall. First, fall as season, the consequence of which is the chapter "Kalendertage" or short "Calender" — from Labour Day to Christmas with all the days of remembrance in between, like Veterans' Day as well as Columbus Day, not to forget Halloween and obviously all parties and invitations, all sales and special offers. Fall turned out to be a fruitful season.

But the seasonal fall is also a personal fall.

It is a personal fall in so far as the protagonist celebrates his fiftieth birthday in a rather special place, the hotel Madonna Inn:

The woman shrugged her shoulders as H. laid down his passport on the counter. She raised her glasses which hung on an amber chain around her neck: "No vacancies." She leafed absently through his passport: "Swiss? That cross there, that's Switzerland, isn't it?" H. nodded. She opened the photo album that showed the rooms available: all the Swiss rooms had been reserved for a long time. That would have been the William Tell room. Here was the man with the crossbow on the window. There were apple motifs even on the bedstead. And this here was the Matterhorn room: the mountain painted on the window.

He didn't care if cow bells were painted on the window panes or if there was a lead statue of a Geisha in the Far East room, if he slept in the Victorian gardens or spent the night in the "barrel," where the stools and the trash basket looked like casks. As far as he was concerned, poppies could be flourishing on the wallpaper, spring flowers on the bedstead and violets in the sinks. What did it matter if the light came not from a birdcage but from an embossed bouquet of roses? And why not chiefs and quivers of arrows like in the Indian room that was recommended for pyjama parties? There were four walls there just as in the Safari room with the leopard and zebra skin rugs and the totem poles for bedposts, carved from a wood like ebony. If not Old Africa, then

Old England, and if not Old England, then Old Mexico or the Austrian suite. The dorm room in "Harvard Square" was just as much a part of it as the mill with the water wheel constructed behind the bed. And why shouldn't the bed be a canopy bed and the canopy not of that Delpht blue that the Dutch love, and why shouldn't the "Romance" room be pink? You could just varnish the furniture or leave it natural like the logs that served as supports for the sofa in the country cabin. What was the difference between a love nest with a circular staircase and one without.

I chose this passage from the chapter "The Staged Nights" because it can be used as a bridge, leading to the third kind of fall. But what kind of fall is this? Certainly it has to do with the geographical, historical and cultural conditions of the situation I wanted to tell. Here in California, more specifically in Southern California and in the Big Orange, the West ended. The West that started once as a Mediterranean world, that became an Atlantic world, that crossed the Atlantic, begun as an Atlantic world again, but crossed a continent coming to an end at the Pacific coast.

There was no more "go west young man." There was no longer the big beyond with new unexplored land. Having arrived here, your dream had to be realized, and if it did not happen you had to fabricate your dream. The neighbourhood of Hollywood is not a purely geographical accident.

Remembering this, it is a fall of memento, of souvenir and reminders. A revival of all epochs with all styles and all modes, a total simultaneity. H. could go once more to Venice or to Naples, he crossed the Rubicon in two directions. The Big Orange as a stage set of all possibilities reflects a state of consciousness: Where everything plays a role nothing plays a role. As a repetition, this fall is a fare-well, at the same time a hello and a good-bye and a new hello.

In the back of the Big Orange lies the New World, the well known America, and in full view the ocean, and beyond this ocean a new world with old cultures. It is this ocean that H. paid his last visit to.

If H. had continued going westward H. would have come across the date-line where you lose a day. But H. had a ticket in his pocket for the opposite direction. Thinking about the date-line, he had a line in mind, beyond which it is senseless to count the dates.

This way our collage comes to an end, too. By crossing the continent we discovered America; the United States as a Pacific nation that sounds banal to you, for us, it is all but self-evident. The situation I wanted to describe is a specific American situation, but as the Atlantic world is involved, it is also a European subject.

(Translated by Renée Schell)

HERBERT MEIER

Herbert Meier

Born August 29, 1928 in Solothurn. Studied history and German literature. For several years *Dramaturg* at the "Schauspielhaus" in Zurich. 1986 Writer-in-Residence, Max Kade Institute, USC. Translator. Received several literary awards. Lives in Zurich. Short stories, novels, poems, plays: *Ejiawanoko*, 1953; *Die Barke von Gawdos*, 1954; *Dem unbekannten Gott*, 1956; *Siebengestirn*, 1957; *Ende September*, 1959; *Jonas und der Nerz*, 1962; *Der neue Mensch steht weder rechts noch links, er geht* (manifesto), 1968; *Stiefelchen*, 1970; *Anatomische Geschichten*, 1973; *Stauffer-Bern*, 1975; *Rabenspiele*, 1976; *Dunant*, 1976, *Bräker*, 1978; *Die Göttlichen*, 1984; *Der Fähnrich von S...*, 1991; *Mythenspiel*, 1991.

Terrence

Terrence, a playwright who occupied three rooms in an old palazzo on Windward Avenue in Venice, Los Angeles, abandoned his home when it seemed about to collapse. Earth tremors had badly shaken the old structure, and a network of cracks had appeared on walls and ceilings, but he persisted, even when gale strength winds sprang up during the night, blowing off the decking of the old pier from which local Mexicans and their children used to fish on Sunday. Even when the electrical power began to fail, Terrence persisted in his work on the last scenes of his latest play. He disconnected all electrical appliances, including his typewriter and the lamps, and, battling fear as he had never experienced before in his life, continued his work with pencil and paper. He rose at daybreak and worked all day until dusk. Then he took a walk along the beach, past the roped off fishing pier, to grab a bite to eat at the seafood joint and watch the skateboardists go by. Then he went to sleep, to be fresh for a new day's work starting at dawn. That was Terrence's life during his last days in Venice, and when he left, fear of earthquakes and storms was only one of his reasons.

He settled in a loft on Franklin Avenue in Hollywood, near a Methodist church that was distinguished by a plausible late-Gothic design which made it a landmark, where he continued to pursue his plan. The important thing for Terrence was the attached auditorium, vacant and complete with a workable stage he could rent for a few dollars. In this room, Terrence started his work on his pioneering play, with the help of three unemployed actors who donated their time. Only a few of his many friends knew about the project. The plot was advanced by walking, standing and sitting. Lying down was reserved for the closing scenes, in which the plot called for a fall. But it was still to be decided whether there should be an end at all. Here is what had come to pass to motivate Terrence and his collaborators: A shortage of wood had developed, caused by air pollution and clear cutting; a shortage of wood for the production of newsprint and paper for books. As the production of newspapers and books dwindled, so writing dwindled. And as writing dwindled, so did reading. Understandably, because the venerable practice of resurrecting endangered words by recycling them in new newspaper articles and new books ceased. The phenomenon was carefully documented by philologists. There was no doubt, the active vocabulary diminished quantitatively and qualitatively from year to year. However, the linguistic phenomenon, in itself bad enough, had devastating, practical consequences. Because people were no longer able to read as before, they were no longer as able to follow written instructions. Airplanes crashed in ever increasing numbers and ships sank, because the crews, unable to read the detailed technical operating specifications at a sufficient level, were unable to operate the vehicles safely. Where airtight closure was called for, they just clammed the door or gate any old way. In many cases, the pressure specifications in airplane cabins and ship hulls were disregarded, with devastating consequences: For want of paper for printing and the consequent deterioration of the reading levels of the population, airplanes crashed and ships sank. People communicated only by talking and could not make themselves understood beyond the auditory media. Medical and linguistic experts added to the list of dire consequences. The ability of the people to express ideas at any level was diminishing at an alarming rate. According to one entirely plausible theory, promulgated by competent authority, a virus feeding on language had entered the environment. The many faceted problem and its possible solutions were competently examined in many duly convoked congresses, but no credible proposals for its solution had yet emerged.

This ominous development necessarily affected the theater, especially the speaking stage. In operatic productions the damage was minimized by "vowelization," that is to say, the presentations were purged of consonants. Film and television relied entirely on speaking pictures. Announcements and discussions were limited to the absolutely essential. There was talk about the only solution to the crisis: return to silent movies and, inconceivable to most, television without an audio track. Radio stations had already eliminated verbal presentations and limited their programming to the long popular music, rolling out day after day a kaleidoscope of tonal creations. Excepting pantomime and dance, the avoidance of the use of the spoken word was not a viable option for the speaking theater. The catastrophe manifested itself here in its full pernicious force. Actors of the speaking theater began to exhibit vexing symptoms that defied explanation. Some of them became unable to follow assigned scripts. It happened increasingly that dialogue learned by heart failed already in rehearsal in a way that was aptly characterized as a tonal shattering, a breaking up into tonal fragments, a disintegration of the fabric of the tonal medium. This failure could not be remedied even by the most adept prompting. Early attempts to explain the phenomenon upon various theories of fatigue were soon discarded, since the syndrome manifested itself even in young persons who were properly rested. For a short time, the problem could be managed by simply striking from the script all parts that did not want to roll off the tongue. Recasting became necessary in some instances. Notwithstanding such expedients, it soon became impossible to present acceptable evening programs. The problem cut to the quick, as the saying goes. It affected the essence of theatrical performance. It was not a matter of personal failing, known in the métier as "hanging up" and traditionally handled by compensating collegiate live improvisation. Increasingly, there was simply no one to save the afflicted actor and no hope at all of maintaining dialogue. The conclusion was inescapable and inexorable that the malady would eventually afflict all.

No audience will humor an actor who cannot get his lines out longer than a few minutes. There is first an uneasiness, a stirring in anticipation of the actor's recovery. Then, if the recovery fails to materialize, comes the mild form of release, laughter, then come whistles, catcalls, the raspberry, or a nonplused walk-out *en masse*. It is believed to have happened, that disappointed audiences stormed the stage and physically attacked hapless actors. The people at large did not yet know that all of them, every one, carried the virus at least in the incubative stage and would eventually be affected in the same way as the actors. That misperception, however, is commonly observed when epidemics break out suddenly, producing victims with strange symptoms that are initially misdiagnosed. Thus, in this instance, in many cities, the theaters were simply closed because of the pathology afflicting the actors. At least that was the official explanation. In some instances, especially in Europe where theaters are often the heritage of a bygone age inconveniently located in the eyes of modern planners, there were those who quickly seized the opportunity. The ornate edifices, with their columns and caryatids, were put to the wrecker's ball. Underground garages topped by pedestrian zones took their place, which proved to be the politically viable thing to do. Mute presentations on the streets became common and were tolerated. Most speaking actors, as they came to be called to distinguish them from congenital mutes and pantomimists by choice, were on the dole. Theater doctors were willing to certify afflicted speaking actors as speech impaired, as invalids entitled to disability benefits. No one was aware that the actors were only the early victims of the broadly advancing viral epidemic.

At the time of Terrence's departure from Venice, the epidemic had been accepted as a fact of life that had to be accommodated. While the experts carefully charted the progressing loss of the verbal substance, the remaining language potential still allowed most people to go about their daily business. Some of the lost words were found to be expendable. Essential concepts that had lost their tonal manifestation survived by means of the well known sign language, the use of signets, numeration, abbreviation, and the like. Things were tough, to be sure, but not yet tough enough to force action by public officials. The work of concerned citizens who, like Terrence, were laboring to intercept the approaching catastrophe, received no public attention. Terrence had only the encouragement of a few friends as he conducted his experiment in the back room of that Methodist church in Hollywood. The neighbors paid little attention, if any, when he and his collaborators drove up in the early morning on Franklin Avenue, parked, entered the building through the clanging iron gate, when they later ate their brown bag lunches on the whitewashed balcony; and hardly anyone noticed their departure late at night. Terrence's collaborators, including Joan, a modest beauty from Costa Mesa, were categorically dedicated to the idea that the linguistic virus had to be stopped at any cost. One evening, while he was taking his evening meal in a Korean restaurant, friends asked Terrence what motivate him and his collaborators in their continued pursuit of their theatrical ambitions in the face of the prevailing conditions. His reply: It is the will to resist the viral decomposition of the linguistic faculties — it works like a powerful antibody to offset, cancel or zero-out the destructive thrust of the virus. That sets the stage on which the recreation of the linguistic faculty can take place in each actor by working a set of words and sentences prescribed by him, Terrence. The actors do not simply learn to spell, as might be assumed, but they re-experience the concepts by listening to stories told by Terrence — stories which lead to the words and sentences. The process is tedious and involves an intellectual retracing of the emotional journey which led to the original acquisition of the linguistic stock subject to the viral attack, a process of re-remembering, and extrapolation, as it were, of the potential of the genetic hardware. Terrence said that he was greatly encouraged by the progress: The apparently empty theater space begins to fill with life, as we proceed, with forgotten, invisible life. Its figures acquire more and more presence. They are among us. In the morning, when we start our work, they are already there, invisibly of course, but clearly immanent. The beneficial effect results from this immanence. One might say that the figures that so pervade the space of the theater teach the actors, or reteach them the use of the lost language. They are driven by their unbroken play instinct, as it were. Indeed, yesterday in the morning, the playful setting escalated into spontaneous ejaculation of word pictures like: "Only he who plays, lives; lives only, he who plays; plays only, he who lives ..." and suchlike transports of verbalized emotions. The actors were seized by enthusiasm that manifested itself in loud laughter and exclamations with such force that a cleaning woman who was sweeping the balcony, opened the door and called out in terror: "Eh there!" And one of the actors replied: "Nix 'eh there'" and happily laughed at her. That was too much for the cleaning woman; she went into verbal shock and barely managed to close the door again. As he spoke, Terrence reached with his chopsticks to the middle of the table, where the meat on the Korean charcoal barbecue sizzled, slightly charred at the edges. One important development was that the actors, having rediscovered their own linguistic potential with the help of his imaginary figures, had begun to converse among themselves. The project proceeded in great strides, the reciprocal understanding growing with the recreated linguistic potential. Upon his observation so far, Terrence believed that his actors were beginning to shed the viral affliction. "We are on the way," he said. "What way?" asked a physician among his friends. "Soon we will be able to give public performances," said Terrence.

And that day came, in November. The audience filed into the theater in the Methodist church with the faux Gothic face as the parting light of the sun filtered through the ocher dust blown out to sea by the desert wind. Then the performance started. It ended only minutes later. The audience, by now entirely affected by the virus, sat at first quietly and attempted to follow the action on the stage, but was not able to understand anything. The virus had destroyed its ability to perceive language. It heard a tonal melange which did not carry meaning, word fragments without linguistic content. There were the actors' gestures, movements, glances, but they were meaningless without connected dialogue. It seemed that the receptive capacity of the theater audience had atrophied. For that reason, it was impossible that Terrence's production might have its healing or cathartic effect, as he had, in sanguine moments, envisioned. Instead, the actors' efforts enraged the audience. The audience turned into a mob that rose from the chairs, shouting, driven by insane impulses, rushing to the stage to attack the actors. Terrence was seated in front of me at the aisle. "Kill! Him!" the man sitting next to me shouted, pointing at Terrence. Since these words expressed a simple idea in a simple way, they were understood by the crowd and immediately made their way through the auditorium. They shouted in unison: "Kill! Kill! Kill!" I jumped up and, in order to protect him, grabbed Terrence by his shirt collar. I dragged him through the crowd, as though I intended, like the rest, to do him in. Terrence was limp and heavy, as though unconscious. The back stage door gave way as I pushed him out ahead of me into the yard. The bloody, mangled corpses of the actors remaining behind on the stage would later be classified by the authorities as the subjects of a sacrificial stage ritual. I drove Terrence, not knowing that he had moved, to his old Windward Avenue address in Venice. Not having spoken a word on the way, he assured me that he was alright. I did not press him. He thanked me and got out. I watched him as he slowly walked into the arcades of the Venetian Palace, turning once or twice to waive at me. I believed that he just wanted to be alone and would make it safely home.

Years later, I heard that Terrence, the playwright, had died. A young man on his skateboard workout found him on a bench at the beach in Venice. People familiar with the local scene told me that he had been a regular among the homeless of the city for many years. He was known as Terry the Mute. No one could remember hearing him utter even a single word. "Was mute, he," one transient told me when I inquired. No personal effects were ever found.

(Translated by Sandra and Ewald Schlachter)

ADOLF MUSCHG

Adolf Muschg

Born May 13, 1934 in Zollikon. Studied German and English literature and philosophy. Guest professor in Germany, Japan, Switzerland and the US. Since 1970 professor in Zurich. 1985 Writer-in-Residence, Max Kade Institute, USC. Member of literary academies. Received several literary awards. Lives in Männedorf. Short stories, novels, essays, plays, film scripts: *Im Sommer des Hasen*, 1965; *Gegenzauber*, 1967; Rumpelstilz, 1968; *Mitgespielt*, 1969; *Papierwände*, 1970; *Liebesgeschichten*, 1972; *Albissers Grund*, 1946; *Kellers Abend*, 1975; *Entfernte Bekannte*, 1976; *Baiyun oder Die Freundschaftsgesellschaft*, 1980; *Leib und Leben*, 1982; *Unterlassene Abwesenheit*, 1984; *Das Licht und der Schlüssel*, 1984; *Der Turmhahn*, 1987; *Der rote Ritter*, 1993.

New Rights

On April 4, the southern Baptist minister Martin Luther King stepped out onto the balcony of room 306 of the Lorraine Motel in Memphis, Tennessee and was shot and killed across two backyards by a man who had steadied his left foot in an empty bathtub.

That very night in the university town of Tompkinsville, New York State, the following buildings went up in flames: Ted Kluszewski's industrial chemical cleaners, the farmer Harmon Killebrew's barn, the Chez Rocco pizza parlor, and fire station no. 5 in Tioga Street.

On December 22, the white student Johnny Vander Meer crossed the rather solitary Cascadilla Bridge on the west side of campus and was beaten up but not robbed. He stated he had no enemies.

On December 25 was Christmas.

The university's film society showed the film: Paris Burning? A Volkswagen could be bought for $1,799. The spring model was expected soon.

At the campus store, one could buy stationery that mothers supposedly liked and used frequently.

On January 10, Afro-American students demanded their own study center for Afro-American studies.

On January 12, an unidentified Afro-American student danced on the desk in the reception of the Dean of Business School holding a water pistol in his hand. The same day, some unidentified Afro-Americans broke into a number of soft drink machines on campus and later burst into the reference section of the library and emptied some rows of index cards from the filing cabinets onto the floor.

The student Ida Simmons, class of 71, called this Mickey-Mouse-Terrorism.

The sorority Alpha Delta Tau forbid the visit of black fraternity members at their inaugural party.

The book "Don't cry, scream" was much sought after at the university book store.

On January 19, five Afro-American students whose participation in the events dated January 12 was considered fact were cited to appear before a multi-racial university disciplinary board but had no intention of appearing there. A minority of the board believed that the presence of the accused students was not necessary for the issuing of a reprimand. The majority voted on a new date for a hearing.

On January 20, the Student for a Democratic Society Steve Gold delivered a speech on medical imperialism.

The same day, shortly before midnight, the white student Don Nottebart was assaulted when crossing Cascadilla Bridge. The white policeman Jim Closkey, who happened to be on patrol nearby, succeeded in catching the perpetrator by shooting him in his left thigh. The perpetrator was the black kitchen hand Leon Goslin, who could not give a motive for his act. The policeman Jim Closkey is a father of five who had had to undergo a stomach resurrection the previous September and who by no means considered himself fully recovered.

On January 21, the Tompkins Daily Sun published a job opening for a female riding instructor at a summer camp for underprivileged children and offered a race-ready Elva Formula C race car for as little as $1,500.

During that and the following week there was a lot of snowfall. Salt corroded the bottoms of cars and the welding seams of the car bodies of older models turned into rust etchings.

On January 25, the student Prentice Snipe, class of 71, required the auto club's help at 234 Oneida Place to have his car jump started.

On February 1, a guest professor from the Philippines made a remark during his lecture on teacher recruitment in developing countries that was considered racist by the Afro-American students in the auditorium.

On February 2, a number of Afro-American students occupied the office of the Dean of Education, but at 1:00 p.m. allowed sandwiches in for the secretaries.

The student paper *Dialogue* ran a series in which managers from important US corporations gave intelligent and understanding answers in two columns to one column long probing questions from students. That edition also carried advertising of the specialized dealer The Jolly Camper for jump ropes, water basket balls, boomerangs, butterfly nets, repair kits for diving suits, and glow-in-the-dark frisbees.

On February 7, instead of the six cited Afro-American students, one hundred and fifty Afro-American students appeared for the hearing of the multi-racial disciplinary board. The board retreated and decided to issue the reprimand in the absence of those reprimanded.

On February 10, the Pittsburgh Symphony Orchestra performed Anton Bruckner's Symphony in C minor.

On February 13, a religious advertisement in the town's paper proclaimed that there was nothing sadder than a former idealist, who now lives in the gutters and pretends to enjoy this.

An increasing number of Afro-American students were awakened by anonymous phone threats.

A new tampon called Playtex promised safety right from day one. The advertisement read: That is why we call it the first day tampon. In every laboratory test, the playtex tampon was more absorbent than the old cardboard-like types. On average, it is truly more absorbent than the leading regular brand because of the unique way in which it is made. In reality, it adjusts to you. It protects every inner square inch of you. Where you are the most woman, Playtex is the most tampon.

Professor of constitutional law Ralph E. Walterlynn slept with his golf club at hand.

The restaurant Steaks Unlimited promised to make every guest a Clark Gable; you only had to grow your own mustache. Hai

Karate After Shave promised that anyone using their cologne would be assaulted by numerous beautiful women.

Sale figures for "Don't cry, scream" slowly started dropping in February.

On March 3, Charlie Brown sharpened a pencil made of Bavarian clay and Madagascan graphite and thus spoiled the fun he received by sharpening pencils.

Some taller trees formed their first drip stains in the area of their roots.

On March 23, Robert W. Dowling, University President, was dragged by his collar away from the microphone by the Afro-American student Ira Reid. In reference to his liberalism and the student's difficult overall situation, the president refused to press charges.

On March 30, the multi-racial disciplinary board officially reprimanded four Afro-American students and acquitted two others.

The same day, Chartair offered flying lessons for students and pointed out that one would be amazed at their prices. Maltese, Miniature Schnauser, and Pomeranian puppies would be availiable within a week at telephone number AR-2756.

On April 4, parents arrived for the university's parents' week and were accommodated at Clara Dickson Hall.

The same night, there was a cross burning in front of the dorm for Afro-American co-eds in 115 Catherine Street. A police patrol extinguished the cross and returned to police head quarters in 12 Warring Lane to await further alarms there after talking with the intimidated students.

On April 5, 4:15 a.m., ninety-five black students stormed Clara Dickson Hall, removed the parents from their beds and barricaded the doors. Over the student radio, they announced at 8:00 a.m. that they had decided to occupy a university building and prove to the university the continual engagement of black students against the illegality of the multi-racial disciplinary board as such and against their insisting on sentencing black students without peer representation and against the fact that they considered themselves the legal body to deal with matters of such political reach.

At 8.25, a group of white Students for a Democratic Society armed with banners and ready to fight assembled in front of the building to show their solidarity with the Afro-American students.

The black Doctor Marsha Carr who was among the spectators said that white guys had been messing around with black women for a long time while black men were kept standing impotent on the side lines.

The laundry owner Ned J. Chow said that he was no racist but this time these Blacks had gone too far.

The black student Obadiah Cleveland said that what the university community here had to understand was that the situation of the Blacks would have to be as good as that of the Whites or else their situation had to get as bad as that of the Blacks.

At 10:08, a group of white students from the Delta Epsilon fraternity tried to get into Clara Dickson Hall. During the following scuffle, three white students and one black one were injured, one of them with a hammer.

As their motives, the Delta-Epsilon students named athletic inclinations and camaraderie.

An unidentified black student shouted from the window that another raid like the one they just had would be dealt with in a way that could lead to a great number of innocent people getting hurt.

In the increasing rainfall, banners like WELCOME PARENTS and SUPPORT THE FIGHT IN THE THIRD WORLD started to become saggy, heavy and illegible.

A rumor clinic was opened on campus. Whoever called AR-6772 and asked if it was true that the Eta Psi Tau fraternity building was on fire, or if the particle accelerator had started to leak and if the board of trustees of the Chase Manhattan Bank had taken over, got as an answer that it was not true, absolutely not true.

Professor Kenneth Bebee of the agricultural department said the Blacks were fighting for much more than a reprimand, they were fighting to free a people from a system that had taken away their right of self-determination.

The Tompkins Daily Sun published a comment by the Jewish student community about the burning of the cross saying that they as Jews had also been victimized by the Ku-Klux-Klan or other groups with prejudices and they wanted to emphasize the nature of this burning as a traditional threat of oppression on human life.

The league of student homophiles cancelled its meeting that day.

The rumor clinic could neither confirm nor deny the rumor that the president had retired to the boat house to think the situation over.

The following day, the rumor clinic collapsed under the rumor that eight cars full of armed fraternity members were on their way to Clara Dickson, although that rumor was probably not true. Although it couldn't be explained how they got there, fire arms found their way into the hands of those Afro-American students who had seized Clara Dickson .

When the talk "The Stability of the University" which President Robert W. Dowley had planned to deliver was canceled, some professors began to evacuate their families to motels in the area and some parents considered recalling their daughters of which only the smallest number was on hand.

That night, 50,000 flyers were printed.

Addressing an urgent inquiery, the police chief of the county declared that his forces were too weak, that a great number of his men had just overcome problems (one stomach resurrection), that they only had fifteen loudspeakers altogether at their disposal, and that if the Blacks shot at their loudspeakers, their effect would drop to a whisper with which order could not be maintained, to the contrary.

At 3:00 a.m., the president's receptionist had a break down. As she was irreplaceable, a hushed jubilation arose among the Students for a Democratic Society.

In the rain, the temperature had fallen to about 32 degrees.

The Students for a Democratic Society now considered taking over a university building but the radical student Dave Burak reminded them that they could not leave the black students without their protection since they had been denied protection for three hundred years.

A group of girls dressed in old military coats carried a banner through the cold saying: FREE CONTRACEPTIVES NOW.

A group handed out flyers that read: The seemingly impossible has happened at this university. All the groups currently involved in this crisis have acted either irresponsibly, undecidedly, ineffectively, or in some combination of the three.

There were differences in opinions whether the Blacks had taken up arms because of arrogance or fear.

Rocco Colavito, class of 70, pointed out that the university was located on old Indian territory.

On April 6 at 5:25 a.m., the president Robert W. Dowling appeared red-eyed at the entrance to Clara Dickson accompanied by a secretary who carried a white flag. He said he had spoken with the board members Hardin R. Glascock and Roger G. Turnball over the phone. Hardin R. Glascock had told him he thought that it would be in order if after all the confusion the reprimand was dropped. Roger G. Turnball was to have said that we had to absolutely preserve the loyalty of the majority of the students, absolutely.

Two female Students for a Democratic Society buttoned up the president's coat. The president said that one principle had to supersede all other principles and that was that no other principle could supersede that of personal safeties.

Professor Ralph E. Fuhrman from the French Department said that if the ship sinks, he, too, will go under as long as the ship represented reason and order but if it was altered by threats and fears, then he would abandon it and take a job as a night watchman in a local bakery.

Professor Stewart L. Brown from the History Department said he thought that those procedures that had led to the reprimand should be nullified and that he had come to this conclusion because of his understanding of the merits of this case and not because of fear.

Professor Lewis Stanton from the Biochemistry Department

218 / Adolf Muschg

said he would not want to teach and could not feel at home in an institution where weapons and white flags were carried openly.

The rain had died down but the south easterly wind blew stronger and the president was swaying visibly. Then he disappeared back into Clara Dickson after depositing his tie with a Student for a Democratic Society since the tie could have been seen as a provocation.

The faculty assembled in the auditorium of the province's Food Office that was built in a Dorian style. The faculty decided that if the president was about to drop the reprimand against the Afro-American students, then this reprimand was to be reinstated.

The Students for a Democratic Society declared all students Negroes.

A moderate ad hoc committee vigorously condemned the president, the Afro-American students, the Students for a Democratic Society, and all parents. Their flyer ended with the following sentences: "Thus we call for a university wide teach-in to show support for the analysis of the situation so that all parties involved can regard themselves as such if they have a mandate for the re-examination of their statements."

At 5:00 p.m., the university's shooting range was filled with 9,000 people. The Students for a Democratic Society declared the shooting range occupied by the students. Some took off their shoes and had them circulate to collect money for a dinner. Among the ranks, intensely fragrant fog-banks started to spread. Parts of the faculty who had split from the rest of the faculty to spend the night with the students attracted attention by waving their hands. The Student for a Democratic Society Dave Mantel took the microphone and said it was impossible for them to ignore 9,000 students who said they would go and stand and fight.

At 9:30 p.m., the president arrived without his tie, put his arm around Dave Mantel's shoulder and said: We have dropped the reprimand, you can go and pick up your black friends. Dave Mantel said: Take your arm off me, we are forming a new society. The student Dottie Felsenstein offered the president a half empty bottle of Coke with a straw and he sat down on the floor with it. Dave Mantel asked the assembly if they wanted to budge an inch before the faculty had turned around and the assembly shook their fists from their sleeping bags. When the president was allowed to speak, he called this movement one of the most positive ones in the history of the university and although the acoustics in the shooting range were poor, he received a big hand as well as some laughter. He said that there was nothing that he said or would say that would not be altered by changes in the circumstances, and he asked for sympathy with the faculty because humans were fragile and should be allowed to change their minds.

At 11:45 p.m., Professor James deVoss, Department for Cultural Engineering, entered the shooting range and stated that the faculty, in light of their humanity, had first agreed to reconsider their decision concerning the upholding of the reprimand and then repealed it. At the same time, he handed the president 27 letters of resignation. The one of Professor Karl S. Guttmann, Nobel price winner for physics, read: An uncompromising moralism that supposedly endorsed the cleansing of the campus from institutionalized racism and the military-industrial complex, would indeed impair the freedom of the sciences and the creed of honest conviction that a faculty member needed and Professor Guttman was not used to being blackmailed and did not intend to learn it. The president turned white.

The Student for a Democratic Society Dave Mantel called for a joint march to Clara Dickson to free the Afro-American students.

The Afro-American students appeared dressed for battle at the entrance to Clara Dickson.

It was generally noticed that they did not accept greetings from the Students for a Democratic Society or any other group for that matter, and that they clenched automatic weapons in both their hands in front of their chests. Their speaker, Ed Whitfield, class of 71, only declared emphatically that he did not want anyone to think that his position was anyhow less serious than it had been before the occupation of Clara Dickson.

While the Afro-American students were disappearing in an orderly procession behind the near horizon, the Tomkins University police force reinforced by mobile units of the district kept photographers and parents at a distance.

Over breakfast, parents for a few brief moments got closer to their student sons and daughters.

On April 7, the papers wrote about Tompkins University that it would never be the same again.

But the Afro-American students with their battle gear made the title page of Newsweek and were the same who had left through the Clara Dickson gate on Sunday morning.

The weapons in their hands, that had frightened the nation, were the same we had seen the Afro-American students clench in their hands.

The sentence, following this title page America would never be the same again, was the same sentence we read in the Tomkins Daily Sun on Monday.

The advocate Richard Nixon, who in a televised speech promised a drastic improvement in the American quality of life, was the very same one.

(Translated by Gene O. Stimpson)

ERICA PEDRETTI

Erica Pedretti

Born March 25, 1930, in Sternberg (Czechoslovakia). 1945 moved to Switzerland. Studied arts and crafts. 1950 emigration to the US. 1952 return to Switzerland. 1989 Max Kade Writer-in-Residence, Washington University, St. Louis. Sculptor. Received several literary awards. Lives in La Neuveville. Short stories, novels, radio plays, children's stories: *Harmloses, bitte,* 1970; *Badekur,* 1971; *Catch as Katz can,* 1972; *Heiliger Sebastian,* 1973; *Veränderung,* 1977; *Sonnenaufgänge, Sonnenuntergänge,* 1984; *mal laut und falsch singen,* 1986; *Valerie oder Das unerzogene Auge,* 1986; *Die Tischplatte,* 1988.

Holy Sebastian

Anne lies on the bed and thinks
of what? Of Coney Island OPEN ALL YEAR, and goes from
one thought to another, from Stanton to Stratton Mountain FINE
SKIING, Mount Washington, to Frank, hi Frank!

Pulled her from the bushes at the bottom of Tuckerman's Ravine
after a dangerous skiing accident.

— Lucky once again! She awakes after being unconscious, sees
Frank and believes, that now she is really dead.

— Where did we last see each other?

— In Sihlbrugg, went by bike to Lucerne. The *Vierwaldstät-
tersee*: looks exactly like a color-postcard, doesn't it? He learned
German in order to read *Untergang des Abendlandes* in the original.

She remembers her surprise at seeing him again and later in

— have you been to Greenwich Village? the old Greek asks.

— Fine, let's go there, says Frank, let's go to Milton's New Year's
Eve party.

The apartment door is open. Splashing in the next room, the
bathroom door has been left open a crack. A girl gets out of the tub
and without drying herself off, she comes, I am Dickie, takes
Frank's and Anne's coats and leads them, dripping, into the living
room. The room, darkly paneled, is illuminated with candles. Men
on the many sofas, in deep leather armchairs and on large silk
cushions, some young fellows also on the deep pile carpet, backs
against the sides of the sofas. Dickie carries the coats into a side
room, and appears again.

— About time to get dressed, Milton says.

— Why? someone says. Nobody seems to notice that Dickie is naked. She serves cocktails and later lights the punch, now dressed, elegantly. Blues. The men dance, alone and with a partner. Somebody yells, bye, dear! and goes to another party.

Hush, somebody's calling me, now.

Hush, somebody's calling me: from the phonograph,

It sounds like the voice of the Lord.

In the meantime some girls have arrived.

Oh, you hypocrites, somebody's calling you

Hypocrites, somebody's calling you

It sounds like the voice of — shut up! Milton turns off the phonograph.

— Ah, there you are! yells one of the girls and sits down on Frank's knee, *baby baby I'm so lonesome for you!*

Say where you want my mind, don't care what I do

occurs to Milton:

When I wake up in the morning, my heart it feels like lead

When I go to bed at midnight, sometimes I wish I was dead.

Anne has retreated to the very back of the breakfast nook and watches, as if she were at the theater, at a play she doesn't understand.

Lord, Lord, can't rest no place I go,

sings Milton, his eyes light up, he leans back in his armchair, expands his chest by his singing, like a celebrating bullfinch, Anne thinks, he spreads his arms, moves his large hands with great expression, he is singing for a blond man, who is sitting across from him:

Blues is driving me crazy, must be reaping what I sow.

Then, as the song is finished, he collapses, becomes like he was before, makes the impression of a pedantic, elderly teacher.

— You liked the picture? The blond man, leans over to his colleague: That is an early work from the time with Max Beckmann. Yes, I was with him a while, Brooklyn College, yes.

Around a round coffee table some people are kneeling, chins

resting on the table, admiring a young man in a jersey, who is dancing above them.

Girls force themselves between the couples on the sofas, new guests arrive, already drunk, from other parties, the girl on Frank's lap throws her arms around his neck, and as he attempts to fight her off, she screams:

— *say where you want my mind, don't care what I do!*

Somebody cries and cries, can't stop crying, Dickie hands him a handkerchief.

— How did you ever get involved with this group? old Frank asks the following day at work.

— I had no idea that there was such a thing, Anne says

And from Frank, who during the taxi ride home cries and laughs and cries, God, I'm drunk, again to the other, to the old Frank, you really should, you must absolutely go to Coney Island, and Robert, Anne carries on, loses himself

— Who was Robert?

> flies   *there*
> *Through the clouds endlessly*
> *Wherever the wind carries him*
> *No man can ever say*

— Once someone said, that is a horrible children's story: to be simply swept away!

— Flying through the clouds, carried higher and higher, beautiful, Anne thinks: to go higher and higher, the houses below become smaller and smaller, disappear.

— Who was Robert?

— Morning Miss! 10th.?

Robert in the rain. And the white haired Negro Robert, liftboy in Maiden Lane 1, corner of Broadway:

— 10th. floor, Miss Anne.

Morotti Brothers & Co. Jewelers: two popular Italians about sixty, a secretary, just like one imagines old secretaries, and Frank, specialist in platinum work with diamonds, it's called *ajour*.

— I wouldn't touch gold or silver anymore, it just doesn't pay, custom work is platinum work, that is, unless you work for a miserable salary.

Anne had taken over this job for minimum wage from a chauffeur who had been trained to assemble and solder together the soldiers' bracelets, during a time, when these were still used in quantity.

— A disgrace! curses one of the brothers

— Curse the President! adds the other Morotti

— not to keep on fighting the war properly

— to order McArthur to return!

— Who understands better how to wage war, a general or a politician?

— That will ruin us!

Identification bracelets, tens of thousands in silver: for Korea.

— Now they want to end it, that just can't

— want to kill us!

Nevertheless, the brothers don't give up hope: if it's not this war, it will be another, it's always been like that, why should it be different now, without war we can't, the world cannot be.

— But of course they mean, what they say! Frank says to Anne.

The bracelets consist of a massive elongated silver plate, on which later serial number, name and date of birth are engraved. On both sides Anne solders a hook, then on each end of the chain a piece of the clasp.

— Be careful when soldering!

The chains, thinner than the plate, glow and melt much faster than the latter,

— whoever planned that, doesn't understand the profession, and the spring in the clasp weakens if it gets too hot.

— Careful, the flame is too hot!

Anne pulls back, still not used to acetylene, and the chain links slip on the soldering plate, she tries to readjust them with the tips of her fingers and burns herself, where are the tweezers, the pieces fall apart again and cannot be held fast.

— the chauffeur did better work, a Morotti looks over her shoulder:

— twice as much in the same amount of time.

One bracelet = one solider. Maybe he's dead.

The chain slips off the plate, Anne has to look for the soldering rod.

This way one at least knows who he was and how much time he had. She's finally able to retrieve the solder with a borax brush from a crack in the charcoal and to secure it to the soldering plate.

Frank's friend was killed in France.

— a long time ago, in World War I, but for me it's like yesterday, Frank says. Anne won't tell anybody about the war.

— Can you show me how to regulate the gas?

He hands the readjusted soldering iron with a small soft flame from his spot over to her.

The Morottis and Miss Alice don't know what war is. And the chauffeur, Anne's predecessor, probably didn't know either.

The dozen finished bracelets are decorroded in a vat of boiling acid, the fumes also corrode the eyes and throat, and collect as a biting stench in the workshop. Frank has gotten used to it, like to the whirring of the polishing motor. Every fourteen days a little woman comes, exchanges her street coat for a high necked black work coat, ties a black scarf around her hair, deep over her forehead, pulls on black leather gloves and sits down with a box full of bracelets, Anne's fourteen day production, in front of the motor and begins to polish. The rotating brushes and felt pads throw out metal particles with polishing paste against the woman, color her, her face, black, up to her nostrils.

Anne sees children's shoes hanging under the woman seat, legs, which don't reach the floor.

— Bye, bye, Miss Anne, Robert opens the elevator door, it's raining: You should take my umbrella.

— Thank you, Robert, I'm afraid, I lose umbrellas.

— 10th floor, Miss Anne, here we are again!

— Reims, beautiful. Paris, beautiful. Fontainebleau, Versailles, I'm not saying anything against castles, says Frank, I actually like them better than cathedrals, and you don't see things like that here, I mean: have you already been to The Cloisters? Beautiful, but not as beautiful as Coney Island.

— And Chartres? Have you also been to Chartres?

— Yes, very beautiful, but nothing compared to Coney Island. Next to her, Frank is filing facets while talking, a small glistening spot next to the others. In front of Anne, small glistening points against a gray background are moving in a square space between the walls of some buildings. Now a ship's bow pushes itself through the water between the concrete

— get back to work!

(For Cartier I would gladly, then again maybe not)

one porthole after another appears

— France is very beautiful in general, at least the areas that I know.

— Can you speak French?

— No, only English.

(He could hardly do there)

A smoke stack comes into view; (that is a very large ship: if it has three chimneys, it is possibly the)

— you're not allowed to look out the window so often. Yes, the view is beautiful, but Coney Island, when you see Coney Island, that is the most beautiful.

(Behind Manhattan, behind Williamsburg Bridge, behind Brooklyn, behind)

— too bad, that there's war in Europe so often: everything of beauty is slowly being destroyed.

(There are still some things remaining.)

— We have tried to spare everything that is considered beautiful, and the castles and cathedrals are considered beautiful. Before I could never understand, what on old, crumbling

(that could, it is now 10:45, according to the schedule in the New York Times she should arrive at 11:00, that could be the Liberté)

— should be so special, until I was there, but they really are

two smoke stacks (or has the front one disappeared behind 37, Broadway in the meantime? Working: cut 75 holes *à jour* then file = 75 x 4 facets = 300 tiny facets to cut and file precisely)

— and in general are most things, which are considered beautiful, really beautiful.

(so that with 4 facets from a small circular hole a square is made, 75 squares placed at right angles to each other results in a diamond pattern, 7 horizontal rows of portholes, that must be the Liberté.)

Daily, on the trip to work, Anne holds a newspaper as a screen in front of her, memorizes daily in new variations the arrival and departure times of the transatlantic steamers.

— you should work a lot faster, and in general, if you keep on going like that

now only one smoke stack remains from the steamer.

— I cannot, however, understand, why one makes such a big to do about the cathedrals, but about Coney Island

and past the deck of the Liberté, that must be the Liberté, a small black pilot boat is traveling in the opposite direction. (One like it brought me here, one like it should take me out again.)

— Don't keep constantly looking out the window!

Now Frank is finished with his piece, puts it in a small box next to the others, takes a new platinum plate, marks it with a ruler and a compass, takes the hand drill

— Coney Island, the most beautiful thing that you can imagine, fantastic, and you still haven't been there!

(I just arrived and came for good, therefore I have enough time. However, I don't want to. I will take the Liberté, won't stay here, will simply)

— and if you keep going like that, sooner or later they will throw you out, you won't find another job that easily.

(As soon as I have enough for the passage, I'll)

— you absolutely must take enough money for Coney Island

(I'll take the Liberté. However, before that I want to take a look at Coney Island.)

It's dripping from the roofs, the entire honkey-tonk sparkles in the drizzle. Bright neon snakes from the dance clubs-, theaters-, fairytale-facades wind themselves, thrash about in the puddles between the legs of the visitors, are trampled, torn to pieces, flinch, constantly renewed, strike at the wet feet.

Here is Adam and Eve's paradise! The thousandth reproduction of long forgotten memory. Yeah, right

— Here the future is shown to those, who have already come to terms with their pasts!

— Here, next door, behind the black curtain: Shelter from the cold and wet with death & all the evil spirits & horror!

— You're wet, are you cold?

We eat hot dogs, standing lonely between abandoned tables in a bar bathed in infrared light.

— Drink a glass of wine, or three or four!

— But, I think, here's only beer.

Then your head dances, and the facades, the buildings dissolve, tremble to the music, to the tom-tom, which moves the legs, moves the body, your voice, your senses

and the merry-go-round spins you, away, away, rotating high

above, you lie flat in the air, in colors, watercolors, water, in

how the sky presses, circling it moves downward, slower, out of the shining colors downward and into the dark alleys and stands, finally, still.

And then Adam shoots, your Adam is shooting at dolls, which are grinning at him, a wall of identical dolls, which grinningly seduce him, not in a dream, not for fun, no really he rests his elbows on the counter,

— you can't possibly!

aims: laughs. Rests his elbows, aims, squints his eyes, aims carefully: a doll. Laughs.

— There you have a doll. Be careful, the rain will make her wet, like you. A doll with golden curls, blood red lips, with long eyelashes, which click open and shut, be careful, that she doesn't get wet.

— What am I supposed to do with the doll?

— Carry yourself through a sky, which is completely green. My green Adam, green doll. Shove, swing the ship, swing, rock yourself into a sky, which is completely red, don't laugh, don't laugh like that, red doll! Long eyelashes click open, don't close anymore, red eyes starring into the sky, which your skirt covers from you, swing yourself, rock high into the sky, which is now yellow, high into the sky, which hides, which is now green, now red, now yellow. Long eyelashes click, fall shut.

Shivering on through the streets of trivial pleasures, Hammon organ streets, isolated blasts of joy from trumpets, through alleys of booths, which cross the entire island, which lead you to the sea, where they mirroring, colorfully glistening lead further, lead you into the sea.

Between two shining cities, between two rain showers, they walk with their arms around each other along the beach. Rain again, runs into the eyes, left and right along the nose into the mouth, onto the collar, along the neck, down the collar bone, drips cold and wet onto the chest.

And the bright mirror breaking, sinking the pieces into the sea.

The rain washes your doll, which lies shot on the side of the road which leads home, slumped across the pavement, Eve from Coney Island with yellow curls, blood red lips, eyelashes lifted up and seduces whom?

(Translated by John W. Arensmeyer Jr.)

KUNO RAEBER

Kuno Raeber

Born May 20, 1922, in Klingnau, died January 28, 1992, in Basle. Studied history and philosophy. 1951/52 director of the Swiss School in Rome. 1952-57 assistant at the Leibniz-Kolleg in Tübingen and Europa-Kolleg in Hamburg. 1967/68 Poet-in-Residence at Oberlin College, Ohio. 1980 "Werkjahr" in Lucerne. Lived in Munich. Poems, novels, essays: *Die verwandelten Schiffe*, 1957; *Gedichte*, 1960; *Die Lügner sind ehrlich*, 1960; *Calabria*, 1961; *Flußufer*, 1963; *Mißverständnisse*, 1968; *Alexius unter der Treppe*, 1973; *Das Ei*, 1981; *Reduktionen*, 1981; *Abgewandt: Zugewandt*, 1985; *Sacco di Roma*, 1989.

Alexius under the Staircase
or Confessions to a Cat

"Up to that August 15th in 1968 at five o'clock in the morning on the West Side of Manhattan. The whole previous afternoon, I had dozed away on a bench under the trees in Bryant Park. Although they provided a nice shade, only the tall buildings all around offered me a genuine sense of protection. It was especially the Commercial Bank of New York, towering over me with the partly good-natured and partly threatening insolence of a brick church in Gdansk or Stralsund, to which I looked up trustingly as I would to a gigantic uncle while lying there, the Times page of engagement announcements under my head. In it, a whole column from top to bottom was devoted to extolling the attributes of the charming and well-bred bride-to-be, who was of a good family. Her father, for instance, was the executive of a textile firm; her mother was the daughter of a general and long-time teacher at West Point; she herself had graduated from Wellesley College with distinction (B+) and had later devoted herself to painting in Florence. For the bridegroom-to-be a skimpy mention at the end: assistant manager at I.B.M., Harvard graduate. Only reluctantly and as a concession to propriety did the anonymous rhapsodist take note of him as the little man who was, of course, indispensable, but indeed no more than an appendage to the queen who, with a bunch of lilacs in her arm and with chastely raised eyes, was smiling in front of an icon the size of a postcard. — The engagement page of the Times under my head, the benches in Bryant Park were never free of bird droppings, I was still breathing spasmodically, though it had already been almost a quarter of an hour since I had ducked into the tranquil alcoves along 42nd Street, which greedily sucked in vehicles and pedestrians (how puzzling, this stillness in the immediate neighborhood of a busy traffic's clucking and gurgling), although I had ducked and stolen away, tortured by the lustful anxiety and the anxious lust (the result of the contradiction between the guiding values I was taught and those discovered by myself and tentatively incorporated into my personal life: in times past they would probably have been called duty and inclination, carnal drives and peace of mind), that befell me again and again in this street. Its crude sex films evoked laughter rather than carnal lust. And so did the bookstores with their posters: to the right of the entrance door, life-size and with sizable breasts, pictures in color of roseately blond female nudity; to the left, in the same format, pictures of males with their brown legs spread apart, offering the onlooker a chance to revere their genitals rising from the scrotum's brushwood, but drooping demurely — these and the bookstore's window displays with their endless juicy, sensuous feasts for the eyes no longer could enthrall me ever since I visited Manhattan for the second time. What made me chase up and down 42nd Street, from 8th Avenue to Bryant Park, were the embodiments of those carnal appetites and drives and wishes and anxieties and yearnings that businessmen and soldiers, and college boys, and sailors, and office workers seek to satisfy in front of the windows and inside the stores. It was the primitive materialization which moved toward me and beset me, be it with the mere twinkle of an eyelid, or with a smile, or with an angry look, or with the movement of a hand, or with the stomping of a foot. Dull and colorless by comparison were the motley posters, the magazines and the books that portly gentlemen, glancing downward through their eyeglasses and feeling conscious of doing something forbidden (forbidden by whom?), furtively picked up from the tables ('Everything about Sado-Masochism,' 'Inexpressible Love,' 'Scouts' Tales') and, title page pressed against their chests, carried them up to the cashier. Once there, they would perforce hesitate and wonder whether they should not think it over — for on the walls of the stand on which the cash register sparkled and resounded were pasted the samples of the boldest but also the most expensive pictures: sex acts performed by two or three, in one or more colors, heterosexual and homosexual (both kinds of homosexual) — in the end, however, they paid and carried off their booty in perspiring hands. Outside, they stood in front of the windows, their faces turned toward the street, and they walked, incarnations of carnal lust-anxieties and anxiety-ridden yearnings: wilderness and provocation of velvety eyes, hard eyes (wilderness of the autumn forest with its sleepy pond; wilderness of the primeval forest full of reptiles, insects, and creeping vines; wilderness of barren mountains and sand deserts with the cruelty of cold, heat, storms and flash floods). There they stood and walked, swayed their hips in tight pants, and over their sweaters hung their chains and pendants with the 'Judaea capta' and the seven-pronged candle holder. They swayed their hips, dressed entirely in leather, black from head to toe, sporting the terrible runic SS on the lapels of their jackets and skull and crossbones on their caps. 'Am I not like Himmler, exactly like Himmler?' Chains dangled from their shoulders, nipples shimmered through their mesh shirts, and spurs clinked when they stomped the ground: 'You know, I am a sadist, but I can also be someone else; it depends entirely on what's being offered.' Day and night he leaned against the wall near the blood bank entrance — 'Collect payment right away' —, the Indio, constantly gazing at what he did not see: the old tribesman, who sat there silently, smoking his long pipe. Spread out before his motionless face were the painted leather shields and the many-colored boats that had been brought here from the warehouses, the storage places of the tribe, and laid out for the marveling eyes of the onlookers to behold. And the old man was proud, but did not show it. He owned five thousand shields, each having its own design, and he owned five hundred boats, each with different ornamental stripes, wavy lines, sun wheels, flowers, and painted-on masks. He did not show his pride: he just sat there and smoked. Half of the day and all of the night he leaned there by the entrance to the blood bank. His shirt, which had been white once but now was closer to black, his sneakers — 'West Side Story' — were gaping for lack of shoelaces. His motionless eyes glimmered from under his helmet-shaped hair. 'No, today it's ten dollars, yesterday it was nine, but today I need a larger dose.' What I experienced here was the plunge, the dizziness of the plunge from the skies of Tiepolo, from the gilded halls of the Doge's palace, from the mosaic heavens of San Marco. The heavy cosmic matter, long since slipped from the hands of its Creator, so that it only once in a while released a spark, struck and blinded me and burned on my hand (the glimmer and flash seen in water spouting upward, which I, strangely enough, never remembered here, not one single time), a cigarette accidentally touching the back of my hand, as might easily happen when people greet each other as they do on 42nd Street. The heavy cosmic matter, God's viscous effluence, so far removed from Him that not a trace of His glimmer fell on it anymore — it was the plunge into this state, the fall from the zenith of Venice into the abyss, into the bowels of Manhattan, that again and again enraptured and intoxicated me. However, it did not take long for me to feel again the lure of tranquillity, of greenness, and the bench under the New York Commercial Bank. There, with my head on the engagement page of the Times, I no longer was the dethroned Doge Alvise Mocenigo, remembered nothing, did not run away from anything, and no longer was searching for anything. There I felt equally indifferent to what was up and to what was down. The birds flew about above me, twittering frightfully.The girls from the Bryant Library sat on the steps in the sun and calmed them with crumbs from their sandwiches, but they found happiness only in the puddles that were left there as a mirror for them by a dark hour that was in no way comparable to the present brightness. There I lay, just as far removed from the sucking force of 42nd Street as from the ecstasies of San Marcos and found myself watched over and protected by the big red uncle and his gigantic friends and brothers all around. If I, enthralled by a face, a smile, a demanding look and then by a new face, a new smile, a new demanding look did not see them from the chasm of the street — 'in hac lacrimarum valle' —, I did look into their large faces and the countless quiet eyes here: 'Stay with us, for evening is drawing near!' And I noticed that the princes of Manhattan became aware of me, recognized me and spoke to me, that they wanted something from me, that they were not content, as I had believed until now, to turn their red and green lit ad-signs toward the red and green twinkling of the airplanes. (It would have taken no more than an inviting counter-twinkling to make the winged fishes forget about landing at La Guardia and set down here in the island-slumber of mid-Manhattan, amidst the twittering birds of Bryant Park; but the silent and noncommittal response to the twinkling remained unaffected.) I noticed that the princes of Manhattan recognized the Doge, and I was startled. What was there about me that gave away my identity to them. Had I not done enough yet to get away from it all and be no longer a definite someone they could address by name and ask to stay with them because evening was drawing near? Were the evenings I had spent here not already too much? Was it not enough that the sleepers on all the other benches around, when nightfall wakened them, shoved their caps up over their black foreheads, smoothed out their crackling plastic covers, pulled the bottles from their jacket pockets, uncorked them, took a swig, got up and came over to me, all of them, invited me to join them in a drink, begged me to drink with them? And I ran out of the park, fled panic-stricken back to the maelstrom of cravings and anxiety to let myself again be seized and carried away by 42nd Street, as if I hadn't just a short while ago sworn never to see it again. And all this because it was now nighttime and no longer daytime. As if that would make the least bit of difference in Manhattan. But I mistrusted the giganting princes, the senators, and above all the red uncle. They might maliciously withdraw their protection at night, when they no longer have to answer to anyone, and want to hang on to me only so they could revel in my distress from afar and from above. I had better leave, submerge, descend to the subway, IRT, Times Square-7th Avenue: Downtown. Jesus said: 'I am the resurrection and the life. He that believes in me, though he were dead, yet shall he live.' With all those other dead people who were humming to themselves and whispering, who embraced each other, bickered and quarreled, who, giggling, showed pornographic pictures to each other, I waited in limbo for the train that would take me to paradise, going underneath the building at number 28, 28th Street, where the naked angels, searching for someone to devour, ran tirelessly up and down the stairs and, causing an endless pattering of sandals, down the hallways of all three floors, past three hundred rooms with doors ajar. 'In my heavenly Father's house are many mansions. Have I been chosen by Him, or been rejected, will the angel enter or pass by?' But already we stopped at 14th Street, at Christopher Street. Resurrection in Greenwich Village, where people went about carrying flowers, wore chains of shells around their necks and ten-

derly stroked each others' hair. 'Make love, not war!' But I wanted
to go on, I knew where, and I did not. I entered a cellar bar and
let myself be treated to a beer, but I turned down the two spenders'
offer to torment me. What they had in mind was to roast me, like
Saint Laurentius and Saint Vincentius, on a grate. First they
would singe the hair in my armpits and on my chest, then proceed
to my abdomen, my pubic hair and the hair on my legs and finally
burn me up limb by limb in small but constantly renewed, inextinguishable flames. 'Today you shall be in paradise with me.' But
I declined nevertheless, took off and went to the Hudson Bar,
corner of Christopher and Washington Street, paid my own beer
this time but only had a sip, then hid the beer can behind the
music box. That way I would save 50 cents, should I happen to
come back. I didn't want to stay here either, although a law
student offered to lash me until I bled. That wasn't enough for me.
I wanted more, something different and didn't know what, and yet
I knew. Nor did I find any peace down by the Hudson River, as
much as I enjoyed the lights on the other side, and I again was
curious to know — I had never come here in the daytime — what
they might indicate, radiate, illuminate, signify. Were any factories there, any shipyards, or just freighters riding at anchor? But
that I could have ascertained, if I had really wanted to know. Be
that as it may, I stood around half-heartedly for an hour in front
of the open moving vans that were parked here every night, and
watched the men and young fellows who climbed in, jumped out
and left in a hurry, glancing nervously around, as if they were
afraid to get stricken. For an hour I watched, but that was not
what I wanted. It must have been close to daybreak. I was looking
for something else, but did not know what I wanted. And yet, I
knew exactly what I wanted, what I was headed for, what lured
me, as I went further and further up the West Side, Downtown.
'You got a cigarette?' That's what I wanted to hear; it was this
horribly banal question I was waiting for. I never carried cigarettes, undoubtedly to be prepared for the moment of decision, to
be ready and justified to say no and with that No pronounce the
longed-for sentence upon myself ('I was hungry, and you gave me
nothing to eat; I was thirsty, and you gave me nothing to drink; I
was naked, and you did not clothe me.') I had been eager to be

sentenced and had run around all night looking for a judgement. 'No, I never have cigarettes.' 'No? Just for that, take this!' Then a blow and a fierce pain. And there it was again, the glimmer of August 15th, 1797. Suddenly I knew that it was only this I had wanted to see once more: the flickering of the Grand Canal at the bow of the 'Virgo lacrimarum' which I had sought for more than a century and a half, had wanted and found in the Last Judgement and in the irrevocable sentence. The golden peacocks spread their tails on all the bridges in Venice, retracted them just to tease me, let their ocellated tails droop lamely at every landing, where the 'Virgo lacrimarum' tried to dock. 'No, I have no cigarettes; I never carry any.' 'All right, then take this!' They surrounded me, letting their motorcycles idle, since there was no point in turning them off.Somebody must have cigarettes. My trial did not detain them long; a kick in the shinbone, a blow and a stab, and once again the flickering of August 15th, 1797, but sharper, more precise; the glistening surface pierced by the impact of the ring, water shooting upward, wedding with the sea, sinking away in the light of the August sea. And the peacocks on the bridges, the 'Virgo lacri-marum,' the carpets with the golden tassels, and the mosaic sky of San Marcos, all of it was there and immediately forgotten again, this time forgotten for ever, submerged in the great motionless serenity of the inextinguishable light. 'No eye has seen it.' And the motorcycles started to howl as if they thought that I still cared to listen to them: I, the Doge Alvise Mocenigo, deprived of my Mithras, my gloves and my emerald ring removed, unrecognized and unknown to myself ever since I laid down my impotent dignity, since I unfolded the paper to announce and admit what had long been kept secret, the death of the republic; since I had stepped up to the window to read the proclamation and declaration of death in a loud voice aimed at the square and the tumultuous scene around the tree. As if I, the Doge Alvise Mocenigo, were still interested in hearing the motorcycles that were roaring away. After searching and wandering about for a long time, after many rides and walks between 8th Avenue and Bryant Park, after innumerable subway trips to the Village (sometimes I got off at 28th Street, other times I didn't, but after midnight I found it hard to resist the temptation), after countless night-hikes along the Hudson, Downtown and Uptown, I had found myself again; myself and the glimmering, the blinking light of August 15th, 1797." — Not the slightest trace of a reference to Doge Alvise Morenigo was to be discovered in the basement of the archive in Constantinople. The respective file must have been washed away by the waves of a big flood, unless it was, marred too badly by mildew and dampness, sorted out and, marked "Illegible," put aside in the hope that some day science would discover rays with which to revive the documents. Thus, it regrettably remains a moot question whether Alexius was identical with the Doge, or with the cat, or with both.

(Translated by John Frey)

WALTER VOGT

Walter Vogt

Born July 31, 1927, in Zurich, died September 21, 1988, in Muri. Studied medicine and psychiatry. Physician and psychiatrist in Muri/Bern. 1979 Writer-in-Residence, Max Kade Institute, USC. Member of PEN. Received several literary awards. Short stories, novels, poems, plays, essays: *Husten*, 1965; *Wüthrich*, 1966; *Höhenluft*, 1966; *Melancholie*, 1967; *Spiele der Macht*, 1971; *Der Wiesbadener Kongress*, 1972; *Briefe aus Marokko*, 1974; *Der Irre und sein Arzt*, 1974; *Die roten Tiere von Tsavo*, 1976; *Schizogorsk*, 1977; *Booms Ende*, 1979; *Vergessen und Erinnern*, 1980; *Altern*, 1981; *Metamorphosen*, 1984; *Maskenzwang*, 1985; *Die Betroffenen und andere*, 1988; *Schreiben als Krankheit und Therapie*, 1992; *Schock und Alltag*, 1993.

Aging

T uesday, December 26th

Reminiscent of the likewise horizontal, then, however, roaring, rising Southern California sun, of Corral Beach, where on three consecutive intense days in February I got my first sunburn. Concerned about my crab red skin, a young girl freed herself from her boyfriends hand and knelt down next to me, — I should cover myself, she implored me, *believe me*, otherwise I would burn my skin. I know my skin very well, knew, that it could still stand two or three hours; however, you cannot contradict such a young American girl, who touchingly shows such concern for an older man. I put on my shirt and froze.

Strange, how Los Angeles already exists for me out of a few, always similar scenes. Can hardly tell anything anymore without quoting myself. Still wearing the same worn out jeans from the clothing store in Santa Monica.

My favorite place soon became Venice Beach, the yellow beach directly in front of the last houses of the city of ten million, on the canal, in which the sail boats from Marina del Rey make their way to the ocean. Where you can watch how every twenty seconds a big jet takes off from Los Angeles International Airport. Where there is a black sea duck with a bright beak, that is called a Surf Scoter. Dive bombing brown pelicans. Flocks of small golden plovers, which follow the retreating surf in order to spear sand crabs in the wet sand, then scurry toward the shore in front of the returning wave. Only in an extreme emergency do they leap, crying and trilling, into the air for a few yards.

When I was sad, melancholic, lonely or simply in a bad mood, I would sit down in the sand for two or three hours, and everything was alright again.

Often I waited on Venice Beach for the sunset — here and there crouched a solitary, lonely figure in the sand and stared toward the west. It reminded me inevitably of Frank Kapra's wonderful happening from the crazy fifties, the golden sixties: Service of the Dead. In the protection of a concrete bunker, which didn't contain anything but public toilets, some girls and young men sunbathed in the nude. Nobody paid attention to them.

The most moving scene that I saw, here on my beach: A fifteen or sixteen year old boy with a guitar goes out, stands in the surf, plays with his head held off to the side, listens to his instrument and to the sea. Later his girlfriend comes. Both children sit down on a sand dune and study from a book.

Perhaps I should explain, why this scene struck such a special chord in me. My own children, when they were little, called that: *having my most beautiful life.*

The young man wanted simultaneously what was for him the best and the greatest: the guitar and the surf.

For a while such young men were sent to Vietnam.

Time and time again I wondered, without success, how such a monstrous apparatus could evolve from these kind people, who are a little scared of themselves. And wondered about a specific problem of American youth: their roots reach back historically to Europe, topographically to the Indians.

I couldn't speak about this with my students.

On the beach at Venice at the beginning of May, young men marked off a field, as if for some game. On small signs you could read what was going on: the nesting site of a small sea swallow (California Least Tern), which is protected under state and federal law. It impressed me that first of all the small terns actually started to nest inside of this marked off area, and secondly that one could obviously count on it, that a marked off area with explanatory signs would be respected not only by the few guests during the week but also by the weekend crowds on the beach.

[. . .]

Wednesday, December 27th

In Los Angeles there are these weather conditions, in which it is always hoped that they will *finally* pass by; change, it doesn't matter in which direction: desert climate, gloomy drizzle, red smog.

Los Angeles is a sickness, like malaria, every three days a rise in temperature, and always present, right under the thin skin of memory.

Why can't one speak rationally about this city?

Beauty cult.

The beautiful youth on the beaches, in the discos, completely natural, bred, not made.

Beauty cult for the dead: Forest Lawn

Fair swans on dark ponds — expressly declared as symbolic of the life's victory over death.

Porno addicted Hollywood Boulevard, between the 5000 and 8000 blocks. A few feet away the respectable middle-class in little houses.

Everything constantly hectic-nightmarish *and* of Southern Californian calmness. The disgust on the faces of the Celtic youth, when they have to touch something, have to *work*.

(They then do it anyway.)

The Beatles line You never give me your number, you only give me your situation from "Abbey Road," for the first time really understood in L.A.:

When somebody says, that he lives in Silver Lake, that in no way means he lives on Silver Lake Boulevard, and besides Silver Lake Boulevard is many miles long. On Hollywood Boulevard, with H.G., the young man from Munich, at night. Thoughtlessly I throw an empty pack of cigarettes out of the car.

Heh, here that costs five hundred dollars ...

(With this measure, they have actually gotten the streets in

California clean.)

Driving on: Heh, that was pretty red already!

OK, another five hundred dollars saved.

The traffic lights in the States hang or stand a little differently than what we are used to, confusing, in the beginning it is easy to run them.

Replay, slow motion: what for that complete silver laughing, silver fish glowing, golden-state-sparkling, ringing, tinkling, day and night, dreamy arousing bustle.

The twenty-four-hour-noise.

Everything, in order to overcome the *terrible emptiness* of the most widely spreadout city in the world, the horror of an *uninhabitable* landscape, which, at least for us, is without a history?

In this town you can travel hundreds of miles, overcoming huge differences in elevation, unnoticed, from somewhere to nowhere?

The dimensionless light of Los Angeles also contributes to it ...

Between ocean light and desert light lies the light of L.A., flat like a piece of paper; Canaletto light only as an exception, for minutes; *and* the flaming yellow of the sunset on the large boulevards, there, where the houses are low, the telephone poles high.

The citadel Downtown Los Angeles —

From my daughter's transistor radio comes: When I'm sixty-four ....

The golden sixties passed by, soon also the arduous seventies.

In five years and five days: New Year's Day 1984.

In 1984, the Summer Olympics *shall* be in Los Angeles ....

The citadel Downtown Los Angeles, one of the most beautiful city building complexes, seen from the Harbor-Hollywood Freeway, mostly at night, with the rhythm of the illuminated windows in the skyscraper complex.

The Chicanos though look up from the east out of their slums and holes onto the massive palaces of the Yankee divinity.

The same in San Francisco, once from Sausalito, once from the east. In L.A., even a skyscraper can stand lonely and abandoned, *mourning,* on a hill with little grass.

Good, on a golden late summer evening L. and I visited Tim and Rosemary Leary in Wallis. We drank a sour Waadtländer wine together. There is even photographic proof of it.

I wanted to see what somebody looks like after three, four hundred LSD-trips.

He looked like somebody after three, four hundred LSD-trips.

C. by chance met someone, who in a bar in Hollywood came to sit next to Bob Dylan, and who had gotten drunk together with him. Once I sat for an entire evening next to one of Dylan's guitar players, was so drunk, I believed I had understood *everything* from Dylan.

The next day, sober, *spaced*, I would have liked to know, *what* I had understood.

Nothing.

One certain spring evening, from Griffith Observatory in the Hollywood Hills: the entire expanse of the city already sunk in a blue dimmer. From the west the last rays of the sun illuminated only the highest building in Downtown L.A., the skyscraper of the United California Bank, UCB.

Glistening golden like an upright giant bar of fine gold, 999.9.

Like an Inca divinity image, says C.

We are silent for a long time over the darkening city; the boulevards, which blossom like rays from stars in neon light, the bank, which is sinking into darkness after glowing.

[...]

Saturday, December 30th

Probably one of my main difficulties in Los Angeles consisted in the fact, that I was unable to impress my stamp upon my apartment in the hotel in Santa Monica. For that, the rooms were too big, all too arbitrarily furnished. I, with my forty, forty four pounds of airplane luggage.

I simply could not do anything against it ....

After some weeks I was far enough, that upon waking up, the first thing I did was listen anxiously whether the car tires were driving over wet or dry streets.

Pacific rainy days, the most miserable thing one can imagine.

This city is not made for rain, said the Angelenos about their city. By the way, they never knew if they should say "city" or "town."

If the tires sounded dry, a bearable, probably pleasant day lay ahead of me. If the tires sounded wet, an unmeasurable, unrectifiable despair awaited me: a wet hotel patio, saggy palms, wet miscolored beach, possibly catastrophes.

And the angels of Los Angeles, sad, with wet hair.

Nobody leaves the house on rainy days in Los Angeles, unless he *has to*. And on the freeways something strange comes about during these Pacific cloud bursts — you move forward, uniformly, slowly, like a wet herd of lemmings, nobody hears anything, because you must close the windows, nobody sees anything, because the windshield, besides the rain, is smeared with the smog; you begin to *sense* each other — cars among cars, as if they had made themselves independent, self-sufficient remnants of a decayed civilization. That is how Los Angeles appeared to me on rainy days: like a city which had sunken into the ocean long ago ....

The *most moving* things were, in February, as the sun still dove into the open ocean, on clear days, the sunsets. The young Celts came down from the hills, out from their caves and holes, stared longingly to the west, where *their* sun was going down — in their wanderings, which had lasted two and a half thousand years, abruptly stopped for ever.

When the sunset was over, they freed themselves from the hypnotic rigidity which had overcome them, smiled like someone awakening, exchanged trivial words, disappeared into the oncoming darkness: *Wasn't the sunset great — !*

So I laid, half asleep, hyper-alert in my king sized bed. The bedroom didn't offer much space beside it: two nightstands, colonial style-imitation, flanked the bed, across from the foot of the bed a dresser drawer, likewise imitation; a large sliding glass door to the balcony, covered with heavy curtains. The balcony faced the south, was, however, covered by a large hardwood tree to such an extent that hardly a ray of sun could penetrate through. This tree was my first friend in Los Angeles. And from the balcony, I saw a bird on the lawn that I was able to identify: the robin, a thrush, a red breasted beautiful animal. Robin in German is called "little red throat" — and it allows insights into the immigrants, who gave the first red bellied bird they encountered this homesick name. On the north wall, a giant closet. My poor articles of clothing, my pitiful little pile of property didn't fill up *anything* in California, not even this one closet.

On one of the nightstands, some books — "Birds of North America," the first book that I bought. When I had it, I didn't feel so completely foreign anymore in L.A.

On the other nightstand, a blossoming branch in a water glass. On the dresser, a small Araukarie tree, bought in the afternoon on Easter Sunday, a hot, leaden day, in a supermarket out of desperation and loneliness.

On the dresser lay the large photo of L., black and white, 9 x 11.5, stuck in a A4 seethrough cover; the rolled up canvas that I had actually wanted to tack to the wall, but where do you get thumb tacks in L.A.? L. and the children, each had painted something for me on the canvas. One picture was always on top, from time to time I changed it.

Next door, the bathroom with shower and bath tub, in which you had to climb down into. Next to the hotel patio a kitchen with a large refrigerator, gas stove, sink. No dish washer. I hardly used the kitchen. My supplies consisted essentially of alcohol, fruit juices in small cans and plastic jugs, whiskey, incidentally in two litre bottles — cheese and crackers, bananas. California vodka. European wines, likewise from the supermarket, solely intended as party gifts, miserable by the way. It is said the flight over doesn't become them.

California burgundy I found, tastes like coated aspirin: first sweet, then sour, then bitter.

A large living room leading to the patio, with rectangular, dark

A large living room leading to the patio, with rectangular, dark wood furniture. When I had finally made up my mind to push the writing desk in front of the window, I felt better.

A likewise dark brown fold out couch of enormous dimensions, with a brown and white striped upholstery.

Television.

A green wall to wall carpet covers the floor — or do I just think so?

Dining nook jammed between the kitchen and bedroom-bath-room-unit, cheap furniture. On one of the dressers, the transistor radio that U. loaned me; as soon as I entered my apartment, I automatically turned it on.

The entire hotel gave the illusion of an ocean liner, with super-structure, masts, nets, ropes, life preservers — the doors to the apartments are like those of cabins. The blue kidney shaped swimming pool, yellow chaise lounges. Moss green artificial grass.

In Los Angeles, artificial grass is something so *natural* that one forgets to mention it in letters and texts. It is cleaned with a vacuum cleaner, is probably seen as hygienic — the sick health consciousness of the Americans alone would be worth an essay. Or their sick need for security, the mixture of paranoia and trustful-ness; I don't claim to have understood it. At night after eleven you had to ring the door bell and call out name and room number, even though the night porter saw you in the meantime through a cleverly placed mirror — only: the elevator from the open garage functioned without problems around the clock.

In one corner of the patio, a blooming red Bougainvillea.

In an orange tree on the patio was the hummingbird nest that supposedly should be there year after year. Two young birds left the nest during the first days of May. C. had seen them when they were still in the nest as he came to visit me and called it a *paradise-like condition*.

Often also cooing pigeons. On the roof of the hotel occasionally a mocking bird that sings like a nightingale.

Palms peeked over the roof into the patio.

Everything is huge in L.A.

Even the imported palms are larger than in Africa.

(Beside fan palms, which you naturally don't see in Los Angeles, all the other palms have been imported. Fifty-seven types of eucalyptus, too, you read.)

The manager or one of her more or less helpless helpers stands at the counter in the lobby. There were always new difficulties with my cash and travellers checks or the opening of the safe. If there was a letter in my box, they said: They still love you.

On the promenade in front of the hotel under eucalyptus and palms blackbirds: similar to African starlings; imported European sparrows; European starlings; Southern California sparrows, which are much more beautiful than the imported house sparrows; whistling squirrels in the bluff, the steep slope on the ocean — and in February still, almost tame enough to touch, a wonderful dark sea gull, Heermann's Gull, which later disappeared from the coast and sought out Pacific islands for breeding.

During the first days the birds still meant something to me, could be, I saw in them my only friends in the foreign city; later they became *too Pacific* for me, too uniform, too foreign — and: I couldn't come up with their German names.

One of the cutest scenes from the bird life: A pair of swifts while mating spun down out of the sky to the Colorado River, on Hoover Dam — like a bouquet of flowers sinking in a spiral, blackish blue and white, trilling and crying, in the weird desert daylight.

Oh, in the beginning I hated my small hotel. There were only long term guests, financially secure retirees. The men sat rigidly in their chairs, an open newspaper in their hand, in front of the flickering TV screen. The women waited on them. Kitchen smells penetrated insipidly and vomit stimulating into the patio. Over Easter, the first hoards of young surfers descended upon the hotel, the children of rich parents, and from then on the hotel swelled over with young people.

C. felt more at ease by the pool than at the beach: There wasn't any flying sand in the hotel patio.

Breakfast in a gloomy, damp small room underneath the artificial grass by the pool, called the Galley; horrible instant coffee with equally horrible powdered milk, sugar, odor- and tasteless jelly, toast with margarine. South American women served; you meet fewer Chicanos from East Los Angeles in the hotels. In the beginning, I had tried to at least do some small journalistic work, texts for my students about Los Angeles, later the city was stronger than I: I expired.

Next to Los Angeles in its enticing strangeness, the East Coast, New York, seemed somewhat European and *very aged.*

Alfred and Regina Jensens, Glen Ridge, NJ: My God, what a gigantic "Muri"; under dripping trees, in full green grass — small wood houses, small gardens: nothing left of the California flashiness.

Oppressive, damp-fertile May.

(Could be that one day the Rockies will prove to be the more significant dividing line than the Atlantic, as it is with the Sahara and the Mediterranean.)

In the attic of one of these middle-class houses Al Jensens' studio: a lot of light from a large sky light, still far too little room for his panels, which stand stacked on the walls. Some covered all over with numbers, silent witnesses of a spiritual process, of a strange mathematical investigation of the world.

Two of these pictures fall completely out of context. In the square landscape of Jensens' mature work, the profile of a girl on the one, of a boy on the other picture. Both have little wings on their shoulders like ancient heroes, which upon closer inspection are more like the little speech bubbles in comic strips, which rise from the young bodies; for the boy heroic, for the girl domestic words.

Al gave his metamathematical, for me completely unintelligible, explanations to his pictures. The erotic force of both of these ephebus bodies, it seemed to me, he didn't notice. He once again seemed to me like a retired, high ranking Danish civil servant, who grows his own vegetables and paints more *inwardly.*

After three days of Glen Ridge and New York, Regina took me, completely drunk from the fare-well-whiskey, to Kennedy Airport.

I needed weeks until I felt at home again, it finally happened in summer at the Murtensee. I dove into activities, negotiated with publishing houses, wrote about Los Angeles and God and the world, reluctantly came to terms with certain aspects of the Swiss cultural scene — felt worn out *and* filled to the brim with bits of memories of Southern Californian gold. My *body*, however, it seems, experienced its return home: during the whole three and half months, it had never gotten used to the time zone in Los Angeles.

(Translated by John W. Arensmeyer Jr.)

URS WIDMER

URS WIDMER

Born May 21, 1938 in Basel. Studied German and French literature and history. For several years editor for publishers. 1984 Writer-in-Residence, Max Kade Institute, USC. Member of PEN. Many literary awards. Lives in Zürich. Short stories, novels, plays, essays: *Alois*, 1968; *Die Amsel im Regen im Garten*, 1971; *Das Normale und die Sehnsucht*, 1972; *Die lange Nacht der Detektive*, 1973; *Die Forschungsreise*, 1974; *Schweizer Geschichten*, 1975; *Vom Fenster meines Hauses*, 1977; *Züst oder der Aufschneider*, 1979; *Das enge Land*, 1981; *Liebesnacht*, 1982; *Indianersommer*, 1985; *Der Kongreß der Paläolepidopterologen*, 1989; *Der blaue Siphon*, 1992; *Jeanmaire*, 1992.

In America

(Introduction)

I wrote this text in 1971, in a time that today seems very distant to me. Back then, in Europe at least, there appeared to be a period of political change, and even in texts that had no direct political objectives, there was often a feeling of carelessness and optimism that up until then would have been credited more likely to the Americans, and would also have sometimes been associated with the "pop-art" concept. Indeed, "In America" was, in all innocence and without program, such a "pop-art" text. Today, it certainly does not matter whether it is or was that or something else. I have, however, rediscovered and reread it with some enjoyment, and since it fits in exactly with this collection, it will once again see the world, the American one this time, of which it also speaks, or at least tries to.

(1)

So this is America. So here I come in my blue overalls. America's train station is enormous, and the bullets whiz over my head. In America, the people have quicker reactions than we do in the high mountains. I go into America's bar. I order red wine. The ice clump floats in it. America is a good country, says the Sheriff on the barstool next to me, big and flat and brave. I know my way around America right away, I also want to grow a crew cut and broad shoulders. Over there sits a girl with skin like snow, hair like ebony, and lips like two pieces of sugar. Could you, I say to the bar tender and slide a dollar bill over the counter, write down the telephone number of that girl there on this slip of paper. He grows pale as death, hurriedly pockets the dollar, and his hand shakes more than a little.

(2)

Well, I think, one lifetime is not enough to describe what it is like in America. For instance, Joe Bananas sets his machine-gun to single-fire when he meets a car with Negroes so that he can get more out of the whole thing.

(3)

I could, I think, call up a lady in lonesome America and say words like fuck and screw into the receiver. I wait for how the lady reacts when I say words like fuck and screw. Sometimes, the lady hangs up right away when she hears words like fuck and screw from the receiver, sometimes she listens quietly, and I, as I am saying fuck and screw, hear how the lady listens to fuck and screw, and pants. Some ladies also say fuck and screw to me. I can call them again the next day in lonesome America and say new words to them that I have made up in the meantime. Other ladies only pretend to want to hear, as I, standing in a lonesome telephone booth, say fuck and screw to them, at the same time they are dialing the nearest police station on the second phone that they have and are saying, Sergeant, there is a man on the telephone who is saying words that I cannot repeat to you. It is the long-searched-for pervert, says the Sergeant. The call comes from Oak Park, but the mysterious caller has already left the telephone booth. In the brightness of the headlight, the police see through the open door the torn-off receiver lying on the floor. Once again, the pervert that is terrorizing America has escaped. But one day, the Sergeant knows, he will catch the guy, and then America's women will be able to sleep in peace again.

(4)

When Mr. D. Gottlieb and I walk into an American joint, the Negroes and Chinese jump back from the pinball machine and let the balls roll where they will. Mr. D. Gottlieb and I hang our suit jackets on a hook, Mr. D. Gottlieb wears red suspenders and I carry two Brownings in a shoulder holster. I play the first ball. Ahh, shout the Negroes and Chinese. A round for the whole gang, I shout, it's Prohibition and we're drinking hundred proof booze from coffee cups. Would you like to play a game of imaginary chess as well, says Mr. D. Gottlieb to me as he plays his first ball? O.K., I say, take it. C2-c4, says Mr. D. Gottlieb. I see, I say and flip my second ball up, e7-e6. D2-d4, says Mr. D. Gottlieb very quietly and comes to 2,397 points with his second ball in play. I see, famous opening, I say, shooting the cigar out of my friend Chris Ventura's mouth for fun while I flip up my third ball in play and move Sg8-f6 in my head. Mr. D. Gottlieb lets a silver dollar spin like a top on the glass, moves Lc1-g5 on the board in his head and wins a freeplay. Tf8-f6, I whisper, uncork a whisky bottle with my teeth, flip my fourth ball in play into the "special when lit," and yell 2,000 on red, 1,000 on odd before the croupier at the next table can say "Rien ne va plus." Mr. D. Gottlieb, as he nails the five hundred with his fourth ball in play and plays castles in his head, asks with his eyes the blonde girl standing at the bar behind me if she will go with him afterwards. I let a Chinaman stuff the winnings into my pocket, finally get my freeplay with my last ball in play, and with my eyes say to the blonde girl, as I give the Chinaman a drop-kick to the knees for short changing me a ten-spot when he stuffed my pockets, that Mr. D. Gottlieb may be a good player but was for sure a bad lover and that after I deal the opposing King its death blow with Sd6-d4, I would show her something much better, since I came from the high mountains and Mr. D. Gottlieb was only a third generation from Dusseldorf. That's it, I say, let's go, and leave with the blonde girl, who had understood everything I said with my eyes, while Mr. D. Gottlieb still has to pay for the round of drinks for the Negroes and Chinese.

(5)

I have done myself up for Jane and am holding a red rose in my hand for Jane. I step carefully through the revolving door of America's bar and am wearing an elegant mustache where I normally do not wear an elegant mustache, and mother-of-pearl colored pants where I normally wear gray pants with a fishbone pattern. I do not recognize Jane. There where Jane has long black hair, she has long blonde hair. There where she has doe-brown eyes, she wears dark sunglasses, there where she wears a bra under her light blouse, she wears no bra under her light blouse. She signals me discreetly with her little finger and for a fraction of a second takes off the dark sunglasses. She is not Jane at all. Her name is Daisy. Say darling to me, says Daisy to me. Darling, I say.

(6)

I see my future in America before me as clear as glass, you see. First I am a good-humored shoeshine boy, then I am a fast newsboy, then I am a trustworthy security guard at the Chase Manhattan Bank, then I am noticed by the wife of Mr. Henry Rockefeller who is in the bank withdrawing a portion of her dollar empire. Then I run an errand for her to her complete satisfaction. Then, Mr. Henry Rockefeller entrusts me with the custody of a portion of his dollar empire. Then I will be invited more and more often to Mr. and Mrs. Rockefeller's for dinner. I am a basically descent fellow. In the morning, after Mr. Henry Rockefeller has gone to the office, I still get to join Mrs. Rockefeller for a little in the double bed. After his unexpected death, Al Capone will leave me $97,000, 2 quarters, 12 dimes, 7 nickels, and 9 cents, I say to Jane.

(7)

In America, I need men and no cowards. I can tell instantly with whom I can deal. With me, you make it the first time, or you don't make it at all. People with clammy hands don't stand a chance with me. I take only top people. I am a master of bribery, I don't just slip a hundred bucks over the table. With me, the other guy's in it before he even knows it. Every complaint goes to my sottocapo, from there to the capo, from there to the general, from there to me. If a complaint gets all the way to me, then its bad news for the guy.

(8)

Well, I say in America, in Sicily I go into a restaurant without a woman so that I can talk about women. In Germany, I go into a restaurant ahead of a woman because I want the better seat. In America, I go into a restaurant behind a woman because I need her to shield me from bullets.

(9)

In America, the murderers are hanged. The execution takes place one minute after midnight. The man who is to be hanged receives his suit, his shirt, and his tie a half an hour before the beginning of the execution so that the man who is to be hanged has time to change. If two murderers are to be hanged, they must decide between themselves who is to be hanged first. If the two men who are to be hanged cannot decide between themselves who is to be hanged first, the prison priest must flip a coin to determine which of the two men to be hanged will be first to be hanged. The prison priest urges them both to decide between themselves, as it makes no difference whether they are to be the first to be hanged or to be the second to be hanged. The murderers are happy about their last meal. The first murderer stands in his blue overalls over the trap door, the hangman slips the noose around the neck from which the murderer is to be hanged, and now he gives the horse a slap in the rear, and already the man hangs.

They are now hanging all ten of them from America's only tree. The citizens of America are happy that the notorious gang is finally silenced. The bandits have their hands tied behind their backs and look like large, black apples on the horizon, now that the sun is sinking blood-red behind the prairie.

(10)

Bee poker is played by the castaways in America. The castaways in America can only save one bee and two pieces of sugar. The winnings of the castaway in America is the wife of the other. The one castaway in America must say to the other, my wife, whose

name is Jane, is delightfully racy, so that the winner has something to win. She has red lace panties, her hair is like ebony, her
skin is like snow, and her lips are like two pieces of sugar. The
lonesomeness of the sailor in America, you see, is hard to endure.

(Translated by Tom Schnauber)

GERTRUD WILKER

Gertrud Wilker

Born March 18, 1924, in Solothurn, died September 19, 1984, in Bern. Studied German philology and literature. Lived for two years in the US. Short stories, novels, poems, essays: *Der Drachen. Ein Gespräch*, 1959; *Elegie auf die Zukunft*, 1966; *Collages USA. Ein Bericht*, 1968; *Einen Vater aus Wörtern machen*, 1970; *Altläger bei kleinem Feuer*, 1971; *Jota*, 1973; *Blick auf meinesgleichen*, 1979; *Nachleben*, 1980; *Leute ich lebe*, 1983; *Zwölf Ansichten des Fujiama*, 1985.

Flashbacks

Two years. That is a long string of days. Two years "over there," in the language of the initiated, "I, too, was a couple years over there." How was it? The way you feel when you sojourn in a foreign country, indefinite, eager, observant, questioning. Storming in, uninitiated, trying to find out what is what, yet fully determined not to be taken in like any greenhorn 'just off the boat.' Not I. I was sincerely determined that this arrogant "Stars and Stripes Forever" hoopla would not get to me. I was fortified by my dedication to European values: *Europe, je maintiendrai.*

(Six hours from Zurich to New York, flying against the sun, over billowing clouds, in solitude, the airplane pursuing its course over the ocean with the certainty of fate. Newfoundland coming up, a brown landscape of craters, with patches of snow, uninhabited, empty, desolate. And then, one hour later, the hustle and bustle of New York. One hour later, America.

Heat, different time, taxi drivers, glass everywhere; women decked out in black hats and gloves, ice tea, popcorn, apes, smoke, Negro women tending toilets — is that America?

Everything different: the money, the language, but where is it, this America? Is it the soldier lounging about in uniform, gum under the tongue, or the machines dispensing Coca-Cola? Or the Bermuda shorts going to the knee? Justice? Liberty hewn in stone, with torch held high? Is that it?

And hamburgers, Budweiser beer in cans, neon lights advertising DuPont nylon stockings — is that the real America?

Three more hours in the air and we make Kansas City, a place as far from the Atlantic as from the Pacific, as far from Canada as from the Gulf of Mexico. That must be it, we thought, the center piece of America.)

The comparison between "over there" and "here" was quite troubling upon the first impression and remained troubling throughout. To be sure, there are differences between Europe and the U.S.A., but they converge. They do not collide. They are mere nuances. And I would have been happy to find columns of fire or some such impenetrable thing to separate us from America, — not these flimsy, ambiguous, irrelevant variations of a common theme underlying human existence. What scared me from the first day was this family resemblance in the appearance of here and there. Such common features are readily explained on historic grounds. Yet, it is embarrassing to find that the transplanted offspring of the old continent is so much more robust than the ancestor and has made its way in the world so much more successfully.

For two years, waking as well as dreaming, I did not succeed in shaking the feeling of not being at home in America. Every word I used was a translation. Everything represented something. I was not a member of, or an aspirant to anything, just a hitchhiker by the roadside packed up for the ride. That, to be sure, is not a bad condition, as the obligations going with such transient involvement are, accordingly, transient. It avoids the need for sincerely felt responses to events perceived by others as national calamities, or successes, or as mere nuisances. One lives in the inchoate phase of the awe attending the practice of freedom in liberty, enjoying the freedom without paying its price. I made sure of not being drawn in, pleading that I was otherwise committed, "otherwise" being hastily subsumed under the notion of "homeland" and the requisite set of plausible emotions.

Where did I come from? — the land of alpine passes, watersheds, the heartland of an overcrowded continent, the land of tree lines, industrial villages, dammed rivers producing electricity; the land that welcomes guests, jealously guards the secrecy of bank accounts, boasts of its citizen soldiers, cantons, municipalities, its Confederation — and what does all that mean to the American? "Switzerland," he asks, "then you live in Stockholm?" For him, I come from a part of the Europe that is semi-real, like the landscape of a fairytale, bedeviled by all sorts of incomprehensible notions of division into parts defined upon nebulous histories by unnecessary borders which defy American understanding and thus, understandably justify American reluctance even to try to understand. The result is a curious inversion: As America is urged on by the compulsion of political and historic obligations toward the old world, American strains avoid emotional involvement. It is willing to go for broke in business, but avoids the risk of disappointment in emotional commitment. America pumps dollars into Europe to pay off devout gratitudes and to pare the relationship back to the realities of economic and military agreements. This is the way America sees Europe: A place to conduct military maneuvers, a business competitor, a stock exchange, a buffer against the Russian block, a pawn between the panic horror of communism and the Western perception of a freedom that has been reduced to the ideal skeleton, without blood and muscle.

The question is whether they, on the other side, have the wrong perception of the old world, entirely removed from its reality? Are we indeed much more than a pawn in the ideological struggle and a business competitor? Are we indeed resolved to execute in Europe a destiny other than what they, over there, expect of us? Are we more than dutiful customers of American mass products, more than enthusiastic victims of their advertising, of their market research, more than well-paid lackeys of a philosophy of human freedom pumped up with Christian pretense? Now really, can't we do better than turn handsprings before a philosophy of freedom that does not even motivate us to reduce our business connections with the Russian satellites? We deliver what we are paid for. Are there any in present-day Europe, who can be said to conduct themselves with the dignity holding out the promise that their souls are not for sale, that they might indeed be willing to die for the ideals they profess? As a matter of fact, there are more people of such quality in Europe than America expects, but no one is writing about them. We no longer serve as the Alma Mater from whom new insights, new impulses and moral authorities emanate for the guidance of the remaining world. But do we insist that we are to be regarded leaders on account of traditions which, though once won with blood and tears, now constitute our sacred treasure which we must guard? Fate has placed us in an advance position, but do we find it worth maintaining? As things are now, have we not allowed ourselves to be separated from one another into ideological, economic, political blocks, thus arriving where Robinson Jeffers sees us, when he says:

> I have seen the United States grow up the
> strongest and wealthiest
> of nations, and swim in the wind over bankruptcy.
> I have seen Europe, for twenty-five hundred years
> the crown of the world
> become its beggar and cripple.

What really troubled me about America is the fact that what appears to me as its public character is reflected in our conduct as Europeans. That is the deplorable thing from which I like to distance myself.

I am offended by this mass of mediocrity, defined by carefully groomed reports by Gallup and Kinsey, its banal ideals (I want to be like everybody else), its better business ethic, the progress through investment philosophy, the hype (education is your bank account).

We, in Europe, have not only become a branch, a subsidiary, an offshoot of the new world, but our self-esteem is even raised by that fact, when we should deplore having become American lackeys.

For two years, I have made shift, living free like a bird, waiting for the blessing of the shock attending my return into the bondage of my home and, where again I could be obligated, involved, a citizen, a member, a concerned constituent.

(Translated by Sandra and Ewald Schlachter)

Parting Between Window Frames

Good-bye to Lawrence. It has been ten months now since my arrival, and I still have not come to terms with this place. Yet, I am parting as a friend. I am parting from the dried lawn of our backyard as it lies in the heat of June, parched and brown. Parting from the trees, the mimosa and the American beech that gave us a thin shadow during the day and the rustling of leaves at night. In spring, a cardinal perched in its high branches and entertained us with songs that evoked memories of the European ouzel with its twittering. In winter, gray squirrels chased one another vertically up and down the trunk, for hours on end.

I am parting from the view of our neighbor's house in its snowy whitewash and from the neighbor herself. One evening, a few days after we arrived, she showed up in our kitchen, uninvited, and handed me a giant tomato.

"Hello," she said, "I am your neighbor; just call me Bunny, if you don't mind. And I sure hope you will like the folks around here." A few weeks ago, a little tornado brushed by and knocked her TV antenna into our tulip bed. It is still lying there. The dogs sniff around its spikes and raise their legs against it now and then. I am parting from the sad view of our back alley. From my bedroom window, I look into an alley, one of those characteristically American back alleys: dirt, dust, rocks, lined with tall garbage cans of aluminum from which dogs drag their delicacies; crushed butter cartons, Pepsi bottle tops, assorted scraps of meat, vegetable peelings, rotted melons, plastic cups, and whatnot. Once we had to call a tow truck to pull our Ford out of the holes the wheels had dug into the ground that had been softened by a sudden thunderstorm. There is no pavement to keep the right-of-way passable when it rains.

Every city in the Midwest has such back alleys. They are crisscrossed by ugly wires; here and there a pipe sticking out of a building gives off puffs of steam. Everyone dumps in his back alley the refuse that would detract from the contrived nicety of the front side. Restaurants, stores, factories discharge liquid waste, solid waste, vent their air conditioners. The back alley readily accepts everything, dead birds, skunks, and rats. The back alley is an open garbage can, the open grave for the refuse of daily life, a museum of conspicuous consumption. A trite history is recorded in the deposits on the back alleys, layer upon layer.

I look through my bedroom window to take leave of the lighted advertising boards: "Light and Power Company," "Allstate Insurance," and "Standard Oil," flicker throughout the night in many shades of red, and cannot be kept out even by the closed Venetian blinds. There is the rusted fire escape of the three-story apartment house in which children are left to cry for hours on end; and the same children then get even with their parents by locking their dog into a wooden shed where he whines for hours. I look over the multi-colored roofs of the houses in the neighborhood and remember that winter morning on which I, bedridden, had drawn the drapes to find everything shrouded in freshly fallen snow, everything clean and new, the roofs, the crisscrossed cables, even the rubbish looked clean; and the freshness of the scene paradoxically accentuated by the noisy garbage truck and its Negro crew on scheduled rounds. My eyes take leave of the tiny house across the street from our kitchen porch from which music and the voices of men drifted across the alley every night in the summer. But for the laundry on the plastic line, it seemed deserted during the day. We never discovered when the red panties, black brassieres, colored wash rags and bathroom towels, petticoats with fancy lace appliqués and gaudy rose designs were hung or taken down. A few times, I saw two Negro women, young and quite beautiful, drive up in a taxi, walk up to the house, open the door and casually walk in.

I take leave quite easily, even though I have used up almost one year of my life in this place. That one year passes through my mind as I look through the windows. One year with nearly unbearably hot and humid days in the summer and dust that permeated everything and accumulated even under the beds. I recall the events of this year in order to implant them into my memory. There was the ocherous yellow of the leaves of the beech tree that turned in fall, a strangely incongruent splash of lively color, like Sunday's best dress, pristine amid the tired drabness of the familiar surroundings. As I stand here, straining to remember details precisely, I become aware of the blending of images whereby this neighborhood came to be a familiar place. I do not know when this blending started; it must have been when I got tired of my initial touchiness in reacting to every one of the many strange images that challenged me. Everything was new and strange: the language, the food, the temperature, the toilet paper, radio and newspapers; habits in the use of water, the way letterhead and envelopes are printed, the deskside manner of pediatricians. This touchiness was without any substantive significance, an irrational resentment of a different way of doing things that arrogated the place of the accustomed way which I had left behind and, thus, lost. And, indeed, I would have been hard pressed to state precisely what I had lost. But the feeling of loss was there and it lingered for a few weeks, until I came to understand what was happening within me. I had just sat down one day to read the newspaper, when, turning the page, I saw this eye catcher in the advertisement of a travel agency — a view of Zermatt against the silhouette of the Matterhorn; carefully prepared with all effective ingredients, the chalet on piers above a rippling brook in Valais, a generous helping of gentian and dandelions in living color. It was the Swiss counterpart of the "Oh, Shenandoaaah, I long to heeear you ...." The typical, absolutely blatant kitsch. I broke down in tears, spontaneously. (I could hardly believe it myself.) That picture, that banal contrivance of a cunning promoter laid bare the wound: I suffered from a bad case of homesickness, ached for ..., well, for what? Not for the Alps of Valais, but for mountains, "mountain views and sylvan fragrance," as the poet puts it. That promotional device had triggered genuine emotional substance transcending the cliché. It was a yearning for intimate contact with nature, with the landscape, lush vegetation, a horizon with cloudy character; it was a longing for the coniferous forest, the boisterous brook, hay on the meadow, stacks of firewood, indeed even for the fragrance wafting from the manure pile behind the barn; I longed for the archetypal landscape showing European cultivation of the land.

To what extent such elemental undercurrents affect the physical functions is hard to judge. They may very well explain a certain hostility vis-a-vis just about everything within the broad category of the typically American.

But that pent-up emotion manifesting itself in the attack of homesickness vanished. It was gone one night in December.

We were returning from Kansas City. I sat in the back seat with the sleeping children and looked out onto the wet road. Our headlights scanned the oncoming roadside. I knew the route and anticipated its features, the curve before the exit to the toll road. There was the toll gate. We slowed down to pay the road toll. The toll taker pushed his window up: "Hi, pretty cold outside — everything O.K.?" He took the 60 cent toll. It was all so familiar, that man and his routine inquiry. Another five minutes and we would be home. Home? Yes, home. The idea came quite naturally to me. Home in Lawrence, Kansas, where we were making a living on our sojourn in the United States. Home was the roof over our heads, a place of security, where I knew the folks, the milkman, the Negro behind the counter in the post office, the girl who tended the tables in the pizza palace, the neighbors and their children, dogs and cats. We called the mailman by his first name. Yes, that earlier feeling of longing for some other place had dissolved.

Indeed. But what had taken its place? The relationship to the new place and its people? Honestly, I had not warmed up to the folks of Lawrence. There was a definite sense of distance toward the people, the lifestyle, the city. But, then, warmth was not wanted. Yet, there certainly was something unique. There was a feeling of ease in dealing with people. I did not seek close contact with anyone and no one came too close for my comfort.

Freedom of the person — I have never experienced and cherished it as during these ten months. I was free to resort to the comforts of my own resources, my personal collective past. I did not owe anyone for the experiences and insights of my past which constituted the emotional capital that sustained me. I did not owe anything to anyone for friendship or social advancement. And the circumstances of my current existence afforded me nothing but an opportunity to engage, or not engage myself, as much or as little, as might please me.

When I try to imagine a lucky break a person of forty can enjoy without reservation, then I must think of the opportunity to savor the happiness of such unconstrained relationship to the world to augment the satisfactions arising from the inner constraints which define identity. To be sure, such luck is precarious in its dependence on isolation, but every person ought to have the opportunity to cherish it, at some juncture in life — this heady satisfaction of personally experiencing that unique stock of emotional and intellectual substance capital which makes an individual whole upon these unique resources.

Writing in my own language, my mother tongue, illustrates that point. Everyone around me spoke, read and thought American. However, I had my German language all to myself and, because of this isolation, I learned it again, now not merely as a means of communication, but as the mirror image of my share of life, as the guardian of my identity. My language gave me my name, a linguistically defined principle, as the distinguishing token of my separate existence within this strange world. I became aware, as hardly every before, that the life that passes from my language is my very own against the background of the whole world, filled as it be with other people.

The individual words cast shadows, possess an aura and evoke an echo. I was sensitized as never before to its rhythm and tonal qualities, its fragility, its overtones and undertones, its effective range. The individual words embody the essence of the being of the language. Words could inspire or have absolutely no effect, they could attract or provoke a defensive attitude. I became quite selective. Some words became my protégés, because I understood the problematic of their meaning and cherished it like the sudden discovery of the secret of a strange life.

I developed a particular affinity for the word *Wehmut*. I rediscovered it quite accidentally when Goethe's *Wonne der Wehmut* was mentioned in a context that emphasized the dampness of the original setting *Trocknet nicht, trocknet nicht, Tränen der ewigen Liebe* (which might be translated "Don't dry, tears of eternal love, don't dry"). I appreciated the turgid symbolism, pointing into two directions thinly veiled in the guise of tender mourning. There are actually two monosyllabic words joined, each poignantly clear in its demand for exclusive attention: "Weh" and "Mut." Their combination produces a hermeneutic, rhythmically trochaic hybrid of an import which is unique to German. There is no equivalent in the English language, not in the form of a word, nor in the form of a concept. "Sadness" points in the general direction, but does not strike the essence. "Wistfulness" does not do it, nor "melancholy." There is an element in it of "sorrow" and "brave endurance." An element of "ambivalence" must be added. The solemnity of the occasion fuses the otherwise irreconcilable elements into a clear, emotionally trenchant concept.

I bid goodbye, leaving behind what I could not reach to incorporate into my being. I do not have regrets, because I take with me what is mine to keep and preserve. I leave behind what escaped my grasp — the secret that is America. I have no roots here, no obligations, nothing to tie me down or hinder my departure from Lawrence. I am free for whatever is waiting for me.

The highway to California stretches out ahead of us.

(Translated by Sandra and Ewald Schlachter)

UELI ZINGG

Ueli Zingg

Born April 15, 1945 in Bern. Teacher for media sciences and German. Lived in the United States and France. Lives in Bern. Novels, essays, documentary films: *Zwischenstand*, 1980; *Vision America*, 1981; *Wörterkasper*, 1983; *Huser*, 1985; *Sterbenswörtchen*, 1989.

Interim Report

What is your purpose for coming to the United States? The colored customs lady will ask him while examining his passport at the airport.

A woman was shot dead on the same afternoon at Kennedy International. The police sealed off the area HERMETICALLY. But he will land earlier and read the next day in the newspaper that the young murderer DREAMED he had to kill the woman. He had not known her.

He will not understand the customs lady at first and will give a perhaps typical answer: We come from Switzerland. She will repeat her question. With emphasis. His answer will this time be the RIGHT one: He is here to take a vacation. To visit museums and galleries. To meet a married couple, primarily acquainted with his mother. To speak English. To get away from the stress of the university. To recover from the strains connected with his dissertation.

With that the prejudice from home is from the outset unpleasantly confirmed: NYC, the city in which one can be shot to death without apparent motive. His wife will say that she did not come here to get shot. He will laugh, but nevertheless be shaken: by the fact that a woman was shot to death in the very place where a few hours earlier he stepped onto American soil for the first time; he will attribute this emotion to his weariness, and that his wife gave voice to her fear of such a death.

The "Maiskolben" they like to eat so much are called COB. The "Kamm" he inadvertently did not bring is called COMB.

Many times on the street he will think for a second that people want to speak to him, but will soon get used to the fact that it is not uncommon for people in this city to talk softly to themselves in public, so completely occupied with themselves are they. Already by the second day, a security guard in the Museum of Modern Art can thus no longer surprise him: The black is always making, *it will bother him that his wife points to the NEGRO*, the same swinging motion with his right hand, in intervals of seconds, at the height of his head, moves at the same time through the crowd as if he did not see them, without, however, running into anyone. F will be fascinated by the recurring monotony of this course of movement, and he will be reminded of POLAR BEARS.

If F by chance visits this museum on a Tuesday, *he likes the Calder in the Art Museum in Zurich better,* he must decide himself how much admission he will pay. On all other days the price is fixed: two dollars. Only on Tuesday is it left up to the discretion of visitors. He will not care much for this situation. The exhibition is naturally worth more than two dollars to him, but everyone in line in front of him, as far as he can see, gives less. He will stick to the amount applicable on all other days. It could surprise him that the cashier thanks him for that. *He was told before his departure that people in NYC are impolite. He will be able to convince himself of the contrary.*

"Hilfsbereit" means HELPFUL.

In an air-conditioned bar he suspects that there are no unair-conditioned ones. In the course of an early evening drink, the name of which he never heard before and which he forgets again immediately after ordering, an American will ask him whether he likes it here. For an almost rude length of time he will not answer the question, because he considers it unanswerable in this form. Finally he will try to explain: What does he mean, living here, here on vacation, here with cultural interests, here because of climate ...? Here, just the way he's here now, will be given him as answer: Well, in that case he likes it here. A coherent conversation does not come about as a result of this.

He had always wanted to sleep with a black woman. But does NOT do it DURING THESE DAYS because he does not want to buy himself this favor.

Rather accidentally, he will notice that a sightseeing agency has an office not far from his hotel. He decides, a little also on account of urging from his wife, *he is unusually inclined to listen to her during these days,* to take a tour through Upper Manhattan. During this tour it becomes all too clear to him why his vacations become increasingly shorter. The planned three weeks, *a trip overseas must be WORTH it,* are already really too long for him. The illusion of NYC was perhaps better than the reality of NYC anyway. A group from Ohio is along: MOSLEM MEMBERSHIP RELATION is written on their fezzes with glass beads. They are probably sewn on, glued on they would move less. All robust people. Sturdy too in their inner conviction, it seems to him. Only that way can he explain to himself this loud outer certainty. After a stop one of them comes back with five cans of beer, starts to distribute them to other fezwearers. Someone declines. TWO FOR ME, the beer-bringer laughs. Quite unexpectedly he looks at F; Want a beer you, guy? F likes beer, is also thirsty, but will decline. A conversation does not develop here either. The Moslem will want to know further where he comes from. I am Swiss-German he will understand as GERMANY and grinning very broadly say JA — JA. Afterwards he tells a joke about his wife, as far as F can tell. The wife waves it off and indicates that it IS NOT LIKE THAT.

The bus passes through Harlem. Here then a potential source of aggression. The people he can see through the tinted window-pane during the trip appear peaceful. There, an elderly White in the midst of Blacks. Chatting. Some very beautiful young people. Black is beautiful originated here as a slogan, the tour guide says. Judging from the reactions in the bus, he can be very funny. *Later: Big Henry Kissinger graduated from high school here. But the most famous man now living went to school here, too. Timy Times. Silence. He's right in front of you. Howling laughter.* And there "Westside Story" was filmed. Here, this very square was used in it. F finds the situation more and more unpleasant. He will not find here the otherness he has been seeking. Nothing is really new. His own cultural environment is merely presented to him in concentrated form. The advantage over Europe in all that is temporally manifest in this kind of civilization becomes increasingly smaller. *What one sees in the great museums of Paris and Rome are copies of what hangs as an original here in the Frick Collection. We are ALWAYS the first to create something new. The others imitate us. Americans and those overseas.* Here F is the one overseas. A banality that he becomes conscious of during the commentaries of the tour guide. *Consider the concentration of different art forms in Lincoln Center. Other cities have begun in just the last few years to take on a comfortable appearance, in the way we realized it in Rockefeller Center in the thirties.*

F will take pleasure this evening in his steak and the huge sour cream potato. In the cheap self-service restaurant on 49th Street. He will be particularly pleased that this simple pleasure can bring him pleasure. After the meal he will probably also desire, as far as it is linguistically possible for him, to swear in American.

Perhaps already on the next day: Fifth Avenue, St. Patrick's Cathedral, funeral ceremonies. Only partly understood: A priest has died, Brother George. Or is BROTHER meant symbolically? Numerous priests are present, take part in the rites, have their particular roles. Stand up. Step forward. Step back. Sit down. One from the group opposite reads aloud, the others respond. It is all repeated. Similarly, not exactly. An urbanely dressed man steps up beside the altar and sings a song. His voice makes an impression of worldly beauty and fullness. They stand up again. A prayer is spoken. The congregation stands up for it. Nobody folds his hands. F does. He was so instructed as a child. Everyone sits. A phase of apparent uncertainty sets in. The headgear of an obviously higher-ranking priest, he stands quite centrally in the arrangement of the group, is removed, someone else places a book (the Bible?) on a music stand in front of him. A few sentences, incomprehensible in the rear of the church, are spoken. F has the impression of attending a play. One of them mounts the pulpit, speaks about Jesus and Brother George. He speaks without emotion, with a firm voice. His sermon is divided into four or five HE WAS segments: HE WAS A

FIGHTING MAN ... explanation. HE WAS A TOLERANT MAN ... Whom does he mean? Jesus? Brother George? Both? Is he making comparisons? He makes use of personal recollections. HE WAS AN INTELLIGENT MAN ... He must mean Brother George. In the last two years of his life he suffered greatly. He bore his suffering in an EXEMPLARY way. F does not recognize the word for "vorbildlich" in the English translation, but it must go that way. The intonation of the priest convinces him of that.

Two pews farther forward a young woman sits down: striking make-up, fashionable clothing. She lays down a bag from Capucci New York beside her. The ceremony goes on and on. Organ music resounds, a woman in the gallery sings. F checks any emotion: The voice is again fascinating. A queen of the night? Everyone stands up several more times. Prays. Responds to the priest. Sits down. Sings a hymn. The congregation forms a procession. The representatives of the church in front. Close to a hundred. The faces of grown-up believers. The woman in front of him has leaned over onto the back of the next pew and cries. Her arms move convulsively, rhythmically.

On stage a sobbing woman should be portrayed from behind in just that way.

To his own surprise F will get used to the omnipresence of the POLICE. In uniform they make themselves visible, stand around ponderously, revolver and handcuffs hang on their backsides. Do they doze in the humid summer warmth? Rapid movements get their attention, they look on, first from a distance, put their arms on their hips. Perhaps only one of them. *A New York policeman can draw his pension after twenty years of service.* F will witness them in this way, on Washington Square for instance: Two Blacks are boxing with each other. Bobbing steps, evasive steps, leaned back, lightning-fast combinations of punches to the head. There is no doubt, they are familiar with him, the Greatest, have studied him, imitate him so that one sees that they are imitating him. They hardly hurt each other. Occasionally their hands smack bonily against one another. Headblows that reach their target are checked at the last instant. The two policemen disapprove of the goings-on. They confer, cannot decide to go over there. Remain standing, distract themselves with a playful Great Dane, which a thin, longhaired man is walking. The dog allows itself to be petted, even roughly, and jumps up and down rambunctiously. All the same they keep an eye on the two boxers. A dark brown policeman approaches from the other side at a resolute pace. He is older than the two Whites. Gray frizzy hair spills out from under his cap. His hips flex lightly as he walks. He goes directly up to the two Ali-imitators, forbids them to do what they're doing, and goes on. He is conscious of his authority. Knows that his order will be followed without resistance, without the need for an attempt at explanation. He does not even look back. For the other two, the Great Dane has become unimportant. They decide to go over. Talk together there for a few minutes. One of the policemen even mimics a boxing movement. The scene appears friendly. Then they leave very suddenly, without audible good-bye. Do they maintain their authority in this way?

On the embarrassing excursion through Harlem, F will see an old woman sitting in the window of a residential building. It will not be possible to determine which way her eyes are looking. He thinks that he does NOT want TO DlE in this city.

What speaks for NYC and against the utterances of acquaintances about NYC:

A colored waitress in a coffee shop in Greenwich Village comes to him with a city map, says that it was left behind yesterday by a customer. Would he like it? At the reply that he carries exactly the same edition around with him, she suggests that he should take it with him anyway, in case he loses his own.

A taxi driver explains his German: My wife comes from Vienna, and ICH BIN JUDE, I am Jewish.

The Whitney Museum is incorrectly marked on the map. After a lengthy search, F stands around somewhat helplessly on Fifth Avenue. A young woman, presumably on her way to work, interrupts her hurried pace, offers help unasked. Remarks as well that he is a good hour too early.

An article on Fassbinder in the weekly newspaper THE VIL-LAGE VOICE. Together with references to Herzog, Straub, Schlöndorff, Kluge, and Wenders.

Ever since his arrival, F will have missed the feeling of being in a foreign place, of experiencing something REALLY NEW. It will set in unexpectedly and violently: Perhaps, without getting exact information, they will both board a bus near Rockefeller Center on the Avenue of the Americas. It is hot, they will be tired. They both suffer from the heat and, not after all because of that, often visit churches. *In southern France this became almost a habit for them.* They just want to sit a little, and the bus is headed north anyway, where the Indian Museum with the shrunken heads is supposed to be located, on 155th Street. His wife notices it first, that fewer and fewer Whites are on the bus. He will reassure her: The bus passed by Central Park West and not East, so it's right. Finally, besides them only one other white passenger is sitting on the bus. An old woman, who looks very American. *The image F has of female Americans coincides with the appearance of this woman.* Now and then she falls asleep for a few minutes. Her head falls in the process onto a protest button that she has fastened to her blouse: HEALTH SECURITY NOW! The size of a beer cap. She gets off, too. With difficulty, muttering to herself. He notices: They are alone with Blacks on the bus. There is not the slightest external sign of danger. The bus has left Broadway and enters the middle of black Harlem. It is Saturday, the streets are alive. He looks around for Whites: none. His wife will bring this to his attention as well. A white policeman gets on. Burly. F senses in himself a feeling of relief. There is not the slightest external sign of danger. The policeman gets off at the Harlem Medical Center. *One has read too much, heard too much. TOO MANY NEGATIVE THINGS.* It is not possible for him to act naturally. He examines everything for its degree of dangerousness. Will ask his wife not to stare at people, in order not to provoke them in any way. There is not the slightest external sign of danger. They are alone on the bus. The driver has reached the end of the line, a sort of bus depot.

He looks in his oversized mirror and requests them to leave the bus. He, too, is a Black.

The situation will in retrospect have something of the ridiculous about it. Or something typical: typical of the negative potential of information. Without this stress it would perhaps occur to him earlier that the yellow New York taxis are replaced here by black ones. Only a small sign on the sunvisor CAR SERVICE would still point to their function. On the other hand, it would not occur to them that there were really no bright-blue police cars to be seen far and wide. Also, communication with the taxi driver would come about as usual VERBALLY; they need not POINT on the map to where they wanted to be taken.

In retrospect there will not have been the slightest external sign of danger.

The Metropolitan's collection rivals in scope and quality that of the Louvre, that will be one of the inscriptions that remains fixed in his memory. Or the information that the Empire State Building is the eighth wonder of the world, the only one of modern times. It's true that the World Trade Center is so-and-so-many floors taller, but there are already efforts underway to enlarge the Empire State Building, so that it will once again be the tallest building in the world. Perhaps F will momentarily see only the quantitative concern of Americans. But merely a Sunday stroll through Central Park would be enough to give him an impression of what possibilities exist in the diversity of this people. He will experience encounters with mimes, countless students from Juilliard, painters, jugglers. He suddenly understands his disappointment up to now: In all the museums he has encountered select works of EUROPEAN ART. The realization that the original America by way of its very nature could NOT BE OF THE MUSEUM would probably seem somewhat kitschy to him. It must be more precisely said that this realization could first seem kitschy to him in Europe.

Two nurses are giving blood-pressure tests on the corner of 47th Street and Broadway. The demand is great. A contribution is voluntary.

On the broad steps that lead to the Metropolitan Museum sit people of all ages. A mime in Marcel Marceau get-up appears, takes up a position at the foot of the steps in front of those sitting, inflates an imaginary balloon. His arm motions show the growing circumference of the balloon. It is finally so gigantic, so huge, that the mime is almost carried away by it. He really has to give it string so the pedestrians can get by at all. In the end he gives it to an elderly spectator. This man is appreciative and visibly pleased to accept it.

The day will be perplexing for F: On the one hand, he wants to come to an interim judgment concerning NYC. *He believes he owes this to himself and also to his wife. Although he thinks his acquaintances don't matter in this regard, he will HAVE TO RELATE evaluated impressions to one or the other of them.* On the other hand, he is conscious of the infinite subjectivity of judgments, but he believes nonetheless in a valid worth at least for his own person and the necessity of such processes that follows from that. He sees too the age-old contradiction between expectation and what really is. He does pride himself for his own part on living without FALSE EXPECTATIONS, but now he detects such things in himself, thus flounders on his own lack of flexibility. He makes a conscious attempt to remain objective. *Accomplishments of American scientists, doctors, engineers will occur to him in the process.* He feels the need to be more concretely objective: He feels good in Central Park. In a place then, where he is not supposed to feel good. *A guidebook says: Do NOT go into Central Park.* The Prometheus near the Lower Plaza, the Fountain Restaurant in the Metropolitan, the triumphal arch at Washington Square are imitations from the heydays of other cultures. He himself is torn between, suspects that the real thing is not to be found there, knows that he has difficulty adjusting to that.

It may well be that the encounter with death over a period of millennia, a seated mummy in the Metropolitan, will make the reflections he has made appear pale and insignificant to him.

The gas station owner a few miles from Alloway: No, I'm too proud for this. He turns down the tip, is or acts offended. Says that this is typical for people coming down from New York City. There you have to pay bribe money for any and everything. The gas he sells has its price, he can live on that. But that's enough for him, too. He is not really prepared to accept the awkwardly formulated apology. Describes, however, quite precisely where the next motel can be found. Even names three of them, gives the prices, and afterwards a recommendation, which one he considers the best. Finally, once again the exact directions to this motel. In slow, accented American. F has really already said good-bye, when the gas station attendant says that he is prepared to give out additional information anytime, in case any kind of problems occur. He should even come by again, if it doesn't work out with the accommodations. Turns around without saying good-bye and walks away.

On the same evening he talks with his wife about her childhood. About the time when her family had to exist under meager conditions. The alcoholism of her father, the same father who gave her the most love in her youth. To drive through the States in a mid-sized American car, even when the scenery is for hours more or less boring, means more to her than a week spent in NYC museums and visiting other so-called sights of a city. After the overly sweet AMERICAN PINK WINE, she finds it easy to admit that she has a great need of luxury and loves as well the mere feeling of being more than the others. *She even would like to say that she cannot get enough of this feeling at his side. But she doesn't say it.*

(*Translated by Eric Denton*)

ETIENNE BARILIER

Etienne Barilier

Born October 11, 1947 in Payerne. Studied French literature. 1990 Writer-in-Residence, Max Kade Institute and Department of French and Italian, USC. Translator. Received several literary awards. Lives in Pully. Novels, essays: *Orphée*, 1971; *Laura*, 1973; *Passion*, 1974; *Une seule vie*, 1975; *Journal d'une mort*, 1977; *Le chien Tristan*, 1977; *Albert Camus*, 1977; *Alban Berg*, 1978; *Prague*, 1979; *Le rapt*, 1980; *Le grand inquisiteur*, 1981; *Leẛduel*, 1983; *Le créature*, 1984; *Le banquet*, 1984; *Le dixième ciel*, 1986; *Les petits camerades*, 1987.

The "American Dream"

Dreams lead to reality — but it is not these same dreams themselves that are fulfilled. Columbus dreamt about discovering a passage to India and amassing gold to reconquer the Holy Sepulcher. He was doubly mistaken: about the identity of the continent he had reached and about his own intentions, or at least the ones of Spain and of Chistianity. When he disembarked, he scarcely found that for which he had come to search.

His misadventure continues. In our own right, we, as modern Westerners, dream, too; our dreams, sooner or later, flow into reality. But the more they materialize, the less they attain fulfillment, in every sense of the expression. We have chosen the rather ambiguous word "dream" to disguise with chimerical softness, to glorify the impossible of our desires and our plans. For that which worries us is a jealousy of reality. It is a desire to have and to hold, more than to dream or to contemplate.

Not that our wants and desires are always and have always been basely material. In the past, we have been able to sincerely strive for scientific knowledge, moral perfection, spiritual triumph and pure discovery. The pioneers of the Renaissance were not all materialistic brutes. But did they really dream that much? No, they desired, they wanted. Their dreams were precise images of the future and the beyond. In short, what we today call plans.

Hence America and its ambiguity. What was "the American Dream?" The fanciful worship of a chimera, or the imperious desire to inflect reality? Of course, a number of pioneers were possessed by a, not to say childish, unrealistic dream: they thought to make the El Dorado come to life. Crossing Death Valley, they suffered hoping to find Canaan just beyond the mountains. In short, they lived and died for chimeras.

But their chimeras were only provisionary expressions of a long-term goal. One believed in dreams, and so one marched on; one believed in hope, and so one produced. One believed in prayers, and so one began building. The dreamer, very quickly, has molded the world to his own dimensions, for better and for worse. Thus the El Dorado became a legitimate enterprise, a real possibility, and was even fulfilled by the few privileged ones who built empires in a split second: first the dreams of gold came and then the bars of gold.

This is perhaps what pioneers could not tolerate. Those who had made America by working hard to fulfill their dreams could not bear that their dreams emptied into a reality too unfaithful to their ideals of the American dream. Homesick for their chimera, they wanted to make their country a land of fulfilled dreams, but dreams all the same, merely dreams. Hence their enterprising, often derisive and pathetic, to imitate their own dreams with the means and the materials of reality. Thus started the strange era of the American *sham*.

What is in fact this sham that is so constantly present in the United States? What is this rage of doing "as if" it were true based on falseness to the inverse, of confounding the history of cinema with a base story of film tricks, of producing fake earthquakes in the country of true ones, of populating a fake forest with fake birds, of making a fake barbecue skewer turn over a fake flame in a restaurant which nevertheless serves real grilled meat (I saw it with my own eyes), not far from a fake Pompeian house filled with real antiques, which become fake in their cardboard decor? And all under the innocent light of the Pacific Ocean. So, what is this sham, if not the literal and desperate veneering of dreams over reality?

The dream never becomes reality. It dies while giving birth to something real. And the sham is the refusal of this evidence; it is the refusal to admit that the dream, fulfilled, will no longer be a dream. It is the attempt to transplant, implant it into reality. As you enter the Nevada desert the first thing you see is a castle from the Middle Ages. Yes, a castle from the Middle Ages. You come closer, and see it is no mirage, no more than the palaces of the Arabian Nights, or the statue of Caesar in the middle of the traffic lights of Las Vegas.

This orgy of fraud has a quite avowed and proclaimed function. That is to forbid any more dreaming: since your dream has become reality, since it is present, it is out of the question to look for the impossible, to escape, to glance further ahead, to stake your unsatisfied claim. "Live your dream, smile broadly, be happy," these are amiable yet imperative words of advice.

Disneyland or Las Vegas are not the only places where Ameria claims to fulfill the American dream. It asserts itself everywhere, in all things, in all aspects. So, one may say, America *is* moral, it materializes the dream of a moral state, similarly, it *is* freedom en route around the world; freedom that watches over the world, and all that could contradict this statement would only be heresy. Finally, America *is* El Dorado: the example of Mr. Ford, Mr. Hearst, and Mr. Getty prove it, and these are but a few; the poor, in turn, are only illusions.

The very word "reality" then changes meaning. The American dream at all costs must become American reality. That is why it is a sham; and the reality must pass as surface effect, false pretenses, so when one camouflages it, it collaborates with the camouflage. In certains neighborhoods of Los Angeles, the beggars roll themselves up so well in their cardboard boxes that you can hardly tell them apart from garbage.

But let us not be unfair. I only spoke about the worst of America, the one that claims to have fulfilled the "American dream." Luckily the dream is stronger than the sham. It is constantly reborn from the reality that imitates it; it is reborn first in America itself by the firm desire not to list the dreams with an ironic or passive bitterness, as old Europe too often does.

The human dream does not lay idle for very long. It picks itself up and resumes its progression toward the beyond. However, after California, how can one go farther or further West? Our little globe has been explored from top to bottom. How can one dream of another El Dorado or of a completely new beginning?

When one has lived in Los Angeles for four months, on the

Pacific coast, as I have had the chance to do, one tends to think that Christopher Columbus's dream can continue: Europe, through its daughter America, will find itself by finding its perfect Other, Asia; in short, one sometimes dreams that the United States is only a giant relay, an enormous base camp for an expedition toward the far away West that finally reveals itself for what it is: the Orient.

But, I am, no doubt, the victim of an illusion: the Orient is still unknown to me. And the earth for me has still not been completely explored. It is still not round. Still one trip or two, and I will be more realistic — and then deprived of dreams.

No, it is up to me to remember that the only "beyond" still available is interior: an "inner space", that space that the Americans, after all, have also managed to discover, they who no longer believe in the beyond but in the *future*. If we manage to dream, not of what is out there but what does not yet exist, the dream will continue to make us act and give us life. So we will not risk confusing discovery and conquest, knowledge and possession, reality and simulacrum. Other Americas can be born on the horizon. And America will definitely be the name of the horizon.

(Translated by William & Catherine Broadhead)

DANIEL ODIER

Daniel Odier

Born May 17, 1945, in Genève. Studied art and journalism. 1983 Writer-in-Residence, Max Kade Institute and Department of French and Italien, USC. Lived for several years in the US. Received several literary awards. Lives in Auffargis (France). Novels, poems, essays: *Nuit contre nuit*, 1972; *Les voyages de John O'Flaherty*, 1972; *La voie sauvage*, 1974; *Splendor solis*, 1976; *L'année du lièvre*, 1979; *Le milieu du monde*, 1979; *Petit déjeûner sur un tapis rouge*, 1982; *Gioconda*, 1984; *Le baiser cannibale*, 1987; under the pseudonym Delacorta, Odier wrote the mystery novels *Nana, Diva, Luna, Lola, Vida*.

Cannibal Kiss

"In the end, Bird, naked and painted in blue, slid open the door to the airplane and merged with the azure sky."

I had just put the final period to my novel. I felt transported into the void where I'd left my character floating. Outside my window spread the stark landscape that had given me the strength to go on until the end. The dunes and the beach, indifferent to my rage, solitude, despair, had not even spared the trace of my footsteps.

As if to prove to myself that the book hadn't obliterated me entirely, I stepped out into the icy air. It was dusk and the red line of the horizon enhanced the brilliance of the first stars. I stood up straight and stretched my spine. I walked down the sandy beach covered with tiny succulent plants. The oncoming darkness crackled with infinitesimal sounds. And then something happened that threw the book totally off course, and my life as well.

I know, the writer is supposed to keep himself at a reasonable distance from his work. He's supposed to be the *deus ex machina*. To pull the subtle strings of his marionettes. He's the conscientious architect, who knows every nook and cranny of the glass and steel palace that he's just constructed and, should the occasion arise, he's also there to reassure the reader and guide him toward the exit. But just imagine for a moment that the opposite occurs — that the flesh and blood of the author dissolves into the edifice, and that this edifice turns into a suspended and flexible bamboo structure, whose form is constantly changing ....

Bird was traveling through space, she was merging with my desert and my book, lighter than the darkened sky. She was a fragment of azure and flesh, which I could hear moving through the atmosphere.

There was a sudden shock, a thud followed by the sound of something unfurling. Bird was hanging there suspended, slowly swinging back and forth, purple in her hair. My character had landed right inside my book, adding a parachute to my fiction, with no respect for her creator.

Bird rolled into the dust. The swelling nylon blisters had disappeared. She unfastened the straps of the parachute. The thick blue paint was furrowed with cracks.

Bird: "To quote one of your favorite writers: 'Art is an airplane that doesn't fly.' But I can fly, and I've come into your novel, into the world of the suffering writer. Dazai was right. Writers are pigs!"

I'd left Los Angeles the year before, mattress, records and books piled into my old Dodge. It was a long trip: five days all alone on the road. The bars, the desert in bloom, the tacky little motels, an emptiness that set in little by little.

Two days after my arrival in Pensacola, I'd tracked down the ideal place: a wooden shack in the dunes facing the ocean, lost in a lunar landscape.

A street lined with tall trees, bungalows in faded colors. Bird slams the door of a white house whose left side is caving in. She crosses a patio with a decrepit railing, past a junked Chevrolet that serves as a shelter for the neighborhood cats. Bird is walking fast. Her ferocity explodes into the warm air. The sound of television. Laughter floating through the night. A crushed bird on the grainy slab of asphalt.

"They call me Bird, like that bird, like Charlie Parker. I decided to commit suicide on the day of my fifteenth birthday. When the day arrived, I wasn't able to figure out how. There were too many possibilities. In the meantime, I decided to read a hundred books. The desire to die erases all fear."

Bird walks into Raj's house. Raj is a dealer from Pakistan. He's dozing in a hammock with a girl whose milky body is covered with freckles. Bird touches Raj's shoulder. His skin is the texture of a mango rind. His dark eyes hover in the night. Bird climbs into the hammock and lies down next to Raj. He takes her in his arms.

"Bird ... what the hell are you doing in my hammock? I'm listening to the crickets."

"You owe me twenty dollars."

"I need to borrow your motorcycle."

"The keys are on top of the TV."

"You're going to become 'café au lait' if you keep fucking that milkpail."

There's a steep path leading to a mobile home at the river's edge. The Indian, sprawled on a lounge chair, is eating fish and rice from a blackened pot. Distant, volatile, impenetrable, and always dressed in black leather. The Indian has only a first name, which he chose himself.

"You talk to the alligators?"

"I eat them. We haven't seen you in ages. You been reading Proust or something?"

"I can't get to sleep. It's been too hot."

"There's a bottle of pulque under your chair."

Bird takes a sip.

"I've always wondered if the worm at the bottom is still alive when they put it in the bottle."

"They're suicidal worms."

You could hear the swishing of rushes. A fish comes leaping up and gulps a little air. Screeching, grating jungle music.

"What I like most about nature is the soundtrack."

Bird and the Indian are lying under a red paper Chinese umbrella that diffuses the light. The shadow of their bodies stretches before them.

"Did you register for the course with the new writer-in-residence?"

"Not yet."

"There's a short story of his in the *Village Voice*, there on the table."

"Is it good?"

Bird goes to look for the newspaper. The Indian falls asleep. The door of the trailer is still open. A slight breeze cools the atmosphere. Bird lies down on her stomach, kisses the Indian, and begins to read:

He watches the writer leave his house, get into his old Dodge and take off into the warm night toward the Blue Lagoon. Who is "he"? We'll call him the Chameleon, as Bird will later on, and say nothing more about it for the time being.

Walking up the red staircase, the writer inhales the odor of bodies, the sounds of reggae and his own smell. He walks across a long room lit by candles that have been placed in colored glasses. After a stop at the bar and a few glasses of rum, he lets himself go with the music.

Bird comes toward him. They dance for each other. Fusion, sudden attraction. By the time the musicians take a break they've told each other everything, except for a few details. Bird infects him with a blue-tinged malaria.

The writer sits on a bar stool. She rubs her back against him, swaying to the rhythm of the music. He caresses the nape of her neck, licks her brow, takes her in. She's wearing a black leather miniskirt and the remnants of a T-shirt. She turns around with a swivel of her hips. They smoke, drink, go outside. Even on Lincoln Boulevard you smell the ocean. Bird straddles her motorcycle and follows the writer's Dodge. There's something fragile about the sky. The light flickers.

The writer's apartment, on the third floor, opens onto a terrace shared by all the residents. They make themselves comfortable on the battered, slightly damp couch, exchange a little saliva and a few words that the Chameleon can't catch.

The apartment is almost empty. There's a mattress on the floor, some pillows, a black blanket. In front of the window is a door resting on trestles, used as a table. The writer leaves his clothes on the floor. Next to the bed, there's a stereo and a pile of books.

Daylight filtered into the apartment, finding their bodies intertwined on the bed, in the hallway, in every room, like a series of snapshots. They were gliding through space. At times they tried to pass through the walls. Little by little, the skin on their knees and elbows is worn away by the carpet. The sun is leaving its mark. The light is unbearable. They're under the table, exhausted. Finally, they get back into bed and bury their twisted bodies under the blanket.

So far it's nothing more than an ordinary encounter, the Chameleon thinks. Actually, he would have dozed off himself, just having emptied the fridge of some leftover tuna and a can of black olives, if Bird hadn't slid out of bed. The Chameleon looks at her body, marked by lovemaking, black and white in the ten o'clock morning sun. She pours herself a glass of milk and sits down in front of the typewriter. The Chameleon hears the uneven clicking of keys. He decides to go for a walk. He'll resume his post later on. He goes out, dancing to the rhythms of typography.

When he returns, he hears their cries. The writer is beside himself. Bird, impassive, continues her writing. Looking out the bay window, the Chameleon counts thirteen palm trees. The writer gives full vent to his rage. Since Bird remains indifferent, he grabs her by the arm and drags her off her chair. He collects Bird's scanty clothes, flings them at her, and unceremoniously throws her out. The Chameleon is surprised by this unexpected display of violence, but he's seen it before. Now it's his turn to get into bed for a while. Observation is his passion, but he gets tired too, anyone would. He falls asleep, grateful for the darkness of the blanket that isolates him from the rest of the world.

When he awakes, the apartment is empty. The Chameleon goes downstairs. The motorcycle is gone. The Dodge isn't there either. What does the writer expect? he wonders, with a mocking smile. Does he think he can find Bird in a city like Los Angeles? It'll be even more difficult with the fog. Sides of buildings and fragments of palm trees suddenly emerge in a mercurial light. The Chameleon goes to buy the *Times* and settles down on the couch. He can hear the ocean without seeing it. Things were happening, as they always do. The Chameleon makes paper airplanes and amuses himself by throwing them off the terrace. The news disappears into the mist. The world has been emptied.

The writer returns alone, feeling tired. The Chameleon accompanies him to his apartment. Artists are strange. The writer rereads the thirty-odd pages, has a drink, looks for the tuna and olives in the refrigerator, and makes do with a cup of tea and a bag of cookies. He is pale and trembling. Maybe it's the light, the Chameleon thinks; he who, in general, is not easily alarmed. The only thing to do is to sleep until midnight.

The Blue Lagoon. The Chameleon had fallen asleep as well. Now, he arrives late. It must be two in the morning. The dance floor is so crowded that the Chameleon has a hard time finding the writer, who is dancing alone to get his mind off it all. The Chameleon takes a swig from his flask and meticulously screws it closed. He sits down on the corner of the stage and lets himself be entertained by the Jamaican musicians. A joint slides down to the bassist's feet. The Chameleon slips in between the musicians, lights the joint and returns to his outpost.

Through the ghostly mist, Bird suddenly appears. She's sitting at the bar. The writer hasn't seen her yet. She ends up joining him on the dance floor. Too much music for conversation. All that matters is to hold each other close. Or at least that's what the Chameleon imagines. They're the last ones to leave The Blue Lagoon. It's getting light outside. Comfortably sprawled in the back seat of the Dodge, the Chameleon can read the anguish mirrored on the writer's face. He's afraid that the motorcycle will disappear, and that Bird will take her book with her.

The typewriter clicks away. Bird still has her T-shirt on. Some African music is playing on the radio. The writer peels a mango and cuts it into slices. Between each paragraph, Bird swallows a few chunks. She drinks tall glasses of peach juice and coconut milk while the writer feverishly deciphers what she's written — it's exactly what he himself will write some day, in ten years or maybe twenty. He knows that these pages belong to him only. Bird is ephemeral.

Every morning on their way back from The Blue Lagoon, the writer goes to buy tropical fruit. Sometimes the Chameleon follows him. Otherwise he stays in the apartment with Bird, reading over her shoulder. He has a foreboding feeling. Why all this confusion? Was it really necessary to be trading dreams back and forth? What about solitude? He likes to watch them dance together. In fact, it's the part he likes the best. He could watch that day and night, but the days are set aside for artistic creation. Not to mention the writer is wearing himself out. Curled up under the blanket, full of desire for Bird, he lets her write for him. Those few hours during the night are his only moments of pleasure. Their liquid bodies fossilize at the break of day.

The Chameleon has no sense of time. It must be ten days and nights since Bird began writing.

Her eyes are red, her features drawn. She's getting thin, her breasts are losing their fullness. But it's when they're dancing that the Chameleon really starts to worry. Bird changes shape right before his eyes. Through some strange mimesis, she begins to resemble the writer.

For once, she's followed the writer into the shower. They have gone to lie down, their bodies dripping wet. The Chameleon seizes the opportunity to curl up in a corner of the living room. Their sighing and moaning keep him from falling into the deep sleep he so badly needs. It's unbearable for him, this sexual frenzy. The only thing he can do is drown it out with a steady stream of music. He turns on the radio and their bodies begin to dance lying down. Their cries turn into jungle music.

When he wakes up, the Chameleon realizes that once again it's too late for The Blue Lagoon. He drinks a little more coconut milk and notices that Bird and the writer are still asleep. The finished manuscript is stuck between their bodies. The dreaded moment. What will the writer do now?

They are talking to each other softly. The Chameleon notes how somber Bird's voice is. A shiver of pleasure runs down his spine. Even when she laughs, her tone of voice remains the same. The Chameleon listens and lets himself be rocked to sleep. The words don't matter to him.

What a celebration! She didn't stop talking all night. The Chameleon feels as though he's slept right on top of her black velvet vocal chords.

It's daybreak. He can see them a little better. The writer has dropped off to sleep. Bird kisses him, lulls him with indistinguishable words. She licks him, nibbles him, she begins to dance again in the profound silence of deep sucking.

It's getting lighter. There's practically nothing left of the writer. Just an imprint of a body on the mattress. Bird is dancing in the center of the white light. Her curves have returned. She's bursting at the seams. The perfume of her dripping body fills the room. The Chameleon blissfully inhales her scent. He's a little sorry that the writer has disappeared. It had been a pleasure following him. But he'd been so deliciously absorbed, you could only envy his final moments. That kind of disappearance is somewhat rare these days, when the hunger for one another takes on all kinds of disguises. The Chameleon tells himself that it's fair, even if the creator is consumed.

Even though Bird can't see him, the Chameleon feels as if she's dancing for him alone. She's offering him her voluptuous body.

[...]

The Chameleon hitchhikes as if it were the easiest thing in the world. He's decided to catch up with the writer. Going from one gas station to another, he steals potato chips, peanuts and bottles of soda. He chooses his ride carefully. He can't stand large families, or couples who take advantage of the monotonous trip to pour out their hearts, or the nuts with their blaring radios. He also avoids the farmers, who often take unexpected routes. Actually, nothing beats the trucks — long distances, steady speed, few stops, and the providential bed.

When he got to Pensacola, he caught a ride in a student's jeep. They drove alongside a stretch of ocean, through a pine forest, and arrived on campus. The Chameleon has a snack in the cafeteria and listens to the university radio station:

"We continue our evening of jazz with 'Lonely Woman' by Ornette Coleman, dedicated to our new writer-in-residence, the strange cannibal whom you can see in the flesh tonight, in Room 106 of the Comparative Literature Department. Don't miss this opportunity, there's still room to sign up. Cannibals, cannibals ... I love 'em! Ah ... I forgot. The name of the person who made this request ... It's Bird, obviously."

The Chameleon can't help but smile. They have no idea what's in store for them. After a nap on the grass, the Chameleon wakes up just in time to find a seat in the back of the lecture hall. The writer is there, asking the students to check off their names on the computer listing. Then he takes out his Polaroid and starts taking pictures of them, group by group, so he will be able to recognize their faces more quickly. The students are whispering. They're talking about the writer, his jeans and black T-shirt with no inscription.

The Indian walks in and addresses the writer:

"I have a name, but I prefer to be called 'The Indian'."

And suddenly, there she is, well, almost. An image of Bird, a variation, a budding blossom. Heat, humidity, perfume. The writer recognizes her. His body stiffens. Not because of her appearance, the leather miniskirt. This is more like a hallucination. The Chameleon is amused by the writer's uneasiness. Bird, delighted with her entrance, goes to sit in the first row. She wipes her brow and armpits with a tissue, crumples it into a ball and throws it in the wastepaper basket, at the writer's feet. He takes a picture of Bird. It doesn't feel like a class anymore. After a somewhat shaky introduction, his voice quivering ever so slightly, the writer begins to take Bird in. He wipes out all the other faces in the lecture hall. Only the Indian's presence resists obliteration.

Come here, I've been waiting for you. Write my book for me. I'll bring you mangoes, I'll lick you all over.

The Chameleon wonders who is spinning the web around whom. The Indian is savoring the emergence of each strand.

. . .

Her body is bulging with a future work. They dance to the music of words. The Chameleon comes closer to make sure he's not mistaken. Bird's body is already swaying, and the writer's is trembling.

The last part of the class is chaotic, on the verge of the incomprehensible. A nosedive toward the color of the sky. Nearly all the students have stopped taking notes. They're chasing after the words, seeking the meaning, the meaning. They'll have to get used to this sort of exercise.

The lecture hall is emptying out. The writer walks across the dark, balmy campus. Bird is just a few yards behind him.

"Thanks for 'Lonely Woman'."

"Tomorrow it'll be 'Round Midnight.' It's Monk Month."

She laughs in the night.

The Chameleon is close enough for Bird to sense his presence. Sometimes she thinks she sees his reflection in a shop window. At night, she can hear him breathing.

The Chameleon isn't too fussy. He accepts the conditions that Bird has imposed during the trip. What he's really interested in is Bird's inner thoughts. He couldn't care less about crossing deserts, waiting for the bus that never comes, sleeping anywhere possible, or catching a ride in any car that comes along.

One night, Bird looks in a mirror. The white glare of public toilets in a train station. Suddenly, she has the fleeting impression that her face is sliding into a void. Her features are moving so fast that her eyes, nose and mouth look as though they'd been covered with clear plastic bags. Bird puts her dark glasses and hat back on, then she goes to the post office to collect the writer's money that the Indian has been sending her regularly.

Outside, the Chameleon melts into the landscape, he disappears into the walls, he takes on the colors of the sky, of the asphalt streets, of the night.

Bird walks into a stadium where several thousand spectators are taking their seats for a football game between two teams of black giraffe-women, completely naked except for their helmets — red for the Atlanta team, blue for the one from Chicago. Bird, the only white woman in the stadium, is sitting in the first row. After the parades of majorettes accompanied by a brass band, the eleven players of each team make their entrance from the north and south doors of the stadium. The crowd begins to cheer.

A scrimmage. The kickoff. The giraffe-women run very fast, supported by legs which by minimum standards must be at least five feet long. Their airy, long-legged strides elicit cries of admiration from the crowd. Very soon, the ebony of their athletic bodies is beaded with sweat. Their abnormally strained muscles glisten. Their hard breasts dance in rhythm. Leaps into space. The violent impact of the ball being intercepted. They're tumbling down — another kickoff at lightning speed. Bird can hear one of the players panting as she streaks past her. The moves are so unpredictable and rapid that the ball sails through the sky as if it were in slow motion. The TV cameramen are having a hard time keeping up with them; even the commentators are lost, since not one player is wearing a number. There are only glistening bodies, almost silver under a dark sky of ashen clouds. The sparkle in their eyes shines right through the grids of the helmets. The players are screaming, falling down, getting back up. It's becoming difficult to count the goals scored by each team.

Suddenly, the game is over. It's a tie.

One woman from the red team and another from the blue team take off their helmets. There is silence in the stadium. You can hear the sound of their bare feet crushing the blades of grass. The closer they get, the more Bird is fascinated by their dripping bodies, their slow, heavy breathing.

The two giraffe-women come to a halt just a few yards away from Bird, who freezes for an instant.

Then she rises, approaches the giraffe-women determinedly, and, in the silence, begins to lick them.

It's a nude by Man Ray. Bird has written on top of it in silver ink:

This sentence makes me burst into tears. Why? *He wants to help Angel kill the alligators.*

(*Translated by Lanie Goodman*)

YVES VELAN

Yves Velan

Born August 29, 1925, in Saint-Quentin (France). Studied Greek, Roman and French literature and history. Lived for several years in the US. 1965/1966 and 1968-1978 guest professor of French literature at the University of Illinois, Urbana. Taught French literature at schools and universities in Florence, Zurich, La Chaux-de-Fonds. Lives in La Chaux-de-Fonds. Novels, essays: *Je*, 1959; *La statue de Condillac retouchée*, 1973; *Onir*, 1974; *Soft Goulag*, 1977; *Contre-Pouvoir*, 1978; *Le chat Muche*, 1986.

Soft Gulag

U pon entering, he took off his windbreaker, waited until it flattened out and put it in his jacket pocket. He found the temperature once again to be fine. He breathed deeply and walked over to the announcement board.

IF YOU LITTER
CONSIDER THIS:
OF ONE HUNDRED MILLION AMERICANS
IF THEY ALL LITTERED
THERE WOULD BE NO MORE AMERICANS

That's a good maxim, he thought, perfectly appropriate for the day of the lottery. Seeing Nick, Dick, and Groucho come out of the elevator also raised his spirits. They waved hello to each other, and whenever they worked together there was a cordial atmosphere, even if they exchanged but few words. The memory of "Carrot Top" faded, and Ad was engulfed in the here and now when Groucho clapped his hands at 12:00.

"Okay, children, it's time for lunch."

And so we see them gather in the center of the room, coffee in hand; some sat in chairs, some on the edge of the table. Something was about to happen. And because of the element of surprise, it was hard to say what it would be.

Listen carefully.

Ad had prepared himself for nothing more than a bit of fun with 'the children' by hinting at the lottery, as his three friends were ineligible. Perhaps this was his greatest mistake — it cannot be certain — but that was not all. Even if Groucho could not, by the letter of the law, call his work mates his 'children,' he was much older, comparatively. He was the office manager, and he was their moral authority which was reinforced by his hobby of psychology, though unproductive. So not only was Ad going to talk about the lottery before Groucho did in front of his disqualified friends, but Groucho's use of the word 'children' would have seemed ironically funny. That was his greatest blunder. But listen to this. Just as Ad was opening his mouth, Groucho said:

"So, today is the lottery."

The excitement built, invited conversation, and saved Ad from his blunder. But *it is not over yet.*

The excitement passed very quickly. Groucho, Nick and Dick, each in their own way, wished Ad luck. As he later noted, he had hardly recovered from his near social blunder and was genuinely confused about being the only one with a chance of winning, and so he tried to change the subject.

"I heard there was a big announcement in the news this morning."

It was hard to believe. The moment he had sidestepped one mistake, he tripped into another, and *it was already done.*

But *it is still not over.*

By an extraordinary amount of luck on this anxiously awaited day, Dick had had to go to his mother's, who was busy with her own affairs, and thus had he been able to watch the television. What's more, he responded so quickly that he became the center of attention allowing Ad's blunder to pass by unnoticed.

"It must be about the petition."

"What petition?" Groucho asked.

A petition to abolish verification. In three days, they've already collected more than four million signatures."

"Who started it?"

"The Californians. In California."

"I could have bet on it."

He slapped his thigh. He would have.

"I could have bet that such a petition would come from the West. I would have bet my life on it and even the Constitution."

Nick asked, "What would happen if the petition was accepted?"

"That won't happen. The rest of the Union will never accept it.

Would you sign it, any of you?"

They shook their heads.

Dick shrugged his shoulders.

"In the South," continued Groucho knitting his brows, "they'll get many signatures."

This statement made them all instinctively turn their heads toward Nick. Groucho's accent was from the Midwest and he was inadvertently putting down the South. Nick, meanwhile, had grown up in Alabama and looked Southern. So the legitimate hostility of the groups now turned against a friend at work. With this, now even Groucho had committed a blunder. What could possibly happen next?

The shortcoming of ITI is its delays. Every year, one delay less — *'thanks for your understanding.'* Everyone has the right to go to his or her place of work, his or her parents, or his or her hobby. All possible rights are your rights. But, you would say, only the intelligentsia engage in writing. Consider the number of words that are necessary to describe all the possible circumstances of the moment we have just left! Could you imagine that in certain cases it would take several pages? Multiply that by the number of Americans there are. It would necessitate the destruction of the forests, rendering the air unbreathable because of the resulting accumulation of pollution. At ITI everything is televised, from job offers to work schedules. But because writing exists, one could ask why is it restricted? It is not restricted; it is simply futile. Therefore, it is not a right or a privilege, for if it were, all Americans could therein engage themselves. But there must be nevertheless a reason for its existence! Certainly. And since it is not social, it is, by default, administrative. It is a matter of work distribution assigned through the conception of differences. As a scholar does not seek to become President of the Union even though he or she has full rights to do so, being a social partner, the other partners do not indulge in written work. Aside from the EB, do you bother yourself with the printed word? Writing is thus used to merely set apart the scholar or the civil lawyer from other professions. Now let's turn back to the frozen scenario — and what a scenario it is!

It is a perfect example of my reasoning. Don't you care about the written word? Aren't you anxious to know the outcome? If this were a real narrative, Groucho's intonation, the facial expressions, and Nick's Southern physique would all be recounted at once. The words fix the facts. Would you like to see Groucho again who is considering his social faux-pas? Would you like to see how Nick will react?

Nick laughed, "From what I know of Southerners, indeed, many will sign."

He had reentered the Midwest with the smooth firm tone of his voice. Everyone laughed. It was truly an exceptional day. The sky was blue. Excitement was all around. Close-up of Nick shrugging his shoulders.

"Purely hypothetically, what would the consequences be if the petition was successful, if we weren't verified any more?"

"None," said Groucho, "I know thanks to my hobby. Our program (he meant to say, the program of his hobby) has recently shown the transcript of a telephone prank. You must know to understand my story that the main character is someone who does not always wake up on his own; he needs to be verified. On top of that, his hobby is advanced electronics. So, the first time he woke up late, he met with the personnel manager and was verbally disciplined. The second time, his lucky number came up at IBM; but he was in bed and missed out on five thousand dollars. The third time, he arrived late for his wedding. Then his fiancée got together with the neighbors and everyone took turns ringing his doorbell every morning. And so he was cured."

"The psychological significance is that we cannot fail society without failing ourselves, but at the same time, society does not allow us to fail it. That is why their petition 'irritates' me, but it does not worry me, since we are sure that it won't pass. Well, of course, it is all about publicity, and we all know that the West is the place for vacations, don't we?"

Groucho's outline stands out against the sky of the south bay window where the view renders an infinite complex of constructions. No sound but the continuous fluid but feeble noise coming from the ocular calculators; everyone was back to work. There was nothing of notice; their eyes start to wander.

Then Dick sneezes. He is in the back of the room, near the north bay window. On the left, there is a wall, behind it another office where Ad's enlargements are hung up. And finally, in the far corner there is a sink. Frozen in swan-like whiteness, it stands out against the now grey walls which were once white. Dicks voice broke in.

"Work is flying by."

"It's the lottery. The excitement is contagious," replied Groucho.

The sun , which had been blocked out during this episode by the bay window partition, now penetrated the room. Sunlight falls directly down on the sink, making it sparkle. Its outline, neatly designed, has a beautiful harshness. A golden brown reflection appears nearby leading to a shelf where a bottle of Pepsi-Cola rises vertically. Just then, a bright flash crosses the room.

"What was that?" Nick asked.

"Oh," Ad replies, "the flight to Mars is the 18th of each month, and those are the take-off tests."

"Can you hear it in Urbana?"

"Not hardly. Less than the planes to New York."

Dick has a patch of white hair.

He turned to his machine again with his eyes still fixed to the south where the light had appeared. Nothing happened. The sink glowed white in the back. The golden brown reflection explains itself with a bit of left over syrup in the bottom. Barely a half inch of it remained in the bottle as it stood precariously on the edge of the shelf. The bottle and the sink are now going to come into the scene as Jim, a clerk, enters and hands the omniscient to Groucho for him to set. Groucho inserted it into his machine. As our friends feel passed over by the omniscient, Jim leaned over with his two hands on the table, one thumb over the edge. His chin up slightly. His imperceptible smile; he betrayed a sense of offhandedness that made it clear he was from another department. But we see that he has pressed his left thumb in an ink pad on the table where the calculators are refilled — which was Groucho's responsibility.

Jim took back his instrument, looked down at his thumb, waved, and headed for the door. His casual smile broadened. You may ask yourself why he did not notice. Quickly we shall understand this sensation of anxious delight: Jim, now at the door, glances at his thumb as if suddenly struck by an idea, his expression markedly different.

"You're going to leave fingerprints," Groucho said.

"Dreadfully funny."

Jim put the omniscient in his pocket, moved with quick steps toward the sink. He raised his hand toward the faucet. What has just happened?

Could he be in a bad mood? One might fear as much. And Groucho had explained that a bad mood could lead to certain actions. Or on the other hand, just supposing, did he want to introduce a little humor that he felt he was omitting? In spite of Groucho's remark, the second hypothesis is correct because it takes into account the abnormal state. In the meantime, the scene goes on which is all that matters. Jim turned abruptly around to face the group ...

The bottle crashed down into the basin like an explosion!

We can explain the sink to ourselves. Things do not appear like that without implications. And under these circumstances, here the implication was the danger the bottle represented. The possibility of its fall was too obvious. The spectacle is frightening, and if it may be said, even obscene. A mass of shards collect at the point of impact that jut out in all directions. The basin is full of them, jagged, sharp and pointed. By a stroke of luck, the label covered up the drain and kept all the glass from falling into it. It could have been waste at its worst. The last of the syrup slowly oozes out through the debris.

Our friends recover from the shock quicker than Jim and they jump toward him. They try to calm him down, and they succeeded. Ad brought him a cup of coffee, but simultaneously, Jim realized what he had done, and thus what he had to do.

"I'll have to go and see Mr. Jurgens."

When Nick, Dick, Groucho and Ad did not move, it showed that he was right and that they were powerless. Jim then headed off for the personnel manager; he was ghostly white. Groucho accompanied him to the door, one arm around his shoulder.

When Groucho came back, his three friends turned to face him, they were still standing by the east bay window.

"More events. We've learned," Dick commented, "that these kinds of accidents happen. But we don't always believe them. They are so ... well ... absurd."

"*Seem* absurd." Groucho slowly said, "But consider the case of Natty Hawthorne and apply it to Jim. You will recognize some disturbing coincidences, such as: where Nat Hawthorne's one arm is shorter than the other, Jim is of small size."

Although no one had noticed, no one would have brought it up. But Groucho could.

"You don't have to be a genius to follow the chain of events. He developed an inferiority complex, then an attitude of failure. At first glance, you might attribute it to bad luck. For example, in the last lottery, they forgot to record his number, an extremely rare incident."

They had not known and were shocked by it.

"Jim's hobby is archery. Three years ago, all in the same day, he shot someone in the foot, and then hurt his hand when an arrow broke while drawing it back."

"Really?" asked Nick politely.

"It's as true as I tell it to you. And in December, when we had our accounting exams, it was colder and more humid than now. All week long, he rode his bicycle around too scantily clad. As a result, he caught the flu and showed up with a high fever. He couldn't get any answers to work out. When they had the make up session, he did brilliantly on the electronics section. Then the day before the second section, he wanted to get as much sleep as possible so he disconnected his phone. Thus, no one verified him and he didn't make it to the class until after the deadline. Now he'll stay a clerk all his life. I could give you many more similar examples but just think about this: At the year end reception, he called Mr. Lancaster's wife 'Miss'."

This last little blunder made them smile in spite of themselves. Groucho explained to them that even if Jim had not broken this bottle, he would have eventually broken another.

"But," Ad said brusquely and almost violently, "his case is atrocious with his hobby being archery!"

"I think," replied Groucho with a calm that contrasted with Ad's agitation (though neither the calmness nor the agitation is abnormal), "that you don't quite know the law; they don't amputate the first finger until after the second offense. The first time offender gets off with a warning. Do any of you know anyone who has committed two offenses?"

Of course not.

"I do. The case took place in Chicago with a woman. It's more typical because she drank. Generally, one feels so much remorse that one doesn't take it up again."

Anticipating their objections, he added, "Don't say the punishment is too severe. Take another example: the dream."

No, this was not a blunder, since Groucho did not know about Ev's confession. And when he did know, it would mean that others would know. It would be official and then no one would talk about it.

"We could say that the guilty one is the one who left the bottle there."

"Exactly," Nick interrupted, a bit upset. He drew wildlife for his hobby, "I mean, we didn't even notice it ourselves."

"That's true," Groucho conceded, We share part of the responsibility. And anyway, I shall make a report to Mr. Lancaster. But I'll also mention that we go to work immediately and didn't have a chance to wash our hands, that because we're so dedicated no one got thirsty. Did you know that in some big cities, such as Chicago, people sometimes leave a fragile item in the office on purpose? Life in crowded cities is hectic, difficult in a way, and paradoxically, when the stress increases, the surveillance loosens up. Let me go back to the dream. We know a little about one situation which could become quite important. But from the little we know, it shows that the consequence would be extreme disorder. This is, as

I said before, the most important reason to go against the petition; rest assured that the kind of accident that happened to Jim would multiply, and then the waste, the waste ...."

Nick looked as if he was suddenly struck by an idea.

"I know," Groucho cut him short, "I know what you are going to say. There is no reason to talk about waste since the glass could just be recycled back into glass. I'll take your thought one step further. Why make objects in glass? Only for this simple reason: if there were no glass, there'd be no risk of breaking it. Or if one could recast the pieces immediately, one would not worry about the waste. The conclusion is always the same: we would stop watching ourselves."

They were impressed. Groucho really understood the underlying motivations.

"I agree with you completely," Dick said.

Groucho realized that they had waited too long before going back to work, not to mention that the excitement about the lottery needed to be built up again. Ad offered to clean up.

He threw the debris into the waste-disposer. With the lid open, he could hear the glass shards clinking, "tink, tink, tong," weaker and weaker. He thought that if all this had happened, then anything could happen. He shivered; the intercom buzzed. Groucho's face was expressionless.

"Sure, Mr. Jurgens."

He hung up.

"Ad, Curt wants to see you."

"Me?"

He headed out to the elevator. He walked a little stiffly, his brow furled, his lips pulled taut.

"I never should have thought that any of this could happen. It's just a form of imagination. So something has happened. And still, I don't see anything for which I could blame myself. But if that's the case, why does the personnel manager want to see me?"

In the elevator, he looked over his hands. Employees of IAD do not see their superiors any more or less than in other companies nor do they think of them any more than that except at random.

But, as with any other firm, IAD has a slightly particular case when it comes to deference; Curt (Jurgens) is more impressive than Burt, the director, and yet Curt is merely the personnel manager. He is reserved, distinguished. He belongs to an old family of the state; his is rich through his wife. He has his name even if he lets employees refer to him as Curt among themselves. He does not need to work. In fact, he only comes to his office three times a week, being so busy with the Chicago Symphony Orchestra. And finally, he has a child, while Burt does not. And so Ad, arriving at his destination, stopped.

Ad found himself parallel a south bay window. He turns his head and there is a remarkable view of the surroundings. Everywhere, clear up to the horizon, not a square meter without towers, buildings, houses; on the ground, the lawns are now green, with the frost gone. No sound.

Ad turned from south to east as a man who had made his decision. Dear readers, let us consider this. Though admitting he had committed an error, he did not want to add another by keeping someone waiting.

But when he heard the voice on the intercom, it was pleasant, friendly.

"Come in Ad, do come in."

Ad entered the waiting room with covered walls that absorbed all sound. The temperature was more balanced than anywhere else; everything was order and beauty, luxury and tranquility. Ad's expression turned intimidated; he is plainly dressed. His mind is occupied with Curt's summoning. The signal to "COME IN" makes him mechanically push open the door. He tumbles into an *almost* unbearable light. Not thinking to cover his eyes, he consciously closes the door behind him when the beam of light moves over to Curt. Curt pushes himself up with his arms, stands, then steps over to Ad with his hand stretched out.

"Bravo, Ad, magnificent, splendid, *your number has come up.*"

The light falls back on him with all its force, and it would not be incorrect to say it sets him "ablaze," for his temperature has risen, excessively so, yet, the glow combines an extremely intense clarity with a heat no less extreme.

"I am very happy, Ad, positively thrilled."

Curt continues his handshake, squeezing twice while looking at Ad. And he, though a bit bowled over by the news, had at least presence enough to notice the lights coming from the cameras, the forms he had distinguished on entering; he knew he had to say something.

"But the lottery isn't until three o'clock."

"It was moved up. These two gentlemen brought the news."

The response that Ad gave could seem mundane or weak. But the emotion it reflected Curt understood well. He kept hold of Ad's hand and shook it. The "Gentlemen" mentioned by Curt also understood. The spotlight moved over to one of them. He raised his hands above his head and waved them hardily. What else could that be except enthusiasm! Ad was able to get hold of himself, and he was okay.

"It's marvelous!"

"Were you expecting it?"

"I cannot say that I expected it. But one always hopes since we all have an equal chance in a lottery."

"Smartly done," one of the gentlemen remarked who, like the other, was very young.

The spotlights are cut. The room, however, is still quite well lit by the ceiling chandelier and a big desk lamp. The two men move toward Ad and congratulate him. A third person that Ad had not noticed steps out from the corner of the room pulling a metallic trunk into which he starts to put away the equipment. He was old.

"You were right," said the first gentlemen, "you had no need to warn him."

"You were right nonetheless," responded the other, "if he had fudged the intro, we would have been off to a bad start."

"It was great that he didn't cover his face."

"It will make a great opening shot, a remarkable dive in."

"His teeth are healthy."

"Even though, we'll have to under-expose him. His skin will show up too red."

"Ad is used to the outdoors," said Curt, "he is a member of the Friends of Nature.'"

The first of the two gentleman turned to him and lively said, "Thank you very much, Mr. Jurgens, we couldn't have done it without your help. Your a real professional. You are pleased, aren't you? It's a great success for the house."

"I must agree."

Curt went around his desk, took out a box, and from the box, a cigarette, lit it up, and closed the box again.

"We're going to be late," said the second gentleman.

Aside from the equipment crewman, the whole group was in the middle of the room.

Hands were shaken, the group dissolves, and the two gentlemen dash out. One now perceived that the equipment and the crewman are no longer there.

Beads of perspiration are visible on Ad's forehead. Curt invites him to sit down.

Curt does not sit behind his desk, but on it so that he is right next to Ad, facing him. He pulls out the box he has not yet put away and offers Ad a cigarette.

"No thank you, sir. I don't smoke."

"I know. But on special occasions like this ... Ad, call me Curt."

He smiles in his reserved way.

"You're a good employee, Ad. I'm happy that chance shined on you today."

"I've still not quite gotten back my bearings. The idea of having a child is so extraordinary that I can't grasp it yet."

"Oh, you don't get one yet."

Curt left his mouth open. He shook his head and smiled.

"I mean, between the red tape and the actual event, it takes a bit of time."

Ad really enjoyed the laughter of such a reserved man.

Curt got up.

"Well, I don't want to keep you. But I hope that you and your wife will give us the pleasure of coming to our house for dinner.

For the moment, though, go on home. Nobody knows anything yet, at least we've tried to keep it quiet. I would like you to be the one to announce the news."

With his arm around Ad's shoulder, he walked him to the door, explaining that the two gentlemen had spoken truly, that this lottery win increased the prestige of the company in any case. Curt opens the door; they are facing one another. Curt does not offer his hand right away.

His face is flooded by a shaft of light coming from the south bay window. He has chiselled features and cold grey eyes that mark a man of character with vision. His head slightly cocked, he looks at Ad, slowly rubbing his forefinger over the bone of his nose. He appeared to be on the verge of speaking some words of consequence. Rather, he asked a natural question.

"Tell me, haven't you some pretty large debts?"

"Yes, I was seriously ill the year I started here with the company. The medical bills were considerable and despite insurance, we have never been able to even hope to catch up."

Ad thought to himself that he had just about blundered since Curt had his company file. But little by little, everything was starting to seem lighter for him, the social blunders as well as the debt.

"Oh, I'm sure you have good reasons for going into debt. Yours come to twenty two thousand, don't they?"

"Just about."

"So eight to ten thousand dollars will come in handy, then?"

"Definitely."

"Well, congratulations once again. And until tonight then, of course; I wouldn't want to miss the ceremony."

"Thank you, sir."

"Curt. Don't forget. Curt. Well, get going and make the most of these upcoming moments. And for that matter, it goes without saying that you don't need to come back to work until next week."

He looked as if he were daydreaming. But in contrast with the joy of our friend, he appeared as he always did, reserved.

This time, Ad made no mistake.

"Thank you, Curt."
And he finds himself again facing the south bay window.

(Translated by William & Catherine Broadhead)

ISO CAMARTIN

Iso Camartin

Born March 23, 1944 in Chur. Studied French, Italien and Romansch literature and philosophy. 1974-77 Research Fellow, Harvard University. Since 1985 Professor for Romansch literature and culture in Zürich. 1993 Writer-in-Residence, Max Kade Institute, USC. Received several literary awards. Lives in Zürich. Short stories, essays: *Nichts als Worte? - Ein Plädoyer für Kleinsprachen*, 1985; *Lob der Verführung – Essays über die Nachgiebigkeit*, 1987; *Karambolagen – Geschichten und Glossen*, 1990; *Von Sils Maria aus betrachtet – Ausblicke vom Dach Europas*, 1992.

Maxims for Los Angeles

Maxims are — different than laws or moral categorical impera-tives — subjective rules of behavior. Of the highest sort, however, because the word is derived from the idea of "maximae regulae" — from the highest guiding principals. Nevertheless, they are based more on experience that principals of thought — and since each of us still has to make his own experiences, maxims can be very individually colored norms of behavior.

Los Angeles is the city, in which I will shortly teach for a couple of months. Whoever loves teaching, knows, that it is an adventure with an uncertain outcome. For seven years I have been teaching a so-called exotic subject at both universities in Zurich. In an exotic subject, knowledge is passed on which is considered non-es-sential for the continued existence of society. Therefore, a type of luxury subject, that, however, for those who dedicate themselves to it, seems as essential as bridge building and medicine. These subjects are sometimes also called "marginal" subjects. They cover in the topography of knowledge the peripheral areas. Since one also discovers that on the peripheries lively thoughts can come about, such marginal subjects are not for all entirely useless.

With such a peripheral knowledge, I will shortly travel to Los Angeles. To a completely unknown flock of knowledge hungry young people. They grew up in different linguistic traditions and lifestyles than me. Therefore I'm at least as curious about this encounter as they are.

In advance I wrote down these sentences which I'll take with me on my journey. Maxims for Los Angeles as it were, more for my own orientation than for the teaching of others.

1. What is useful knowledge?

Every fall, when the young students sit in front of me, new arrivals with tiresome school experiences and great expectations for the beginnings of their studies, I feel the same uneasiness: did they come to the right place? They have escaped the subjects forced on them in high school and find themselves on the path to a knowledge of their own choosing. But, is that, what I have to offer, what they really want?

As a teacher one is caught up in the belief in the usefulness of one's own teaching. But also encouraged by the fresh curiosity which confronts the teacher. "You learn from those, who learn from you" the philosopher Gadamer said. When there are new faces in the room, the learning begins anew for the teacher.

Unfortunately the times are gone when studying at a university could be considered an adventure or a journey of discovery. The jostling for position is great, the competition hard, the career prognosis are bad. Those that don't quickly know what they want fall behind. Useful knowledge is called for, knowledge that leads one straight and without losing time to a career, in any case to money. There's no place for the procrastinator, wanderer, or player. If you come too late (also to exams), you will be punished later in life.

Today's students are mostly very realistic and calmly take into account every frustration in their studies. There is a lot of material and only limited time, therefore they ignore everything which doesn't directly belong to their major. They are prepared to calmly cram their way through all obstacles. Everything is avoided if it's not test material. The coercion to study a lot of subjects in high school is imperceptibly replaced by the coercion to just study your major at the university. If you study like that you're admired, and not only by the school officials, because you quickly make room for those following in your footsteps.

I do not want to sing the praises of the eternal student. I also know that our students are old when they graduate compared to the international average. I also think that eight to ten semesters should be enough for a degree. The question is, what should one do with this time at the university?

There is an old fashioned suspicion that what we learn in college we can't use later in the real world. There are enough CEO's who boldly claim that those who come from a university have to relearn everything again with them. The things that one brings from the halls of higher learning are hopelessly far removed from actual practice.

If only that were true! The trend towards schooling has made great advances. The criteria of usefulness and usability of the subject matter have become more and more emphasized in the curriculum. And far too many of our young people at the university head straight for that knowledge which is considered useful.

For what then, would the universities be the right place?

Not for hanging around and wasting time, certainly not, but for curious wandering and circuitous exploration of the ports and treasures where the knowledge of the ages is stored and the experiences of civilization are recorded.

One must take a leisurely Sunday drive in the vehicles of one's own curiosity because the knowledge that will really shape us, not only has to do with desire and mood, but also with decisiveness and responsibility. One must set sail on sea-going vessels and ships of the desert to the islands and oasis where the representatives of a knowledge sit, a knowledge that doesn't allow itself to be changed into the newest products. A knowledge that doesn't just serve to give you something to do, but serves to be something or in any case to become something.

Where, if not at the universities, should young adults find the optimal conditions to understand the relativity of our priorities and our values, our fixations on material goods, to which only we place such a high regard, while other civilizations also have other values?

Knowledge must not only be useful. It must confront us with alternatives. Knowledge is not goal oriented. It must enlighten us about the crossroads on which we are standing. And it must warm our hearts so that we can courageously decide for one way or the other.

When we as teachers at the university educate people without making these other aspects of knowledge accessible and experienceable, then we should quickly change our profession.

2. What is spirit?

To start with, it is a word with an extraordinary range of meaning. With the spirit, we move linguistically from schnapps over nightly spirits to the Holy Spirit. Spirit is the contrasting principal to material and to nature, but also to the legal tender money. Money and Spirit — that isn't the worst formula for that which moves us. When the flesh is weak, the spirit cannot do much. If the spirit is willing, we consider it a servant, the spirit of darkness, we consider the ruler of hell. The spirit of the times is considered shallow, the spirit of the law as that, which is not expressedly formulated in law books, therefore it is missing, although it is the most important. We want the spirit to give us life, but to be possessed by spirits is something nobody wants. If the spirit flees into a foreign language, it can acquire additional qualities: A person with "Esprit" is not simply spiritual, but also endowed with an element of elegance. In the original meaning of the word, the spirit is a breathing, roaring and dubious matter, something that stimulates and excites us, but also scares and confuses us. However, to lose your spirit is obviously something nobody wants to do.

We discover most directly what spirit actually is, oddly enough there, where it is destroyed. "O what a noble mind is here o'er-thrown!" says Ophelia in the moment, when Hamlet snubs her with insults "to a nunnery, go." The spirit which has been cast aside: that was the concrete image of the time for insanity. Therefore spirit has something to do with order — although order fanatics are always spiritless types. The noble spirit of Hamlet is gone for Ophelia because it has been "blasted with ecstasy." In ecstasy, in the going beyond and abandoning of the trusted and reasonable, a border becomes noticeable for that what we are able to recognize as spirit. "You are the peer of the spirit that you comprehend" — it says in Goethe's *Faust*. But is that, what we don't comprehend, already the unspirit.

In Islam it is said that the mentally ill are God's favorites because their spirit has gone to him in heaven ahead of time while their bodies remain with us on earth.

3. When is less more?

"The half is better than the whole." So said Hesiod. Not everyone understands this strange set theory right away. As soon as one knows that it is dealing with inheritance, one suspects the connection. Preferably half, quickly in hand and undisputed, rather than all of it and the battle with the relatives that goes along with it. The joy of the laughing heir is quickly spoiled when someone contests the will. And when the inherited goods are gone, then it is well known that only the lawyers are laughing. Thousands of inheritance stories confirm the tiresome truth.

Is this sentence from the ancient world really dealing with this?

It is found in the introduction to Hesiod's *Erga*, a work written around the beginning of the 7th century B.C. that is considered as a type of didactic poem for our civilization. In fact, an inheritance dispute with his brother Perses appears to have been the cause for the poet to communicate to us right at the beginning his interpretation of what he considers justice and honesty. This brother Perses must have been a real good for nothing. The inheritance of their father had hardly been distributed to both brothers, Perses had already blown his share and now attempted to get his hands on the other share. To this end all means seemed justified to him: he bribed a judge and even perjury did not deter this legacy hunter.

> Not so we shared the patrimonial land
> When greedy pillage fill'd thy grasping hand:
> The bribe-devouring Judges lull'd by thee
> The sentence gave and stamp'd the false decree:
> Oh fools! who know not in thir selfish soul
> How far the half is better than the whole.

The admonishment appears to say above all: be satisfied with the half that is rightfully yours. Don't be covetous of that which doesn't belong to you. Ill gotten wealth doesn't thrive! One knows about the sermon of modesty, which doesn't make much impact on the greedy.

But is the theory of the half exhausted with this?

Hardly. Because the inheritance moral is deeply imbedded with Hesiod. Once — one could say — into a physical science, then also in a theology, which is life affirming. There is still something else which the fools don't understand, namely:

> Oh fools! who know not in their selfish soul
> How far the half is better than the whole:
> The good which asphodel and mallows yield,
> The feast of herbs, the dainties of the field!

Half of the gain, Hesiod thinks, cannot come to us through the inheritance, but solely through work and perseverance by tilling the soil. The fruits of the earth: that is the second half which no caring father can bequeath, each must plant it and harvest it for himself so that he can live happily and satisfied. He who doesn't notice that this half is worth more than all inheritance is a fool and hasn't understood anything. An early plea, therefore, for working with your hands against the idleness of those who only want to live off their inheritance.

But with that it's still not enough. Hesiod's set theory still has another sense. The actual thunderbolt at the beginning of the *Erga* is not — in today's terminology — the defense of work against capital. Above all Hesiod is concerned with a new assessment of the strife.

In his early work, in the *Theogony*, the poet had described how Nemesis, the god of revenge, bore resentful daughters of the night, among them also Eris, the goddess of strife, "whose heart is full of violence." He refers back to this and at the same time, in order to correct a mistake he made in his own theology, he says:

> Two strifes on earth of soul divided rove
> the wise will this condemn and that approve.

Besides the strife, which causes war, tears people apart, destroys kingdoms, there is also the good strife, in which justice is not broken, but which enlivens the forces and promotes competition. It is good for the people if they would spur each other on, if the one potter makes the other, if one singer makes the other, envious through their good work. — He who understands this half of the strife, has more from life than if he would blindly make himself a squabbler. Still, in that which is considered evil, there is the good half to be discovered. He who doesn't understand how to share, brings the entire misery upon himself. The ability to make a distinction obviously counts for more with Hesiod than the virtue of modesty. It is a benevolent wisdom that is being propagated here, not a malevolent moral of renunciation.

Hesiod's set theory has experienced in its history strange divergence and actualization. One of the best was probably by Lessing in *Emilia Galotti*. There, the Prince Gonzaga says to the painter Conti, who unveils a portrait of a bygone lover of the prince:

> Everything that art can capture out of the large, protruding, blank, glassy Medusa eyes of the countess, that you have, Conti, honestly captured — Honestly I say? Not so honestly would be more honest.

Now this is not said by an especially honest man. Nevertheless, we have before us here the actual natural application of Hesiod's set theory in matters of the heart. In our everyday language the phrase is retained from the prince's critic: "Less would have been more!" However, who still realizes that Eros was once involved?

4. Doing the one thing, leaving the other undone?

One should do the one thing, but don't leave the other undone. The sentence sounds so completely rational that it could have been written down either by Eckermann in his conversation with the old Goethe or by a cautious upright Swiss. By someone, at least, who wouldn't want to forgo anything before its time by taking sides.

However, that which seems morally so unyielding in this "this as well as that mentality" originates from the bible and is located there in the middle of diatribes and curses:

> Woe unto you, scribes and Pharisees, hypocrites! for ye pay tithe of mint and anise and cumin, and have omitted the weightier matters of the law, judgment and mercy, and faith: these ought ye to

have done, and not to leave the other undone. Ye blind guides, which strain at a gnat, and swallow a camel. (Mt. 23, 23-24)

How did this tame wisdom come about in such a violent context, surrounded by curses, kitchen herbs and strained insects?

The law demanded, that one tenth of the "seed of the land and the fruit of the tree" (Lev. 27, 30) be handed over. According to another passage the tithe encompassed "all fresh fruit, must and grain." This law still did not seem concrete enough for the scribes, who had the task to interpret the written records for the needs of the day. Therefore they expanded this tithe to also include herbs and spices and obviously handed over embarrassingly exactly even one tenth of their mint, their dills, and their cumin. (In St. Luke 11, 42, mint, rue and all manner of herbs are mentioned.)

Now Jesus did not speak out against this, but about the fact that the scholars ignored the important matters of the religious law and concentrated more on the trivial matters. What they didn't follow was the duty to decide between good and evil, to show mercy to the weak and to live in devotion and faith with God and the world. These pedantics filtered their drinks through a cloth in order not to break the commandment of cleanliness by swallowing an unclean insect, but it didn't bother them, "to swallow a camel," which according to the commandment is likewise an unclean animal. It was against this hypocrisy and reversal of the sense of this law that he spoke out against so impetuously.

Don't the "either-or sentences" seem better suited for Jesus who, after all, was also a zealot? Wouldn't it have been more radical and more consequent if the evangelist would have proclaimed: "To the devil with your tithe of herbs! Remember what is significant and forget these trivialities!" Why then here of all places — the one *and* the other.

The theologians certainly have their explanations why even the fulfillment of the unimportant commandment remains important. However, something else is more crucial here. Even the words of the evangelist are laced with proverbs and statements that go back to the old times and traditions. Traces of this evangelical sentence, whereby the one thing is to be done and the other thing is not to be left undone, can already be found in the Old Testament. Didn't something sneak in here which comes from a completely different understanding of the world?

The wisdom proverbs date back to the third century B.C., the compiler denoted himself the preacher. There it states:

> Be not righteous over much, neither make thyself over wise: Why shouldest thou destroy thyself? Be not over much wicked, neither be thou foolish: Why shouldest thou die before thy time? It is good that thou shouldest take hold of this; yea, also from this withdraw not thine hand.   (Ecc 7, 16-18)

We are confronted with a strange interpretation of life here. That we don't get carried away with our wisdom — this is taken care of by the world wide and life long tendency not to be able to avoid committing stupidities. That one doesn't even take it too seriously with righteousness, this is a rather daring bit of advice for a biblical scholar. He even allows us to be "wicked," not so much though that we end up hurting ourselves. A strange moral apostle, this preacher.

However, when one thinks it over a second time: he's right! Doesn't most misery come from the fact that we have to do everything to the extreme, that we damage the earth with our demands, that we do things, that really lead us to an early grave. We excite ourselves with those things which we consider right and underestimate the quality of those things that we despise. What we desperately need is a moral which goes easy on life.

In this version of "this as well as that," we are confronted with a skeptical, but nevertheless cheerfully uncomplicated philosophy of life! Ancient wisdom now shimmers through our sentence, the wisdom of the middle of the road, may be not paved in gold but at least suitable for people. The inflexibility and harshness of the New Testament in terms of the important and unimportant are blown away. Even the dubious compromise, which is presented in everyday terms as the real meaning of the sentence, has been happily repressed.

Occasionally one only has to go back far enough in the holy scriptures in order to find in a passage a variation of the good message which still fits one's own situation in life.

We don't want to strain out any insects and swallow any camels.

And we also don't want to be fools. In a world, in which one often doesn't do the one thing and would like to leave the other undone, it depends above all on not taking anything to the extreme. For the short term take hold of the one thing that we have at the moment and don't let the other thing, that will soon be reachable, completely out of sight. Or like the preacher says: Don't completely withdraw thine hand from the other. The (easy) hand to be sure, that, which can hold — and when it leads to mercy — can just as well withdraw.

5. The world simultaneously — in Zurich and in Los Angeles

I come from a small town. From a remote one even. I spent my first twenty years there, not really looking at other places, but at the end waiting rather impatiently. When the time came, I discovered surprisingly that there isn't anything in Switzerland that one could call a large city. I went to study in a foreign country and remained there for another twenty years in more or less large cities like Boston or Heidelberg. Then, because of my career, I again took up residence in Switzerland, to be exact in Zurich. In a city of which one can always say that in some regards it has something of a large city character.

"The first violin from Moabit, the cello from Lyon" a gypsy declared in 1915. For me, too, it depends on the mixture. A city must be so attractive that no continent wants to be left out. The ability to attract must extend beyond Moabit and Lyon. Whoever looks into the orchestra pit, discovers faces and profiles from far away countries. And there are places and streets in Zurich, where the people are as colorfully mixed as on the stage of a variété theater. That is Zurich as I like it. Where the languages become as multicolored as the clothes.

And as varied as the occupations. In the end, everybody in a small town does the same, whether pastor, teacher, farmer, construction worker or saleswomen: they follow the rules. At twelve o'clock: close the shop, eat, listen to the news, take a short rest, and at one thirty everybody goes back to work again. In the evening, the same ritual. In the city, things at least fall a little out of rhythm. The hours of the day, the weekends lose a little of their unmerciful power of division. To be sure there is still a certain marching in step, but some things are mercifully moved to a different time. A personal rhythm becomes noticeable. Although so much still remains highly regimented.

"Boumce! It is polisignstunder!" The Joycian formula for the intervention of the uniformed officers in Zurich. Today it has less to do with putting an end to late night frivolities. Closing time comes always when too many people are together who are simply against it and with that ends the discussion. It is most unbearable in Zurich where only the homogenous types are among themselves and when they soon also have the say. It effects all social classes. One must — let me cite a personal example from my own circles — only let a flock of university professors debate which type of high school is the only correct one from the university's perspective and immediately an absolute know-all attitude, visionless thinking, a willingness to restrict others and an intention to prevent other opinions comes about unannounced. Whatever you do, don't look past your own four walls! What seems right for you, must also be right for the others.

Zurich is arduous, where the high middle class ideal of the "Etepetetischen" (putting on airs, snobbery) reigns. The word is supposedly a Berlin transformation and amalgamation of the German word "öde" (dreariness, monotony) and the French "peut-être." To steadfastly insist concerning trivial things that only one way is good and correct. That is unfortunately not an insignificant petty bourgeois fixation, but is a means of how one can keep other lifestyles at bay. How one cocoons oneself in the familiar and secure and therefore supposedly in something better.

There are often for me in Zurich "Hours of Temptation" — above all then, when I doubt that one cannot get any more Swiss even in this city despite the best prerequisites. Occasionally it seems as if the entire energy of this city is used up trying to keep up the facades, in trying to demonstrate properness around the clock, the fantasy is unrestingly used up in the creation of pleasant packaging for chocolates. Or when I feel the coldness, with which the people of Zurich, who supposedly love this city, treat those who are searching for reforms, which they also consider improvements. Then — with all respect — it doesn't look that good with everything in Zurich. I wonder sometimes about the good reputation Zurich and its educated circles had in earlier times and ask myself: Where did this cosmopolitical spirit, this curiosity about the world as a complete and coherent reality, actually go?

The hours of temptation are not there, so that one can adapt or come to terms with them. Zurich does offer possibilities to get out of them again. When one discovers, for example, that in a neighborhood, among the colleagues, among the students, among the youth there is a lot to be found which has nothing at all to do with achieving and maintaining the status-quo. One takes a walk through a part of town and discovers that one cannot only encounter ecological reason but also an openness of the faces and a warmth of words. Or one meets on one of the beautiful bridges in Zurich a woman, who with her arguments and charm can quickly refute the masculine know-it-all attitude.

The daily challenge of this city lies somewhere else, however. Nowhere are — on the basis of economic and political factors — the outward prerequisites for emergency relief so good as here. Could not and must not a lot more happen? For those, who because of poverty and homelessness cannot find the city beautiful. And also for those, of whom we are reminded here daily from the colorful mixture of faces. The world simultaneously in the city: In Zurich one isn't too badly placed in order to experience and to measure those things which are someplace else even more difficult.

Now I am on my way to Los Angeles. There the world is even to a greater degree simultaneous than in ordinary, foreseeable Zurich. Don't we travel first and foremost in order to get fresh eyes for what we are actually looking for?

(Translated by John W. Arensmeyer Jr.)

FLURIN SPESCHA

Flurin Spescha

Born August 24, 1958 in Domat/Ems. Studied French and Italian literature and literary criticism. Lived for several years in the US, Canada, Great Britain, Israel, France and Italy. Schoolteacher, journalist, taxi driver. 1986 "Werkbeitrag" of the canton of Zurich. Lives in Zürich. Novels, poems: *und sei's nur ein traum*, 1981; *quasi diesch poesias*, 1983; *Das Gewicht der Hügel*, 1986.

The Weight of the Hills

Cricket and Ant

Cricket and ant
wanted to have a wedding.

The lovely cricket said:
I want to marry.

So the ant asked:
Is it me you want?

The lovely cricket said:
Yes, that's what I want.

They approached the altar
and exchanged rings.

Then the cricket turned a somersault
and broke its neck.

The ant traveled across the sea
to look for a remedy.

It left after Easter and
returned at Christmas.

The cricket was already buried.

The ant stood at the grave and
cried until it collapsed.

At the Grave

Mother wants to die.

I am here, after she spoke on the phone about the yard, that everything looked overgrown and unkempt. Since he's not here anymore, she says, and it's up to the sons now, at least every few weeks or once a month, even if it's just for an hour or two, maybe for an afternoon, weather permitting. The lawn is still not too bad, she says, the flowers don't need watering yet, either, but the beds and especially the weeds everywhere — you just have to go ahead and bend over. I'm feeling my age, she says. It's usually raining when I'm there, or she's already gotten the worst of it out of the way, once you get going, she says, but that's exactly what's hard for me more and more, and taking care of the grandparents, especially grandmother, she complains, takes a lot of strength, cooking and washing and in the middle of the night the bell rings and grandfather reports that she's out of bed again and floating around the house somewhere or lying on the floor like a piece of wood, heavy and stiff; so that mother has to go over there and pick out the right pill out of the many that grandfather has stored up somewhere. Then they heave grandmother back into bed. Now I can't sleep, grandfather complains.

Grandfather wants to die, too.

Our relatives were here in June. They fixed grandmother up and poufed up her hair a little so that it looked more or less presentable. The village sent drummers, pipers and a band. Later on, the church choir and men's choir. The mayor expressed congratulations and presented the now oldest citizen of Amedes with the highest order, with a coat of arms including the picture of the patron saint. In the restaurant *Sternen*, a hearty country meal was served at grandfather's request: sliced roast of beef or pork and lightly fried potatoes with beans, just the way he likes it. Then the recipient's speech, which wasn't as up to par as he was on his ninetieth. But, in comparison to her, still vigorous. All that was missing, in contrast to five years ago, were the phrases speaking of forging ahead into the future. Grandfather made do this time with a broad "Thank you Lord" to everyone for everything. In the name of all the grandchildren, Herbert von Herrliberg took the floor. He had been the only one to make it to the top in every career: Ph.D., insurance company manager, captain in the military. His wife Doris he calls Dosli. For the rest, he limited himself to youth, health, family, security, etc. in his long speech from which all Romanic trace elements, except for *tat* or *tatta* or *culn*, had been elegantly expunged.

The tables were arranged in horseshoe fashion, as they had been three years ago, only then it had been less formal, there were no place cards or seating arrangements according to sex, age or degree of relation, no speeches either. A few cold cuts, salami, some bacon, with bread, butter and wine. Mother sat somewhere between the grandparents and the immediate family. Sobs and words of comfort. We would just have to stick together.

Advice and tips. Speculations on the cause of death, smoking, alcohol, stress. Lots of what ifs, finally unanimous: when the hour is come, so help us God, everyone has to die, sooner or later. Grandmother's senility pierced the muffled murmuring regularly with the question: *Chi é mort*, who died, whereupon someone — half annoyed at her lapse in memory, half ashamed to have to repeat the name, since you do tend to speak of *him* or *the deceased* — bent over close to the confused *Tatta* and whispered your name to her. Then she began to sob convulsively, which led some to talk about the weather or about sports but made others, more closely related, sob all the harder.

Grandmother still cries today. Almost daily, and almost always to herself, and when she is asked why, she whimpers and answers without raising her eyes, which are fixed on the pattern of her apron: *Mia tatta é morta*, my grandmother died.

It happens sometimes that mother selects the wrong pill and the next day, grandmother suddenly gets going and tells the entire world to go to hell. Later, as she sits like a lamb and, leaning slightly forward over the table, she drinks her tea in leisurely sips with a crescent roll that she consumes with her clattering dentures. She has already forgotten the reason she was angry. At some point, grandfather stands up and commands: *Via!* Arm in arm and supporting each other, they trudge over to their house like two tourists who have all the time in the world. As long as the sun is still casting a few rays on the *Sternen*, they sit on the little bench in front of the house and watch the hubbub on the main street. Grandfather puffs on his pipe while grandmother's hands smooth the pattern of her apron with infinite care.

Grandmother wants to die and cannot.

The yard is of minor importance. An excuse. If it rains, mother is twice as glad and says: Now we can sit together inside. We don't say much. The main thing is that she thinks I'm doing all right. Around six she flips the television on. Could be she's looking for a familiar face, wants to hear a voice, suddenly, after the announcement and station identification, according to the program schedule and your weekly calendar: Thursday, cut; Friday, moderation; Saturday, *Telesguard*, the special Rhaeto-Romanic channel. Face and voice. Maybe she is looking for the eyes that smile into the room, twinkle into the rooms, somewhat impudent and somewhat serious, and then the sonorous, warm, smoke-heavy voice: *Caras aspectaturas, cars aspectaturs, oz ...*, where she can tell herself, not without pride: That is my husband.

It's not like that anymore. She could, of course, have copies of the cassettes sent to her by mail from the archives and partake, slice by slice, of ten minutes daily, almost live. But she would need a video recorder for that, and who, mother would ask, would pay for it? So she must be content with the fatherly newscaster who experiences every catastrophe and the pain of the world in person, or with the brisk sports commentator, full of love for life, he appeals to me, she says, or she asks: Why don't you go out for sports anymore, Amedes, as you used to? She usually falls asleep after the news. She hasn't yet begun to put on make-up for the evening in front of the television, the way aunt Babale used to do. Every evening she sat herself freshly made up, powdered and coifed in front of the screen and waited for the guests. In Amedes she would tell the story: In the evening I converse with the leaders of half the world. Remember, Father?

Mother will get old.

As soon as I'm in Zurich, after a few days, a week or two, the yard will be important again. In the summer, the fruit would have to be picked: cherries, apples, pears, plums, or mother makes jam from the quinces and surplus currants. Only strawberries and blackberries don't produce much, there is only enough for one or two bowls of granola. Maybe it happens to be Mother's Day or it's the weather, as she says, much nicer at any rate, than in Zurich. And always lots of weeds, very many weeds.

Mother misses you at every step.

Of course, you are hanging in the kitchen, on the walls and in the entryway. Some of the photographs are framed and behind glass. Others, taken from the newspaper and small in format, she has stuck to the wall or to a calendar with pins or thumbtacks: you in front of the meadow in a plaid shirt and posing. Another time with your cap pulled low over your forehead, your eyes peeking out slyly from underneath. Here formal, Sunday, a holiday or procession, in suit and tie. I always liked you that way: in a white shirt with silver or white gold cuff links. There with a microphone and interview guest: furrowed brow, a lock of hair, inquiring eyes, lips. Or with the cameraman and sound engineer: arm outstretched, index finger. Or plainly visible, the narrow wrist and the fingers on a table, cigarette between index and middle fingers, the ash burning so long it bent toward the table, next to you a pack of Murattis and a glass of mountain wine.

Or, reading with lids half lowered. Or, laughing heartily. In conversation. Winking.

Mother sees you daily.

I remember: We were going to get together in the evening. In my appointment book under Thursday, October 21: Father for supper (no onions), 7:00 p.m. You came a bit later, the spaghetti was already almost *al dente*. Your face full of furrows, but happy. You sat and talked about your film, about the work in the cutting room, about the editor, but mostly about the film, while I added more seasoning. Portrait of a beekeeper. Portraits, long your specialty. Before, it had been painters, sculptors, rake makers, wood carvers, etc. Later on, psychiatrists and housewives. Now the beekeeper, *igl apiculture*. You had immersed yourself in your subject, as always, curious, books, field studies. Then the first test recordings in the *Bündner Oberland*, attempts to encourage the taciturn beekeeper to speak and rid him of his stage fright. You had great respect for farmers. And for craftsmen. Were almost submissive. Or was it envy? You gave them the feeling, at any rate, that they were somebody. You preferred the practical ones to the gregarious theoreticians. Is that why you told me, years ago: Cobbler, Amedes, that would be right for you?

Friends came for dessert. Now you simply blossomed. After a short time, you had them all in the palm of your hand and talked more and more excessively about your beekeeper and your colonies, about your drones and your queens in images that became increasingly rich and heavy. And this sense of direction, you enthused, and not to mention the nectar. Finally, you reached the honey sandwiches. Then everything once again from the beginning, a few words about ecological balance here and there, spicier and spicier, more and more anecdotal, and like you after retirement, then I'll get my own colonies, you said, my colonies, my drones, my queen, you said that was a science in a manner of speaking and deserved a professorship unto itself; suddenly you had become professor of apiculture, in Pisa or Nimes, we could have elected you unanimously, we even spoke Latin, and you quoted the beekeepers' oath. Not enough. You got your second wind, it got late, they were yawning, they laughed again, laughed while yawning, while you, yawning, kept talking, filled up your glass again, sketched a figure, you see, you said, this is the way an aviary with thirty colonies looks, then you drew the combs and the head gear a beekeeper has to wear, imagine mosquito netting with very fine holes, you said and embraced the air, but our imaginations weren't functioning anymore, the first of them took their leave, you called Latin beekeepers' slogans after them like reminders, praised the bees' hard work once again as well as the nectar and the honey. It's late, Father, I said, but you wouldn't let me change the subject and held onto that one word like a battle cry or a secret, that only you seemed to know, as if you didn't believe that we'd been on your side for a long time: *SI SAPIS*, you said and raised your eyebrows, *SIS APIS*.

A week later you were dead.

[...]

Admission Note

> Entrance complaint: The patient
> could not say why he is in hospital.

Tucson, Arizona: The first ones were called Bruce and Buick. That's my stepfather's car, Bruce yelled after he had picked up Amedes at the airport. Then they drove up. The music was loud and the wind blew in through the open sunroof and swallowed their voices. Cacti, some with one, some with several arms rose toward the sky on both sides of the street like fingers. It's the first time in my life that I see a cactus, Amedes said, and: We have different trees. Amedes also had to yell. That's great, Bruce yelled back, and: Your English is very good.

No, no, in Switzerland they don't speak English, except in school, but we speak four languages, Amedes explained into the wind and music and stretched out a four-fingered hand to Bruce. Vromensh, yes, Vromensh, and Bruce wanted so much for Amedes to say something in Vromensh, please, Amy, and Amedes, who had agreed to the American nickname (I'll just call you Amy, alright?) yelled: *Beinvegni* — welcome. And Amedes had arrived.

London: Alison says: I'm sad. But PanAm means well with them, Amedes' departure is delayed again and again, there's still some time, they go to the park; the farewell is getting greener by the minute, a boat, or there, an oak tree so you can lie in the shade. I wish you could stay, but the wishes go the way of the wind, get caught in your hair, in your blouse, in the blades of grass, in the ants' backs as they clamber up your legs, kiss me, you forget yourself, you're just tongue and skin and twenty fingers and your nose so close to her earlobe rose water and a tumble the crown of the tree and the green of the sky then the earth grass and ants and ants and an ... Not here, Amedes.

Finally in the air. A sky of water under Amedes, then a giant iceberg like a long winter; toward twilight. New York. A short layover, change planes, a helping hand; someone who had taken the same flight and already knew everything: You know, UP WITH PEOPLE. A look through the big window out into the evening, far behind an orange-yellow ball and skyscrapers: That's Manhattan, said Ake, that was the name of the hand that dragged Amedes's backpack over the escalator. Amedes followed Ake with short, rapid steps because there wasn't much time and the return flight home to Houston had been booked. The aircraft dropped suddenly several times as the captain said something about ten thousand feet. The test with the swimming vest, some cold cuts and orange juice, then the landing. Fasten your seat belt, good-bye, Ake, and Amedes stood there, somewhere in Texas with his backpack manufactured by Bonatti, sat down in the huge hall and waited wide awake for the following morning to come. I miss you, Alison.

That's the button for the ice cubes, said Francy, Bruce's mother. You can choose below: the left-hand switch is for the big ice cubes, the right-hand one is for small cubes, but my husband and I usually use the big ones; and that over there is for Coca Cola and that's for orange juice, you just push on it; and here you can get cold water and milk is over here, just make yourself at home, and Amedes said: Thank you very much.

That's the verandah, you can smoke here, but you have to close the door. That is Bruce's room and that one is Marcia's, you'll like her, I'm sure. Your room is on the other side. Here are bath towels and hand towels, you can take this side or that one, as you like, honey, do you have a girlfriend, Amy? In the morning, we eat pancakes and eggs and bacon, and in the evenings, we often stay at home, we have so many channels, and on Sunday, we have a barbecue, friends come over; since we've started going to Marriage Encounter we've made a lot of new friends, I'm sure you have a girlfriend, Amy; but we're also in the New Catholic Church, are you Catholic too, Amy, and Amedes answered: Yes, but ... Oh, that's wonderful, Francy interrupted, we all love you, son.

The ballroom at the University of Arizona was filled to capacity when Mr. Blanton Belt, the President, stepped up to the microphone and shouted out to the crowd: Hi everybody. Welcome to UP WITH PEOPLE. Mr. Belt stretched his arms out (standing ovation). You are lucky people, Mr. Belt pointed his index finger? (standing ovation on the chairs, stamping). A chorus in unison from the crowd: Blanton Belt Blanton Belt Blanton Belt Belt Belt. Roar.

Amedes remembered: Chur in Graubünden. The concert was publicized in newspapers, on posters, by word of mouth. In the evening the city's theater is filled to the last seat. The show begins: Light whips across the stage, faces appear, they laugh, as if everything were light and playful, sing songs of a better world; equality, brothers and sisters, Black and White, a lot of sunshine and light again, like an organ, it's raining light. What sort of people are they, Amedes wonders. He's one of the first to rise after the performance and yell *encore*.

It is getting late. The city's theater is almost empty. Amedes is sitting in a row and waiting for the interview, the all decisive conversation that will determine the future; finally, Amedes thinks, and: Imagine, people from all around, on tour with half the world, here, then there, South America perhaps, or Japan, perhaps China or Poland, and I am here too, thinks Amedes, in one of the five groups that are on tour yearly, I am with them and one of them; oh, I could chirp for excitement; that will be some party.

Then the interview: people like you and me. (But they have something we don't, there is a light in their eyes we don't know). Amedes explains his world in cautious yet decisive words (just don't say anything wrong, for heaven's sake). Peace and the joy of life he says, and translates what he reads in the other person's eyes, deciphers the code that is winked to him from afar, this is what I really believe in, he says, and future, and one world for everyone. I believe.

(I really want to.)

Two months later, the letter comes. Amedes recognizes the envelope immediately. It is shining out from between the daily news and the parish newsletter, my God. Amedes plucks the snow white envelope from the goldish dirt surrounding it and now straight out with it and under the birch tree. He tears open the envelope, unfolds the letter and reads with bated breath: Dear Amedes, It is our pleasure to inform you that ... oh man, oh man, what now, what now, Amedes thinks; finally: a shining ribbon of huge letters floats out toward him, down there, in black and white, there it is: admitted.

Somersault.

On the verandah: Amedes looked down below at the city turning on its star sky. Cacti wherever you look. Amedes turned around. He recognized the silhouettes of the Edisons behind the mosquito net in the slightly darkened room. They were drinking something and staring into the niche from which a color-bright kaleidoscope kept emitting new images. Amedes remembered Blanton Belt's speech as he looked down over Tucson again, and he became aware of the fact that music consists of notes and dance consists of steps. I don't, thinks Amedes, like Marcia.

Four months later, Dr. White says: We'd better keep you here, after he had examined Amedes in counting. Try to count down. Amedes had to subtract, always minus seven, ninety-three – eighty-six – seventy-eight –, sorry, – seventy-nine. When he said fifty-fifty, the doctor said it would be better if he stayed for a few days and added: I guess you didn't have much schooling. Amedes stuttered a few words about middle school and Latin and liberal arts high school. Then he was led to a room, yes, please, and a nurse took off his watch and ring, but his name, she said, he could tell her tomorrow morning: Good night. Amedes could see only the barred window and a small lamp on the wall that was on all night and brought the shadow of the grille up to the ceiling so that Amedes didn't even have to turn his neck to see it.

High School Final Exams: *Ductus Pneumaticus*, and all fish have a swim-bladder. Correct, the Biology teacher Mr. Nuggli nods. But I don't know anything about the fins, Amedes says and thinks: The swim-bladder should get me a D all right. *Je ne me souviens plus*, he says to the French teacher Mr. Sonder, heavens, what's his name again, *Sartre, non, Camus, non plus*. Mr. Sonder, who is almost related to Amedes, changes the subject, *vous avez un point blanc, ce n'est pas grave*. Finally: *Vol de nuit*. Made it after all. Amedes gives a report on Rivière who demands the utmost from his pilots, and on the relationship between man and nature and space. Sonder lets Amedes talk over his time limit so as to compensate for the D in swim-bladders. The History teacher, Mr. Fanot, passes out the long distance bonus, you just have to be friendly while passing, oh boy, and hey, Prof., then the man from Prättigau beams throughout the entire valley and effuses: Oh, those fresh athletic youngsters, well ..., just like when he teaches and compares the number of dead in one battle to the number of dead in the other and is amazed at the impressive difference: The Spartans ... P.E. teacher Mr. Melchior is happy that there have been goals, but they're not recorded in the grade books, which dismays him, who has preached for seven years: if you can't run, learn from the horses.

The principal of the senior high school presents the diplomas in the evening with the smile of a ripe tomato and says, facing the graduates, that they have studied themselves silly in learning to tell black from white, but now it is high time to recognize the gray tones. The school orchestra strikes up once more, then handshakes and bits of flattery.

On that same evening Alison and Amedes went to London where they waited, their arms tightly around each other, we can write, you know, then flying off abroad and Houston; now we can only write. Then the next day on to Tucson by way of Austin and El Paso, where the air is sticky and Amedes had to cough as he stepped out of the airport terminal and looked around and waited for America to come get him.

Amedes had fought against everything under the sun for America. He had been determined to do everything possible to earn the $5,000 himself. In the summer, he worked in the large plant in Amedes as a temporary worker. He had to fill cans with paint solutions and attach the lids and labels to the cans. The labels had the titles WGH, HWG, GHW or GWH, depending on the contents. The supervisor, Mr. Candrian was furious when Amedes sang while labeling the cans. You weirdo, said Mr. Candrian, who had spent the last 18 years in the same room mixing paint and filling cans. At best, the money covered the flight. The rest was parental love and gratitude. The main thing was the dream about a thing.

(*Translated by Renée Schell*)

America: Illusion, Battlefield, Disillusion

As I'm writing these lines, I'm sitting at a table on the second floor of a seigniorial house which is surrounded by a little square with a monument in memory of the victims of World War I, Verdun 1916. The window is open. America is far away. It is February. Next to the house, there is a bell tower which belongs to the church in the back. The bell always rings the hours twice — a custom that is quite frequent in the countryside, not only here, where I am now, in the French Provence about a hundred miles north of Marseilles, in the Valley of the Durance but also in some parts of Switzerland, especially the southern Italian speaking part — but maybe, who knows, also in America, in the United States, in parts of the United States, maybe in the Midwest, maybe in Wisconsin or South Dakota, I don't know — America is huge. The panel discussion planned for Sunday, March 3 at Stanford University is entitled: "The America Image in Swiss Literature." This title provokes in me a certain anxiety. My preoccupation might well be a simple sophistry but then again I can't help feeling somewhat concerned. The title sounds to me like a piece of music with a tremendous crescendo on the first seven notes (The America Image) and an equally tremendous decrescendo on the following notes (in Swiss Literature). You might well tell me that I'm suffering from an inferiority complex and that I am not aware of what the matter is all about. In this case, the title of the symposium at USC would indemnify me for my feeling of deficiency: "How does contemporary Swiss literature view the United States?"

The weather in France is mild. I can see the branches of three trees in front of me, two of them, one on the left, one on the right hand side of the square seem to carry chestnuts in summertime. Behind the three trees, I can see the roofs of three houses. By the aerials on top of the roofs you can tell that the people living in these houses are connected to the "rest" of the world, even to America. On the right hand side of the valley, they have built a new highway to bring the people from the Marseilles Airport to the skiing area of Albertville where the Olympic Games will take place in 1992 as they did before in Calgary and Lake Placid. I don't know whether the Canadians or Americans built new highways for those occasions — I think they did. America. This word, an abstract notion to define or insinuate a continent, is just too powerful for me. It's a word that seems to include everything so that nothing really shows. America has become a cliché. And I don't know if it is possible to have an image of a cliché. Coca Cola, Jeans and CNN have become concrete signs of this cliché. CNN shows many pictures but the image is covered up. It is like a view through a closed window: what you see is glass. The Swiss writer Peter Bichsel wrote the following phrase a few days ago, expressing his sorrow concerning the US-engagement in the Gulf: "It is very difficult for me right now to admit that I like being in America very much, that I like sharing my time with Americans, that I appreciate their kindness. Why are nations something so totally different from the sum of their citizens?"

From the highway of the Valley of the Durance, a constant sound comes up to me. The sound of the chamber orchestra of the Valley — once upon a time just crickets and crickets and crickets — has now changed dramatically. But I suggest that the people living in this area are happy since they can reach Aix en Provence or Marseilles in a short period of time. Behind the highway, I can see the river that delineates its serpentines towards the south. In the background there is a range of hills. In summertime the lavender blossoms all over these ranges and the air is full of a soft perfume. I think you even might forget the highway for a while. I suppose that a long long time ago there was a glacier in this valley. The range of hills in the background, once a moraine, might well be a pleasant and aromatic witness of that epoch of evolution. My eyes follow the hills and the serpentines to the edge of the window. The other half of the picture, the upper half, is dominated by the sky, the sun and some clouds announcing rain or snow or wind. Somewhere far beyond this background, beyond the line of the horizon, beyond the clouds that fade away in the milky color of the sky, there must be another side, another reality, another existence. There will be a day, when all American clichés will have been exported all over the world; and in a certain sense they will be "brought back" to where they came from. Then, I hope, it will be possible to rediscover America, sorry, I mean the American citizens, and to look out of their windows or into their windows while they are open. We know that this day has already arrived.

What else do hills and mountains cover than the sea — the final home of all rivulets and rivers. In the eyes of the mountaineers (and one remains a mountaineer in spite of CNN), the sea becomes the metaphor apt to allow the prefiguration of another reality, of another side. The sea had been named before the continent existing overseas was. Whoever wants to reach the other side has to make a trip. And to make a trip, such a trip, one needs a pretext, a provocation, an emergency.

In Romanche literature nobody makes a trip overseas just for fun. In the seventh verse of the folk-song describing the unfortunate love story between the Ant and the Cricket — a song every Romanche (to be exactly: Sursilvan) speaking child learns in the kindergarten —, the Ant makes a trip overseas to find a remedy for her husband who has lost his mind following his tremendous pleasure of marriage. The continent on the other side of the sea is not concretely named. A few years ago, this sad fable was turned into a cartoon film. The interpretation of the author shows the Ant arrive — in a little nutshell — in the Bay of Hudson River. In the background, he drew a huge and tremendous line of skyscrapers. For the first time the imagination of what might be on the other side of the sea, of the ocean — that never was articulated until then, even though everybody was thinking of America — got visualized in a very concrete way. The other side of the sea had finally gotten a face. The song starts with a harmony of love in the homeland. There seems to be no reason to split the union. But the idyllic reality is shattered by an unexpected accident. The remedy can not be found in the homeland. Who knows, maybe because of a lack of medical technology. Unable to help oneself one goes elsewhere to find the remedy. We don't know whether the Ant found the remedy on the other side of the sea. We don't even know what she did there. What we know is that the cricket died before the Ant came back. What we know is that even America could not help us to save our little singer. But who knows: maybe the Ant was clever enough to know that there was not enough food back home. One cannot only sing and make love and forget to make provision for the winter. Maybe the trip of the Ant is a first subtle metaphor of the emigration. How can we know what she did there, in New York? She left after Easter and only came back at Christmas time. Plenty of time to enjoy life and to make new friends. But all these things are no part of the song and I know that my speculations are nasty. We all know that the Ant, as far as the song is concerned, was anxious to return back home as quickly as possible — traveling in a nutshell takes its time! — and seeing that her lover had already died, she died as well. In this song, America (or to be correct: the other side of the sea) became a relay transmitter. If you don't lose your mind back home, if you behave properly and decently there, then there is no need for any trip away from the place you belong. An unexpected situation of emergency is required to justify the trip. The trip to America serves to find the remedy. The return is highly intended. But the trip turns out to be useless. America is an illusion.

In Bühler's novel *Igl Indian Grischun* (The Grison Indian), written in the late seventies of the last century, the hero Guisep is forced, like the Ant, to leave the country and his family due to an accident. As a mountain guide he had to lead an English tourist across a mountain-pass. Due to a wrong step, the tourist falls into a canyon and dies. Giusep, fearing that the people back home might not believe his story, decides to "escape." After a few stops on the continent, where he always finds work, he decides to take a ship, leave France and make the trip to the "other side of the big water" as the chapter is entitled. Thus he arrives in Quebec, Canada. His younger brother Gion tries to find him. He follows his tracks and after a longer odyssey also arrives in Canada. A war between the Indians and the troops of the French settlers seems to be — dramaturgically speaking — necessary to make possible the reunion of the two brothers. One fights on the side of the Indians. The other one on the side of the French troops. In that sense, the novel is an early Romanche version of the theme of a white man turning into an Indian. Although the Indians are not really characterized, one can all the same say that Bühler tries to draw a "correct" picture of the Indians conceding them their right to rise. But the approach of the two brothers stays in the center of the novel. The choreography for that approach and the later reunion is a battlefield. The element that saves the two from killing each other — since they meet in a duel (one with a tomahawk, one with a gun) in a dark forest — is their native language — the only efficacious "remedy" in that second decision over life and death. Before Giusep, the "Indian," can hit his brother with his tremendous tomahawk, he hears him exclaim: "Jesus Maria e sogn Giusep!" (Jesus, Mary and Saint Joseph). With these words, the two brothers recognize each other, they embrace each other, take a canoe, then a ship and hurry homeward where all ends in a big and romantic happy end. Giusep is connected to the figure of the lost son. His departure — an involuntary act — is an emergency that provokes an equally emergent search for him. He is not gone to stay but to be brought back. That is at least the ideology the text transmits. Who knows, maybe Guisep had become familiar with the Indians, found a new home out there, became a "Dances with Wolves." This suggestion is not very credible. A few words in his native language were enough to bring him back — mentally and emotionally. He doesn't even feel the need to say good-bye to his Indian friends. On that background, the last phrase of the novel seems to be more than logical: "America is nice, fertile and marvelous with its magnificent fields and forests and interesting for its different kinds of people, but it is never, never like home." The remedy is the native language brought by a family-member. The message is an exclamation with a religious touch — as if the "paganized" brother should be re-assimilated to the former confession. The confrontation falls together with the reunion and takes place on a battlefield. Would they have met without a war? Is harmony the fruit of battle? Bühler probably needed to lead the two brothers onto an American battlefield so they could return as heroes, back home, where the army of the Ants had already prepared the party of reunion, not even knowing when or if they ever would return.

Although the novel was written in German, Amedes, the hero of my novel, is also a Romanche figure. In the beginning of one chapter the native language again is a code like in Bühler's novel. But the signs of the code are turned upside down. The code does not attempt a reunion and a return but a clear separation. At the arrival in the States the word *beinvegni* is replaced by the word "welcome". Amedes is ready to assume the new codification and to leave his homeland behind. His decision to leave his home country is not the result of an accident. Amedes is not an ant searching for the remedy for a mad cricket back home. Neither is he a farmer's son who escapes because of a sense of guilt. Rather Amedes is to compare with a cricket that leaves before it loses its mind. But he exports the flip-flap. His view is focused on the new frontier he is ready to cross. Amedes leaves ants and brothers back home. The possibility that he might need a remedy sooner or later does not bother him. Singing and dancing in his mind, he joins the United States. It is possible that he was searching for freedom and that he expected to find this freedom in America. Joining the group UP WITH PEOPLE was the outer aspect of this search. But there the confrontation starts. Instead of enjoying freedom, he has to learn the discipline, the assimilation, and the uniformity. While the people of his age had to serve in the recruiting school back home, he ran into another kind of recruiting school in the States. As time went on, he started to dance more slowly and to sing lower. Not able to cope with the velocity and hectic of the American society, and every transitory slow-down being impossible since the show had to go on, Amedes started to prepare his personal flip-flap.

There we are again: America becomes a battlefield. This time, no war has to be invented. The battlefield is an internal matter and the outer choreography is delineated by the so-called American way of life, where you again have the usual clichés like the orange-juice-machine, the ice-cracker, the superficial friendliness of Francy, the declamatory voice of a president (Blanton Belt), a screaming crowd and again and again a speed that is faster than any thought. And the remedy? Amedes attempts to find one, and that takes him straight to the decision to fight. The fight is a confrontation between the different cultural backgrounds — European vs. American. Talks and approaches. But the show must go on. Amedes just does not succeed in becoming an American. After a while, the fight turns into self-destruction and ends in hospital. America is a disillusion.

FRANCO BELTRAMETTI

Franco Beltrametti

Born October 7, 1937, in Locarno. Studied architecture. Lived in Japan and for several years in the US. Lives in Riva San Vitale. Short stories, novels, poems, plays, essays: *Uno di quella gente condor*, 1970; *Nadamas*, 1971; *Face to Face*, 1973; *In transito*, 1976; *Another Earthquake*, 1976; *Quarantuno*, 1977; *Airmail Postcards*, 1979; *Sperlonga Manhattan Express*, 1980; *El Tibetano*, 1981; *Target*, 1981; *Banana Story Eccetera*, 1985; *Surprise*, 1987; *Nado, Nado*, 1988; *Niente da*, 1990; *Tutto Questo*, 1977-88; *Monte Generoso*, 1991; *10 000 Words Autobiography*, 1991; *13 portraits de trobaîritz*, 1991; *Clandestins*, 1991.

33 Poems Plus One

1.

A blown down
pine branch –
master Fo Yin & Su Tung Po
wrote the fallen-down-pine-branch
lamentation.
2 o'clock night
North Chorro Street
the kitchen windowglass
                went in a thousand pieces.
More air & wind
come in.

2.

WHITE ON BLACK:
                wood & coal & rabbits, for sale

I think of the
good blonde she neighbour,
a strange hoarse voice.
Gone to Alaska.
Must
be cold,
now,
up there.

3.

53 Sparkes Rd., Sebastopol

After all this rain must be 1 o'clock night
Jim is back in the small white smoky room.
Real claws & feathers by a Durer's owl etching.
Wind & dogs howling again.
He pours more red wine. Are you hungry? he says.

29/XII/67
for James Koller

4.

A BIRD ? AN EAGLE ?

if you don't mind it seems to me a condor
Gymnogyps californianus,
almost extinct
(says a birds field identification guide)
a condor, seen with indian eye:
one of those
condor
people

?/I/68

5.

(((north of Klamath river)))

I CALL MY MEDICINE
WHITE DEER MY POISON
SHE ALWAYS COMES BACK
SOMETIMES MORE
SOMETIMES LESS

6.

*

there is nothing special to understand
just pay attention
*

11/III/69

7.

Bank of America College Square, San Luis Obispo
20. 45 nobody around

JERRY MALONE PRODUCTION INC.
presents
LITTLE IRVY
20 tons   38 feet

---

a whale in a truck
frozen on two rails
35 cents to enter
see oncle Americo the misfit killed 1933
            in Santa Maria, California
ten seconds & out
in the chilly January night
shiney cars slide on
highway one

I'M NO MORE A CIVILIZED MAN

* * * *

8a

If dawns have fingers
And fingers have drums
Drums have dreams
And dreams have almost
Everything. If everything has
Dawns
Fingers
Drums
Dreams than
What's the news? Call
The owls — they
May tell you.

7/XII/74

8b

I feel the warmth of my ears close to my head.
I am sitting by an aluminium window.
I am taking up space.
The dark green wooden trunk is occupying space too
    to my right, in front of the couch covered with
    blankets on which I sit.
The aluminium window is to my right, the sky is
    lumineous, white fog behind & around geraniums,
    a driftwood greenhouse & a cypress tree.
The stove to my left is very small & warm & has
    four funny instect's legs, an iron cubic beetle,
    the name CORONA is casted on its lowest door.
The stove's legs shine.
Everything with a body has a volume & is doing this
    space which otherwise
    wouldn't be here

10/XII/74

9.

Dreamed smooth plans: everyone and everything was
Taken care of. The first sun rays play leaves shade theatre
On the wet window. And I forgot the plans.
Bolinas Mesa a green boat: coyote brush parsley hemlock
And rocks woven together. Mud roads puddles mirrors.
Sky and water
Till China and Japan.
All the way down to Chili.
All the way up to Alaska.

17/XII/74

10.

the moon is a lantern
hanging
through the freezing woods)
    (a Buffalo Bill show) (hey, mister
Death, Mrs. Calamity Jane) (a super dakini
of total imagination) (a she-warrior)
sun light reflected hanging through
the freezing woods

?/XII/74

11.

(and then) (and then) (and then) (and
then) (the wolf) (and then the wolf)
(saw) (and then the wolf saw)
(Little Red Riding Hood) (and then) (and then)
(and then) (and then) (and then)
(Little Red Riding Hood) (and then Little Red
Riding Hood) (saw) (the wolf) (and then)

5/II/77 for John Giorno

12.

(più vecchio di Lao Tzu il paradiso perduto) (già) (c'est la
catastrophe) (già) (do your best)
(violon) (try again) (radiateur)
(the sound of) (paradiso perduto)
(più vecchio del vecchio Lao Tzu)

23/II/77 per Steve Lacy

13.

(people who no longer exist
guide my signs)
(people who no longer exist
dictate these words)

17/VIII/77

14.

GEOGRAPHICAL INDIAN NAMES
FOR GIULIA NICCOLAI
LEAVING FOR CALIFORNIA

Cotati Cucamonga Gualala
Lompoc Malibu Morongo
Napa Natona Nipomo
Ojai Olema Petaluma
Tahoe Tamalpais Tomales
Topanga Yuba Yallo Bally

?/II/78 Napoli

15.

(plenty of light & ventilation is
important) (run, sweat, day-
dream) (do not think) (very important)
(Theodora baby blue eyes) (very, very
important) (consider clouds, water, woods,
wolves, words, BOOKLAND is a neon blue
sign) (Smith Corona, your typewriter)
(from the A-frame pitch window I see
I see I see) (where are we)

19/III/78   Georgetown Island, Maine
for Joanne Kyger & James Koller

16.

(totally free this morning) (fog on)
(fog cleared) (fog off) (drove through
hills) (no new tires for the day)
(even if you can pay) (totally
loose, this morning which is getting
into late morning) (and hungry
we are both very
hungry) (pale blue south sky) (deep
blue north sky) (very hungry) (feel so
free so loose) (she holds the car
registration in her teeth) (even the
asphalt the parking lot even the
highway grade a paradise) (so
free so loose so hungry this
late morning) (in your Hornet Wagon
1974) (loose/free/hungry)

15/VI/78
Bolinas

17.

(split words, split phrases, split
images) (split songs, reassembled
split again) (double-faced, many-
faced, with so many
arms) (is this what I want,
what I need?)

23/VI/78
Santa Fe

18.

A VIEW IN THE KITCHEN

(late Sunday morning
in a green nightgown
she practices Dai Chi)
(just like toothbrushing
she declares)

9/VII/78 NYC

19.

they never met, now they do
no piano to sit on (target)
an old man dragging four suitcases
(target) we don't want to discuss the
situation (target) boring newspapers for
drawing notations (target) one girl
comes in one eye goes out the other
(target) *sulle infinite onde della
pelle* (target, target) yes we exist
no we aren't on mescaline
no we aren't on anything
no I don't know Allen about generalizations

12/XI/78 NYC

20.

on the running highways of the mind, mind
you, everything is exceptional :
troubadours palmtrees pyramids the
Pacific along the dunes of a lagoon
Piero della Francesca talks to Jim
Dine – Cy Twombly green bridges yellow
billboards, add all you want
with gestures casual & easy
"donne che avete intelletto d'amore"
an infernal well-devised machine
WHAT DO THESE PEOPLE EAT, WHAT DO THEY
DRINK under the belly of clouds
through Illinois
I read Paul Blackburn, we're in Barcelona
a tree becomes a person, a person becomes
a tree, which kind of tree
7th 6th 5th 4th St. the Bowery
large stretches of fenced-in black
earth - "wanna hear what I wrote," she
says, Cheyenne Wyoming, the through express
coach, 19 / XI / 78, INTERSTATE 80

21.

short cut

——————————————————————————

(the improbable the impossible the unexpected
the sudden) (an operation done with no
haste) (all the possible corners of
the world) (he bows, becomes Monkey, the
wise monkey) (her shoes scattered on
the floor) (even solitude has advantages)
(today the word EVERYTHING recurs)
(one should give it a WHOLE existence)
(ALL OF EVERYTHING, never enough)
(a big bed now very distant)
(a state of grace which comes which goes)
(the same window by day by night)

15/XI/78   NYC
for E.

22.

for and from Demetrio Stratos and John Cage

in a day there are many hours
how many do you put in
how many hours do you put in 24
they cut off Giacomo Giacomo's legs
they cut off Giacorno Giacomo's finger
how many hours can you put in 24
the emptier the nearer one is to the rest
how many hours can you put in 24
mushrooms have 4 sexes
150 types of males
about 75 of females
only a few
found in combination
how many hours can you put in 24
in the next years we can
expect anything
how many hours can you put in 24
in reality people when asleep
are very busy with their dreams
how many hours can you put in 24
the only way to do projects
is when they rise in front of our eyes
how many hours can you put in 24
like crossing a transparent sheet of paper
how many hours can you put in 24
to the land-of-running-waters
how many hours can you put in 24
did he say something
does he consider us stupid? in the country
crickets and other animals of the night
how many hours can you put in 24
ask for the impossible
how many hours can you put in 24
with the voice you can do it too

29/II/80

23.

the movie I would like to see tonight
starts with a big scene of horses
galloping into a dusty main street
suddenly torn from deep afternoon sleep
each horse has a rider of course
but what really matters is horses
from there the movie takes off
without any loss of speed
till the unexpected slow end
which has a still life intensity
though it all happens in the open
under a huge sign hanging on the horizon
which reads: WELCOME & GOODBYE

12/I/81

24.

because I am here and because
you came back from Mindanao
which is a long way away even
flying, and because you stayed
one night and took a shower
I am writing this: Mindanao
has a very specific sound I
never realized before, an island
three times bigger than Kyushu
which has a very different sound
but what I wanted to say is how
you and islands and me and sounds
do sometimes get together like
on this page with many ands

14/I/81

25.

Half of It

Ted Berrigan wrote a list poem called
People who died
Now he has died too
There is no way around it
Outside it is raining
I remember Ugetsu Monogatari
About traveling in time and space
The pilot a ghost princess
A Japanese movie
Today it is full moon
I just finished glancing thru
Vargas, a Swedish magazine,
Where Ben Vautier says
REGARDEZ AILLEURS!
I already said: outside it is raining
But I haven't said: it is past midnight
Now I said it
I can hear my son now seventeen
Breathing in his sleep
A while ago he was
improving his reading
On the Italian comic *Diabolik*
Then he practiced his
electric guitar
I wonder what and how
are doing so and so
Sure I'd love to love her
and I do
I wonder if next year
I should keep a journal
I haven't done that for years
84 sounds good for it
8 is the ∞ *INFINITE* standing
And 4 after all is half of it
Good night Mr. Brian Eno
KING'S LEAD HAT

?/?/83

26.

(ah) (oh) (mh mh)
(ah) (mh mh) (oh)
(oh) (ah) (mh mh)
(oh) (mh mh) (ah)
(mh mh) (ah) (oh)
(mh mh) (oh) (ah)

19/I/84   for Brion Gysin

27.

(spacewalk) (of yesterday during which) (the astronauts)
(spacewalk) (the astronauts) (of yesterday during which)
(of yesterday during which) (spacewalk) (the astronauts)
(of yesterday during which) (the astronauts) (spacewalk)
(the astronauts) (spacewalk) (of yesterday during which)
(the astronauts) (of yesterday during which) (spacewalk)

?/II/84
for Nanni Balestrini
and W. S. Burroughs

28.

KYOTO SURPRISE

I thought she was
Lady Murasaki
and she was
Lady Murasaki
same face
same soul
1000 years later

?/V/86

for Duncan McNaughton

29.

fast lane
slow motion
full moon
empty space
desert rats
no return
big smile

19/X/86
for James Koller

30.

INFOLIO READER
TODAY'S VERSION OF I T
for Tom Raworth

(lucky man
(outside the kitchen window
 on the fire escape
(any politician will eat
 radioactive food
(the sun goes down
(bombs tend to go off
(you have no imagination
(goodbye to the Bay of Naples
(another tattoo
(the last message comes first
(days pass
(human error
(your cute life
(the early bus
 forever to be lost
(there is no trick
(out there in the country
(hard currency preferred
(this is not the way
(begin again

17/XI/86

31.

qualche	some
parola	word
trovata	found
spostata	displaced
reciclata	recycled
diventata	become
incantata	enchanted

25/II/88

32.

THALIA VERBATIM

I tend to simplify everything:
if he enjoys pouring tea
in the pinball machille
don't worry!

25/XII/88

33.

NORMAL DEEP PERSON

there is no separate
   activity yet you
      are I am a person so
         everybody wears his own
            mask it's a classic and personal
               matters do matter beyond artificial
                  separations I do poetry that I never
                     know) (the needed angel or needed
                        angle is always a specific angel or
                           different angle or catalyst) (ritornello
                           possible & impossible why
                              not) (and very familiar syntax
                         synopsis and interrelated
                    speeches in which there is no
                me nor you anyway poetry always
                does something else) (a matter without
            goals without use and that's precisely
         its very use you
      see) (out there in emptiness
   no illusory me fights no illusory
you no thank you) (from that window
   what do you) (normal deep person) (see
      in this here case through horses
      and snow normally you've got
         less than 2/3 of a second) (quote
         and strangeness granted there
         is no
            separateness) (no
            there isn't

              ?/?/89
              San Francisco

BIBLIOGRAPHY

Peter Bichsel:
America Doesn't Exist = "America gibt es nicht" in *Kindergeschichten*. Darmstadt, Neuwied: Luchterhand, 1969. (Sammlung Luchterhand, 1987[20]: 23-24.)
Typically American = "Typisch amerikanisch" and
Waiting in America = "Warten in Amerika," both in *Im Gegenteil: Kolumnen 1986-1990*. Frankfurt am Main: Luchterhand, 1990. (Sammlung Luchterhand, 1990: 125-27, 42-43).
The Despair of the Peaceful = "Die Verzweiflung der Friedlichen" in *Schweizer Illustrierte (SI)*, Juni 1992.
He talks to me = "Er spricht mit mir" in *SI*, April 1992.
The Privatization of Life = "Die Privatisierung des Lebens" in *SI*, Mai 1992.

Jürg Federspiel:
The Best City for the Blind = "Die beste Stadt für Blinde" in *Die beste Stadt für Blinde und andere Berichte*. Frankfurt: Suhrkamp, 1980. (Suhrkamp Taschenbuch 1984: 27-49).

Christoph Geiser:
Desert Passage = *Wüstenfahrt*. Zürich: Nagel und Kimche, 1984: 29-38.

Eugen Gomringer:
At Home with the Missionaries — Almost a Fairytale = "Zu Hause bei den Missionaren – fast ein Märchen." Previously unpublished.

Eveline Hasler:
The Wax Winged Woman = *Die Wachsflügelfrau: Geschichte der Emily Kempin-Spyri*. Zürich: Nagel und Kimche, 1991: 20-31, 69-76, 88-95, 142-154, 202-217.

Hanno Helbling:
Discovering America = "Amerika entdecken" in *Neue Zürcher Zeitung (NZZ)*, 23 March 1992.

Urs Jaeggi:
Brandeis = *Brandeis*. Darmstadt: Luchterhand, 1978. (Fischer Taschenbuch, 1980: 229-259.)

Hanna Johansen:
Ideas. Previously unpublished.

Jürg Laederach:

Emanuel — Dictionary of the Enchanted Loafer = *Emanuel: Wörterbuch des hingerissenen Flaneurs*. Frankfurt: Suhrkamp, 1990: 54-69.

Hugo Loetscher:

From Coast to Coast = Reading at the Conference "How Contemporary Swiss Literature Views the United States." Los Angeles, 6 March 1991. Includes excerpts from: *Der Waschküchenschlüssel oder Was – wenn Gott Schweizer wäre*. Zürich: Diogenes 1983. (Diogenes Taschenbuch, 1983: 159-162 – "Ein unhelvetisches Ende oder Besuch der Freiheit.") *du: Die Zeitschrift der Kultur*. Sonderheft "Chicago" 1972. *Herbst in der Großen Orange*. Zürich: Diogenes, 1982.

Herbert Meier:

Terrence = "Terrence" in *NZZ*, 27/28 August 1988.

Adolf Muschg:

New Rights = "Neue Rechte." Previously unpublished.

Erica Pedretti:

Holy Sebastian = *Heiliger Sebastian*. Frankfurt: Suhrkamp, 1973. (Suhrkamp Taschenbuch, 1982: 34-45).

Kuno Raeber:

Alexius under the Staircase or Confessions to a Cat = *Alexius unter der Treppe oder Geständnis vor einer Katze*. Darmstadt: Luchterhand, 1973. (Frankfurt, Berlin Wien: Ullstein, 1982: 207-16).

Walter Vogt:

Aging = *Altern*. Zürich, Köln: Benzinger, 1981. (Fischer Taschenbuch, 1984: 95-97, 99-102, 108-113).

Urs Widmer:

In America = "In Amerika" in *Das Normale und die Sehnsucht*. Zürich: Diogenes, 1972: 90-94.

Gertrud Wilker:

Parting Between Window Frames = "Abschied zwischen Fensterrahmen."
Flashbacks = "Rückblenden," both in *Collages USA: Ein Bericht*. Zürich: Flamberg, 1968. (Elegie auf die Zukunft: Ein Lesebuch. Frauenfeld: Huber, 1990: 142-48, 139-33.)

Ueli Zingg:

Interim Report = *Zwischenstand*. Bern: Zytglogge, 1980: 81-93. Translation reprinted with kind permission from A. Leslie Willson. *DIMENSION: Contemporary German Arts and Letters*, special issue (The Image of America in Contemporary German Writing), 1983: 520-35.

Etienne Barilier:

The "American Dream." Previously unpublished.

Daniel Odier:
Cannibal Kiss = *Cannibal Kiss*. New York: Random House, 1989 (copyright 1987 by Daniel Odier, translation 1989 by Lanie Goodman): 3-13, 15-17, 40-43.

Yves Velan:
Soft Goulag = *Soft goulag*. Vevey: Editions Bestil Galland, 1977: 70-90.

Iso Camartin:
Maxims for Los Angeles. Previously unpublished.

Flurin Spescha:
The Weight of the Hills = *Das Gewicht der Hügel*. Zürich: Nagel & Kimche, 1986: 7, 9-17, 71-79.
America: Illusion, Battlefield, Disillusion. Previously unpublished (reading at the conference "How Contemporary Swiss Literature Views the United States." Los Angeles, 8 March 1991.)

Franco Beltrammetti:
33 Poems Plus One. 1-7 in *Uno di quella gente condor*. Torino: Geiger, 1970; 8a,b-10 in *Mandala*. Amsterdam: In de Knipscheer, 1975; 11-12 in *Abracadabra*. Luxembourg, 1977; 13-15 and 19-20 in *Target*. Great Britain: Grosseteste Books, 1981; 16-18 in *Airmail Postcards*. New York: Vehicle Editions, 1979; 22-24 in *Ibernazione*. Roma: Cervo Volante, 1981; 25 in *Nice To See You*. Minneapolis: Coffee House Press, 1991. 26-32 in *A Gang Person*. Brunswick/ Maine: Coyote's Journal, 1989; 33 in *The Person*. Berkeley: Poetics Journal, 1991.